HOLE-IN-THE-ROCK

An Epic in the Colonization of the
Great American West

Commenting upon the pioneering experiences my father [Mons Larson] declared always, that the handcart journey in which he made the journey from Winter Quarters to Salt Lake City was not nearly so hard as the journey through the Hole-in-the-Rock.

— ELLEN J. LARSON SMITH

HOLE-IN-THE-ROCK

An Epic in the Colonization of the
Great American West

DAVID E. MILLER

PRINTED IN THE UNITED STATES OF AMERICA
PUBLISHERS PRESS

DEDICATION

This book is dedicated to the men and women of the San Juan Mission whose valiant efforts brought American culture to one of the remotest regions of the United States.

PREFACE TO THE FIRST EDITION

One of the most significant epochs in the history of the United States is the great overland migration that brought American civilization and culture into the Far West. A major factor in this epoch was the Mormon migration to the Great Salt Lake Valley and the subsequent colonization program of the L.D.S. Church* under the leadership of Brigham Young and his immediate successors. Under church direction, colonizing "missions" established Mormon outposts throughout, and often in remote parts of, the intermountain frontier. One of these missions, conceived in the mind of Brigham Young but not carried out until two years after his death, is the subject of the present study — the 1879-1880 mission that took the first permanent settlers to San Juan County from many southern Utah communities by way of Hole-in-the-Rock.

In all the annals of the West, replete with examples of courage, tenacity and ingenuity, there is no better example of the indomitable pioneer spirit than that of the Hole-in-the-Rock expedition of the San Juan Mission. No pioneer company ever built a wagon road through wilder, rougher, more inhospitable country, still one of the least-known regions in America. None ever demonstrated more courage, faith, and devotion to a cause than this group of approximately two hundred fifty men, women, and children with some eighty wagons and hundreds of loose cattle and horses who cut a wagon passage through two hundred miles of this country. Even the wily mountain sheep could not have negotiated the Hole-in-the-Rock before it was given a "face lifting" by these pioneer road builders. Today their feat seems well-nigh impossible. Yet they proved that virtually nothing was impossible for a zealous band of pioneers. The story of the Hole-in-the-Rock expedition is an excellent case-study of the highest type of pioneer endeavor that broke the wilderness and brought civilization to the West.

The San Juan region to be occupied could have been reached by way of Lee's Ferry, Moenkopi, and the Navajo reservation or via the Old

* The official name is the Church of Jesus Christ of Latter-day Saints, although it is commonly referred to as the L.D.S. or Mormon Church.

Spanish Trail — Salina Canyon, Castle Valley, and Moab. But leaders of the mission decided to try a "short cut" by way of Escalante and the almost completely unexplored and unknown country to the south and east of that frontier settlement. The major obstacle on this proposed route was the Colorado River. Scouts sent from Escalante during the summer of 1879 discovered the Hole-in-the-Rock, a narrow slit in the west wall of Glen Canyon, and reported that a road could be built through it and down to the Colorado. A later and more extensive reconnaissance by members of the expedition, both of the Hole and the broken country east of the Colorado, convinced most of the explorers that the route was impassable; however, by that time the company was well on its way, forty miles southeast of Escalante, and the heavy snow of late November in the Escalante Mountains virtually blocked the return route. So the decision was made to push forward at all costs.

It took a month and a half of united effort to construct three-quarters of a mile of road from the plateau west of the Colorado down to the river through the Hole-in-the-Rock, and because of the difficulties experienced at that point the whole trek is called "The Hole-in-the-Rock Expedition."

The story of the San Juan Mission is not unknown throughout Utah and the West; several articles have been written about it. However, since until now no one has attempted a documented historical account, most of these articles are either sketchy or inaccurate, or both. The present work is the result of six years of intensive study of documents, journals, biographies, autobiographies, letters of participants, and church records. Scores of letters have been written and dozens of persons interviewed in an attempt to ferret out details and locate new sources of information. Believing that the hardships encountered cannot be fully understood or appreciated without having visited the sites, I have made numerous field trips into the area and have traversed the whole pioneer road from Escalante to Bluff — by jeep, boat, and on foot. My sole objective in this study is to present a true and unbiased narrative of this outstanding pioneer venture.

In the process of preparing this work for publication I have had occasion to write numerous articles of varying lengths regarding various aspects of the subject. Two of these should be mentioned here: (1) In writing a report of my research in connection with the History Section of the Upper Colorado River Archeological Salvage Project, 1957, I included a brief summary of the Hole-in-the-Rock trek. (2) An adaptation of Chapter I appeared under the title "The San Juan Mission Call" in the *Utah Historical Quarterly*, Volume 26, No. 2, April, 1958.

I would be ungrateful indeed if I did not acknowledge and express sincere appreciation for the help given me in this undertaking. A grant from the University of Utah Research Fund defrayed part of the expense of the field work; a university vehicle was made available for some of the field trips. For this assistance and that of the many individuals who have given freely of their time and energies may I express my deep gratitude: to Drs. L. H. Creer and C. G. Crampton, who have given constant encouragement and assisted with field work; to Mrs. Lucretia Lyman Ranney for her untiring efforts in helping assemble a list of participants, for reading the manuscript, and for granting permission to use and publish that portion of the Platte D. Lyman journal which covers the trek; to Earl E. Olson, librarian of the L.D.S. Church Historian's Library; and to his staff, for making available church archival materials, helping seek out details, assisting with field work and for other aid. Mr. Olson read the manuscript and made several suggestions and constructive criticisms. Others to whom I wish to express appreciation are Albert R. Lyman, for supplying valuable information and constant encouragement and for accompanying and guiding me on one field trip; Charles Redd, for his constant support and for having read parts of the manuscript; Mrs. Rhoda Wood, for helping locate some important documents; and Lynn, Henry, and Edward Lyman for guiding and assisting in the major field trip. Scores of other persons, to some of whom I have referred in the footnotes, bibliography and appendixes, have been most generous in answering letters of inquiry and in making available letters, life sketches, and other valuable information as well as in assisting with the field trips. I assert exclusive claim to all the shortcomings and errors that may remain in the work.

DAVID E. MILLER

University of Utah, January, 1959.

PREFACE TO THE SECOND EDITION

Contrary to my expectations very little new information regarding the Hole-in-the-Rock trek has come to me since the first edition of this work in 1959. I had supposed that the book, involving so many families, would result in a barrage of letters containing information I may have failed to ferret out before the publication. The small amount of new material brought to my attention since that time encourages me to believe that my original research must have been quite thorough.

The most significant document discovered since the first edition is the very brief journal of Silas S. Smith, President of the San Juan Mission. This account adds some details to the information already available.

As a result of additional new information, a few more names may now be added to the official roster of the expedition. (a) James Harvey Dunton (page 144) who returned with the Four Scouts from Montezuma to the Hole-in-the-Rock evidently joined his family at the "Hole" and escorted them back to the San Juan. His family included Mary Ann Doidge Barker (wife) and the following children: Ellen Melissa Barker, Medora Barker and John Harvey. (b) Joseph Lillywhite's family (page 145) should include the names of Lawrence and John (the babe in arms).

The first edition of *Hole-in-the-Rock* was very well received by scholars of Western American history. *Desert Magazine* recognized it as 1959's most significant history dealing with a Southwest subject and issued an Award of Merit to that effect. The Organization for State and Local History granted it the Award of Merit in 1960.

Copies of the book have served to enrich the experience of hundreds of Colorado River explorers and other groups who have ventured into that wild fantastic country of southeastern Utah. Largely because of the book thousands of people have ventured overland into the area, made their way to the rim of Glen Canyon and peered down through the "Hole" with utter amazement that wagons could ever have gone that way. Yet, incredible as it now seems, for a little more than a year this was the major wagon road between southern Utah settlements and the Four Corners region. Wagons traveled both ways on it — up as well as down through the Hole.

Portions of the old wagon road are now covered by the waters of Lake Powell, but the Hole-in-the-Rock will never be submerged. At its highest level the water will rise nearly to the base of the notch. The great sand slope and huge patch of poison ivy so well known to earlier visitors, will be covered. Jackass Bench (see map page 121) will likewise be submerged. Most of the tableland directly across from the Hole will also be buried; the tops of the Register Rocks will jut out of the lake in the form of small rocky islands. From those rocks the lake water will extend eastward approximately a mile and a half into Cottonwood Canyon. As a result some significant portions of the old road will be covered. But with the Hole-in-the-Rock itself well above the lake surface thousands of people will visit the site each year, by water and by land, and marvel at the achievement of Mormon pioneers who took American culture and civilization to that remote part of the Great American West.

DAVID E. MILLER

University of Utah, March, 1966

CONTENTS

HOLE-IN-THE-ROCK

CHAPTER I

THE MISSION CALL

It is the voice of the Lord to me to go and
I am going by the help of the Almighty.

— *Jens Nielson*

Brigham Young was probably the greatest colonizer America has produced. Under his leadership the L.D.S. Church not only moved to the valley of the Great Salt Lake but from this point branched out in all directions, discovering, exploring, and settling not merely the Great Basin but also the whole intermountain West. The pioneers of this colonizing movement truly made the "desert blossom as the rose" — and a good deal of the exploring and colonizing was carried on in real desert country. A common and practical custom developed by the church was to call members on missions to colonize a region which church leaders wanted occupied. When called, most families gladly responded, often leaving well-established homes, farms and other business enterprises and taking all their possessions into rough, unknown, untried country. There was no assurance that the new home would prove satisfactory, that sufficient water would be available for crops, or that rivers would not flood the settlements once established. But the missionaries called seem not to have been too much concerned about such economic and temporal matters. They usually considered their call an opportunity to serve the church, and once they had accepted there would be no turning back until the mission had been accomplished.

Sometimes the assignment seemed virtually impossible; sometimes the obstacles were almost too overwhelming. But nothing seemed really impossible for the pioneers, and thousands now recount with pride the fact that their progenitors were among those called by the church to plant colonies in Arizona, California, Nevada, Idaho, Wyoming, Colorado, New Mexico, eastern central or southern Utah, and even in foreign countries. Rightly are they proud of these pioneer forefathers, who in conquering the wilderness provided an example and heritage almost beyond comprehension.

When Brigham Young died in 1877 the colonization program which he had launched had not been completed. Among the areas not yet settled was southeastern Utah, although for several years church expansion had been in that general direction. Settlements at Price and elsewhere in Carbon County would be made in 1879; the site of Moab, settled and abandoned during the 1850's, would be reoccupied in 1880; Escalante had been established in Potato Valley during 1875–76; Kanab (established in 1864 and abandoned in 1866) was resettled in 1870; outposts along the Paria River were in various stages of development between 1865 and 1875. The abandoned Elk Mountain Mission at Moab was the only Utah settlement which had been attempted east of the Colorado River.

A study of this colonization program indicates that it was a church policy to plant settlements in all available areas — to occupy all usable farm and grazing land. This expansion was natural and inevitable, since the Mormon settlers were always looking beyond the horizon for more and better acres. It has been truly said that few farmers ever have all the land they want; and the chief activity in pioneer Utah was farming. To acquire more and better land was a major motive behind the whole westward movement, and in this respect the Mormon pioneers were no exception.

For various reasons the church encouraged this natural growth and expansion. It was felt that the economic well-being of the individual would be better achieved through a colonization program; furthermore, the rapidly growing Utah communities needed outlets to relieve their growing pains.

It was in addition to this spontaneous, natural expansion that church leaders found it desirable at times to organize official colonizing "missions" for the purpose of occupying definite areas. Such action was deemed necessary when the region to be colonized was too remote for natural expansion or so thoroughly unknown that little or no interest had been shown in it. Such was the case with the San Juan "Four Corners" area: Mormon colonists were just not moving into it of their own accord.

Church leaders seem to have been quite anxious to obtain the San Juan area before it could be settled by non-Mormons. Mining booms in southwestern Colorado had resulted in rather extensive migration to that region; stockmen were moving into the area and it was also becoming known as a rendezvous for outlaws. But Mormon settlers were slow to go in that direction.

The late 1870's was a period of rather extreme antagonism and increasing friction between Mormons and non-Mormons in Utah, both because of the increase in momentum of the federal campaign against polygamy[1] and because of the struggle between the two groups for political control of Salt Lake City and the whole territory of Utah. It is understandable that church leaders would be very conscious of the increasing numbers of non-Mormons in their midst and would be interested in occupying all available "border lands" if for no other reason than to keep non-Mormons from obtaining them. Although this may not be considered the primary objective of or reason for the San Juan Mission, it certainly must be accounted as an important factor.

That this was one purpose of the proposed colonization is definitely indicated by a letter from Erastus Snow to L.D.S. Church leaders John Taylor and Council. Under the date of November 6, 1879, after the major migration to the San Juan (that is, the Hole-in-the-Rock expedition) had gotten under way, Snow says in part:[2]

Silas S. Smith has started for San Juan with forty or fifty men and some boys and quite a few families, with Boats &c. intending to hew their way threw [sic] the Canyons and open a straight or more direct route to San Juan and as he thinks also to the head of Little Colorado & he needs all the strength he has and more too for the task he has in hand; and less cannot secure the San Juan region in Utah, to say nothing of the region higher up that stream, and its many Tributaries in Colorado & N. Mexico. . . .

To secure the San Juan region for Mormon colonization, to settle it before others could do so, was certainly a major church objective and members of the expedition evidently recognized this. Charles Redd, who obtained much of his information from his father, Lemuel H. Redd, Jr. (an important member of the company), makes this significant statement: "A buffer settlement was needed, it was felt, against encroachment by stockmen from Colorado and the Southwest and Indians of this unpenetrated, unknown area."[3] Possibly incidental but still important was the fact that church members moving to this border country might act as missionaries among the "Gentiles."

Another very definite reason for establishing a settlement on the San Juan was pointed out by George B. Hobbs in his account of the undertaking. He says:[4]

One of the objects of the colonizing of San Juan County by the leaders of the Mormon Church was to select a place where the converts from the Southern States might make new homes in Utah and still be in a warmer climate than where they had recently been settling in the San Luis Valley, Colorado ...

Many converts to the L.D.S. Church who had migrated from the Southern States to Colorado were not completely satisfied in their new homes, as, among other disadvantages, the winters were too cold. It was felt that some attempt should be made by the church to locate sites more suitable for these people. That this was an important factor in leading to the San Juan settlement is indicated by correspondence of church leaders. On May 9, 1878, John Morgan, president of the L.D.S. Southern States Mission, wrote as follows to Apostle Erastus Snow regarding the southcentral Colorado region and problems pertaining to the migration of Southerners to that location:[5]

There will be considerable migration from the Southern States this season to that section and it seems to be a great necessity for some of the Utah Saints to go to them to locate and learn them how to carry on their farming operations and other duties as saints;

The people who go from here are to a great extent almost helpless in regard to caring for themselves in that country and in addition they have not had an opportunity of becoming acquainted with the manner of lives of the saints, and need much instruction on those points, they . . . need a few of the old time saints to assist them in getting in a good foundation temporally and spiritually.

If it could be that a few families could be located in their midst from Utah it would be an immense advantage to them; there is good land, plenty of water, wood, etc. etc., and would be desirable location for those who wished to give their attention to agricultural pursuits, or grazing. . . .

About a month later (June 11, 1878) Apostle Snow wrote to President Taylor as follows:[6]

. . . I would add that from the accounts given me by Bro. Ivins and my Son, lately returned from the Rio Grand, and from other sources, I am satisfied there are many good locations for settlements on the upper branches of that stream as well as on the Tributaries of the San Juan in Southern Colorado and Northern New Mexico and if it is deemed advisable to encourage our Emigrants from the Southern States or elsewhere to occupy that region, there should be some substantial good men sent there to locate them and preside over them.

Additional testimony is available to prove that this purpose was definitely part of the San Juan colonizing plan.

The primary objective of the San Juan Mission, however, was to cultivate better relations with the Indians and lay the foundations for future permanent Mormon settlements. It had always been church policy to maintain friendly relations with the Indians: besides the fact that Brigham Young had found it cheaper to feed than to fight them, one of the fundamental teachings of the church has always been that Indians are part of the House of Israel and will eventually embrace the gospel and become a "white and delightsome" people.[7] This doctrine and mission program certainly tended to dictate a friendly policy, and underlying the whole program of the San Juan Colonization was this basic idea of bringing the Gospel to the Lamanites.

In spite of this attitude of friendliness toward the Indians there had been considerable friction between the two peoples. As Mormon settlements were being established in southern Utah and northern Arizona during the 1850's, 1860's and 1870's, roving Navajos and Paiutes, long accustomed to plundering their neighbors, found the flocks and herds of the newly arrived whites an irresistible booty. Being well acquainted with all possible crossings of the Colorado, small parties of Indians often raided the outlying settlements, drove off stock and disappeared into secret hideouts southeast of the river, beyond the reach of their pursuers. At times this plundering assumed rather important proportions. One writer states that in 1867 a herd of some twelve hundred stolen animals was pushed across the Colorado at the Crossing of the Fathers and that in one year more than a million dollars' worth of horses, cattle and sheep was looted from the impoverished Utah frontier.[8]

A natural outgrowth of this cattle rustling was spasmodic border warfare that resulted in numerous armed clashes and many killed on both sides. During the late 1860's this warfare became so fierce that some Mormon outposts such as Kanab and Pipe Springs had to be temporarily abandoned. The diplomatic skill of Jacob Hamblin, Thales Haskell, and others was taxed to the limit in attempts to bring peace to the southern Utah border. The perseverance of Hamblin and his associates succeeded in winning the confidence of the Navajos, with the result that during the early 1870's peaceful and legal trading replaced looting and border raids. However, in 1874 three Navajo brothers were killed in an unfortunate tangle with Utah cattlemen and the whole southern frontier was threatened with full-scale Indian warfare.

Albert R. Lyman, in "The Fort on the Firing Line," has very effectively described this phase of Utah history and shown the relationship between these Mormon-Indian hostilities and the evolution of what was to become the San Juan Mission. Says Lyman:[9]

> The decision of the Church leaders was to plant a little colony of Mormons in the very heart of all this incipient danger; right on the turbulent border between the Navajos and Paiutes, and squarely on the trail of the fugitive desperado wolf pack from all over the west. It was a perilous venture, as the years were to prove, its objectives to be achieved through great sacrifice, hardship and danger. With few in numbers the little colony would be compelled to hang its hopes of survival on the hand of Providence and the faithfulness with which it could wield the agencies of peace.
>
> Besides the precarious problem of saving itself with its women and helpless children from the wrath and rapacity of these three breeds of savages, its principal purpose was to save the rest of Utah from further Indian troubles by constituting itself a buffer state between the old settlements and the mischief which might be incubating against them. It was to be a shock-absorber to neutralize what otherwise might develop into another war.

By the mid-1870's the San Juan area of southeastern Utah had for some time been known as a refuge for lawless men, white as well as red; it was literally an outlaw hideout, as the settlers would soon learn. A colony there would act as a buffer to absorb any possible hostilities far short of the rest of settled Utah. With the encouragement of the Southern converts to move into the area it would be more important than ever that friendly relations with the Indians be established and that law and order be maintained.

Morgan Amasa Barton, son of Joseph F. Barton (one of the leaders of the Hole-in-the-Rock expedition), also emphasizes this purpose of the San Juan Mission in the following statement.[10]

> And why were these people called to settle San Juan? Perhaps not specifically stated or publicly announced, but definitely apparent, for in settling this part of the country they were an established outpost, detracting marauding Indians from interior southern settlements of Utah Territory as well as being a point of interception of bank robbers, horse thieves, cattle rustlers, jail breakers, train robbers and general desperadic criminals, reducing to a minimum a continuation of their terrorizing and plundering inland settlements in their manner of living while out of reach of law and justice and into which country U.S. officers didn't care to penetrate. These people were to be the shock absorb-

ers of premeditated plots of Caucasian outlaws and Indian renegades and if they failed in tact, diplomacy, mental ingenuity and patience in handling this phase of their mission they would fall in the category of what we term today as expendables, and they performed this part of their mission as any other. Many times I have seen my father, with other men, rushing home and at times out of religious services, for their horses and guns to take up the chase of outlaws. Besides this additional mission duty they were constantly on guard over their own stock, property and families. Basically, not with primary reasons of what San Juan might be a hundred years hence were they called but for immediate protection of different sections of the country from which they had come. Still it was hoped and desired that besides making friends with the Indians there would be the accumulation of stock and property and means for the establishing of schools and churches which, as a natural consequence, would be fundamental in the greater development of San Juan.

This Mormon colony would bring law, order, and justice to a region thus far considered too remote from any settlement for law enforcement.

In view of the expansion program of the church under Brigham Young and the influence of factors already considered, an eventual movement into the San Juan region was inevitable. It is difficult to determine just when the idea was first conceived for a permanent settlement there. Kumen Jones, reminiscing in later life, had this to say about it: "Here is where and when the idea of the San Juan Mission was born, about 1877 in St. George. The death of Pres. Young delayed the execution of the plan until the latter part of 1878, when about 100 men, most of them young men, were called at a conference held in St. George."[11] There seems to be no reason for doubting Kumen Jones' statement regarding the origin of the idea. By 1878 circumstances seemed right; the time had come to put the colonization program into operation; church leaders began laying definite plans for the venture.

At the suggestion of Apostle Erastus Snow, himself a pioneer, statesman, colonizer and patriot, whose prophetic visions pierced the future, the decision was reached to plant a colony somewhere in the neighborhood of the "Four Corners" where the territories of Utah, Arizona, New Mexico, and the state of Colorado cornered together.[12]

The church had given Snow the assignment of perfecting the plan and providing for its successful execution.

Southern Utah settlements, being nearest the new site, would be expected to supply most of the colonists. Consequently, a "mission call" was made part of the business of the quarterly conference of the Parowan

Stake, "held in the Parowan Meeting house" December 28 and 29, 1878. An excerpt of the conference minutes containing a list of persons called at that time is here quoted. I have taken the liberty of italicizing the names of those who went on either the exploring expedition or the Hole-in-the-Rock trek.

The following names were then read by the clerk & presented by Prest. Snow as missionaries to settle in Arizona, or where directed, all of whom were unanimously sustained by the Conference: *S. S. Smith,* S. H. Rogers, Davis Rogers, *H. H. Harriman, Geo. Hobbs,* H. Harrap, Solomon Wardal, *James Decker,* Paul Smith, Daniel Allen, Orson Allen, *Peter H. Mortinsen, Hansen Bayles, Willard G. W. Butt, Hyrum Fielding,* E. M. Dalton, *John C. Dalton,* Christopher Wilck, Henry Wilcock, *Adelbert McGregor,* R. R. Burbeck, *John C. Duncan, John T. Gower,* Christian Tufft, *Kuman* [*sic*] *Jones, Hyrum Perkins,* John H. Adams, *John Joseph Nielson, Francis Webster, Jr.,* Jens Jenson, John Mitchell, *Wm. Robb, Jr.,* John Lister, Jacob Gould, Simon Topham, *Henry Holyoak,* John S. Barton, John Williamson, *Jos. F. Barton, Geo. Robb, J. R. Robinson, Jr.,* Peter B. Fife, Louis Fisher, *James L. Davis, Thos. Bladen, Geo. E. Perry, David Hunter, Geo. Urie, Samuel Rowley.*[13]

In this way people learned that their church was calling them on a mission — a mission that would require many to give up fine homes and move with all their possessions to a site that had not yet been precisely located. There seem to have been no prior interviews, no letters of inquiry; those attending the conference heard their names read from the pulpit much as though they were being called to run an errand for the bishop. Those not in attendance would soon learn from their neighbors and friends that their names had been included among those "called." If this seems a bit blunt today, we must realize that that was the method then used by the church for calling its members on missions, be it for a lifetime of colonizing or two years of proselyting among the Gentiles.

The following March 22 and 23 (1879), at the next regular quarterly conference of the Parowan Stake held at Cedar City, more people received similar calls.[14]

To Arizona:— Jesse N. Smith, *Silas S. Smith, Jun.,* Joseph Fish, Smith D. Rogers, Amos Rogers, John R. Hulet, John H. Rollins, *Cornelius Decker,* Lehi West, Sister West, John A. West, *Z. B. Decker, Jun.,* N. P. Warden, Lars Christiansen, *Jens Nielson, Samuel Cox,* Jane Perkins, Sarah J. Perkins.

It should be pointed out here that not all those listed were called to the San Juan Mission, which, of course, had not yet been named. Many went to other fields, in Arizona, Nevada and elsewhere. Furthermore, some of those called were officially released before the major expedition got under way.

Several accounts of the Hole-in-the-Rock expedition such as the statement of Kumen Jones cited above indicate that the first official "call" was made at a stake conference held in St. George. In fact, most published accounts are probably based on the Jones statement. However, L.D.S. Church records indicate definitely that the conference in question was held at Parowan and it was then and there that people first received notification of their appointment. That preliminary discussions regarding the proposed mission had been held in St. George even before the death of Brigham Young is, of course, very likely. But church records of stake conferences held there during the fall and winter of 1878–79 make no mention of the mission call. On March 16, 1879, at a conference held in St. George ". . . A number of missionaries were also called for Mesquite Flat in the Lower Valley of the Virgen, for Arizona, and for New Mexico."[15] Some of those called to Arizona and New Mexico may have been intended for the San Juan Mission since the definite location had not yet been designated. But no names appear in this report.

The records here cited are the only ones I have been able to locate in the church files that actually supply names for the list of missionaries called to participate in the San Juan colonization. However, an examination of the list of those who eventually went (see Appendix I) will show that only a small portion of the total number are included in these two accounts. It is known that many of those who made the original trek but are not listed in these two conference reports definitely received calls by the church. If complete records were available of meetings held in southern Utah during that time, many more names would probably be added to the list known to have received calls at conferences. Many others such as Platte D. Lyman received private notification. Also, a sort of blanket invitation was later extended to anyone who wished to join the expedition whether or not specifically called. Furthermore, some people are known to have attached themselves to the movement not as members of the mission but as a means of getting to Colorado, Arizona and other points, in company with a large party of colonists. Partly because of the incomplete records and other complications, no attempt is made in the present work to classify the members of the Hole-in-the-Rock expedition into groups of "called," "volunteers," or otherwise.

In the meantime, at a meeting held in the Social Hall, Cedar City, January 2, 1879, those named at the Parowan conference were given counsel and encouraged to express their feelings regarding the "mission."[16] The new colonizing venture was portrayed as being definitely part of the Lord's work; this assignment was to be considered just as important as though they had been called on foreign missions.[17] The missionaries were admonished to put their trust in God and that all would be well with them. Single men were advised to seek a bride and marry, if possible, before the movement got under way. This mission was intended to be a stable, permanent project. In order to further impress the gathering with the importance of their calling, Henry Lunt of the Parowan Stake Presidency "stated that the march of the Saints today was toward the center stake of Zion . . ." The colonists might very well be the first vanguard of Saints to begin the great trek eastward — back to Missouri.[18]

In the course of the meeting Bishop C. J. Arthur informed those present that they were *not compelled* to accept the call. He "required all to use their agency as to whether they went or not, but advised all who were called to go with a cheerful heart." He further announced that additional volunteers would be accepted should anyone not already listed desire to make the trek. The undertaking would require many strong and valiant people if it were to succeed — and there could be no thought of failure.

Although some of those present seemed not too enthusiastic about their new assignment, most of them expressed satisfaction and a determination to accept the call and pledged themselves to devote their entire energies to its successful completion.

Elder James Davis stated that he had been warned by a dream that he would be required to go & live in the Arizona Country . . . & would do all in his power to be ready when the company started. . . . Thos. Bladen, thought be could live where anyone else could & thought he would be on hand when the crowd got ready. G. Urie was not prepared to say whether he would go or not . . . [But he accepted the call and was a member of the Hole-in-the-Rock company.] Elder F. Webster, was willing to go & doe the best he could . . .

Such were a few of the sentiments expressed five days after the call.

While thus admonishing and instructing the newly selected missionaries and learning their reactions, local church leaders also promised to try to get additional information concerning the proposed location of the new settlement. It may be surprising to those not familiar with L.D.S. Church history to find these men accepting such a call to an unidentified location. Indeed they did not know for sure that a suitable site could be located. But the history of the church contains abundant examples of such service and devotion. The Saints had moved from Kirtland, Ohio, to Missouri during the 1830's, from Missouri to Nauvoo, Illinois, in 1839, from Illinois to the Salt Lake Valley in 1846–47. From Salt Lake City many had been called to settle in southern Utah and other places throughout the intermountain West. This colonization, they believed, was the work of the Lord; any sacrifice required to further that work would be cheerfully made. They had complete faith, not only in the divinity of their church but also that its leaders were guided by divine inspiration. Wherever the authorities directed, they would go.

As the months passed and the time approached for the company to get under way, some families dropped out, others obtained official releases, and some new members joined the ranks of the expedition. For those ready to begin the trek Jens Nielson expressed what was probably the prevailing sentiment: ". . . he felt it [was] the voice of the Lord to him to go & he was going by the help of the Almighty . . ."[19] Writing late in life, a half-century after the Hole-in-the-Rock trek, Kumen Jones expressed what was no doubt the sentiment of the founders of Bluff and still is that of most of their descendants today. He wrote:[20]

My purpose in this humble effort in writing about it, is to convince my children and my descendants of the fact that this San Juan Mission was planned, and has been carried on thus far, by prophets of the Lord, and that the people engaged in it have been blessed and preserved by the power of the Lord according to their faith and obedience to the counsels of their leaders. No plainer case of the truth of this manifestation of the power of the Lord has ever been shown in ancient or in modern times.

This humble writer of the story of the San Juan Mission sees now, in looking back over it, the inspiration of appointing Erastus Snow as head colonizer of Arizona, Colorado, New Mexico and Utah. He was of natural wisdom backed up with wide experience, he had more than ordinary good common hard sense, and above all, he had the inspiration of the Lord.

As indicated, the location of the newly proposed settlement was indeed very nebulous, not only to those called but to the general church authorities as well. At the conference of December 28–29, 1878, the call had been to "settle in Arizona *or where directed.*" At that same time (December 29) Erastus Snow wrote to President John Taylor recommending that "Silas S. Smith of Parigona (long a member of the Legislative

Council) . . . would make a descreet presiding officer to lead settlements on the San Juan or Salt River . . ."[21] Six months later at the Parowan Stake conference on June 29, 1879, "Prest. Snow spoke of the importance of making new settlements in Arizona, Mexico and other places. . ."[22] During the summer, letters received by Platte D. Lyman further indicate that there were several possible locations being considered. On June 22, according to his journal, Lyman received a letter from Erastus Snow containing a list of volunteers who were expected to start about September 1 for the "Grand River"; a second letter from the same source dated July 3 refers to the same site. Late in August when Lyman received his official letter of appointment to share the leadership of the colonization effort, church leaders had not yet selected the exact location although the exploring expedition under Smith's guidance had long since reached the San Juan and found suitable land at the present sites of Montezuma and Bluff.

In accordance with Apostle Snow's recommendation, Smith was appointed leader of the proposed expedition. A letter to that effect from President Taylor to Snow, dated January 9, 1879, reads in part: "In regard to Elder Silas S. Smith, the Council voted unanimously that if it be in accordance with his feelings, that he lead a colony to settle on the San Juan river, at wherever point may be deemed advisable . . ."[23] Since Smith was known to favor the San Juan in preference to any other location, he was now given his chance to settle there. Once appointed, it seems logical to assume that in his conversations with other members of the mission he tended to direct their thinking in favor of the San Juan region. At any rate, by the time the exploring expedition got under way in the spring of 1879, there seems to have been little doubt among its personnel regarding the proposed destination; the expedition was headed for the San Juan.

Although Smith had been selected in January to head the mission, Platte D. Lyman was not officially chosen to assist him until August 13, after the exploring expedition had already reached the site of Montezuma. As events eventually unfolded, Smith actually spent very little time with the Hole-in-the-Rock expedition, leaving his "assistant" in active command. Lyman's appointment came in the form of a letter from President John Taylor, dated August 21, 1879.[24]

At a meeting of the Council of the Apostles, held August 13th, 1879, it was unanimously decided that you be called and set apart to assist Prst. Silas S. Smith in the charge of the Saints located on the San Juan, at Manassa, or at such other point east of Green River, as he may direct. It is desirable that you move this fall, either with or without your family and effects, as your circumstances will permit, so as to be fully posted, located and prepared for the Spring labors. You are also at liberty to take with you some five or six of the Partridge families who, we are informed, have desires to make their homes in Southern Country. You will please forward us a list, as soon as convenient, of the names of those you may wish to accompany you, also of your moves, from time to time, as to your preparations, time of starting &c. . . .

Once the site of Bluff and Montezuma had been selected (1879–80) many of the stalwart pioneer missionaries accepted that location as the place to which they had been assigned, although no definite spot had been indicated at the time of the mission call. And once established, many of them refused to move to possibly better locations until officially released from their mission calling by the presiding officers of the church, even though Indian hostilities and the shifting, treacherous San Juan River made the new homes almost untenable. They were devout members of what they considered a divine church, led by divinely inspired leaders; further instructions would come from those leaders.

FOOTNOTES

1. The L.D.S. Church considered this campaign an unconstitutional violation of religious freedom and justified resistance to the Anti-Bigamy Act on that ground. In spite of the ruling by the United State Supreme Court upholding the Act (*Reynolds v. United States,* 98 U.S. 145–169) another decade of conflict and ill-will (see B. H. Roberts, *A Comprehensive History of the Church of Jesus Christ of Latter-day Saints Century I;* [Salt Lake City, 1930]) elapsed before the church modified its view regarding the practice of plural marriage and in 1890 adopted the Manifesto forbidding the practice.

2. Letter on file in the L.D.S. Church Historian's Library. Italics supplied.

3. Charles Redd, "Short Cut to San Juan," *Brand Book* (Denver, 1950), 5.

4. Cited from San Juan Stake History.

5. Letter on file in the L.D.S. Church Historian's Library.

6. *Ibid.*

7. The basic Mormon philosophy regarding the American Indian is contained in the *Book of Mormon.* According to this account America was peopled by Israelites, the major migration having occurred about 600 B.C. under the leadership of Lehi. All were white-skinned at the time of settlement, but as time passed dissension developed and a segment of the people strayed from the true teachings of Lehi and degenerated into a warring, dark-skinned people. The *Book of Mormon* refers to these people as Lamanites, after their leader Laman, one of the sons of Lehi. This tribe eventually overpowered the other descendants of Lehi (the Nephites, named after Nephi, another son of Lehi) and, spreading throughout the whole land, were ancestors of the American Indians found by the discoverers of America. The church believes that these "Lamanites" will eventually receive the Gospel of Jesus Christ as taught by the L.D.S. Church; consequently it has always been part of the church program to send missionaries to the American Indians.

8. Albert R. Lyman, "The Fort on the Firing Line," *Improvement Era* (Salt Lake City, December 1948), 797. Careful examination of the Crossing of the Fathers convinces me that it would have been very difficult to drive a herd of twelve hundred cattle across the Colorado at that point, unless perhaps they were driven across on the ice from the mouth of Kane Wash. This practice was sometimes followed by the Indians when the river ice was thick enough to provide safe passage. Perhaps the whole estimate of rustled cattle is too high, but there is virtually no way to obtain accurate figures.

9. *Ibid.* (January 1948), 44.

10. Morgan Amasa Barton, Back Door to San Juan, 9.

11. Kumen Jones, Preface to the Writings of Kumen Jones, 23. As suggested here, plans for the colonization of the Four Corners area were no doubt in the making before Brigham Young died in 1877. His death merely put a temporary halt to the movement. In another account entitled "San Juan Mission to the Indians" Jones accurately states that this mission call was made at the Parowan Stake Conference held in Parowan, not in St. George. The term San Juan Mission used here and throughout this chapter was the name ultimately applied to the movement, after settlements had been established at Bluff and Montezuma. The name had not yet become current during the formative stages of the undertaking.

12. *Ibid.*, 2.

13. Parowan Stake Historical Record, No. 22125, 174. Some of these missionaries were unable to go with either of these first two expeditions but later journeyed to the new colonies on the San Juan; no attempt is made here to identify these people, although they fulfilled their mission as well as those who went with the first company.

14. *Ibid.*, 178.

15. St. George Stake Manuscript History, March 16, 1879.

16. Parowan Stake, Cedar Ward Historical Record, No. 22183, 332.

17. In a general sense the term "foreign mission" refers to a proselyting mission outside of Utah, either in one of the other states or in some foreign country.

18. When the L.D.S. Church established itself in Missouri during the 1830's there was created at Jackson County what was called the "Center Stake of Zion." However, due to persecution the church was forced to leave Missouri before this stake had been thoroughly established or the proposed temple built. Since leaving Missouri the church has consistently taught that there will be a return to the "Center Stake," which will eventually become an important Mormon center. This ultimate migration back to Missouri is still part of the long-range church plan; three-quarters of a century ago it was believed by many to be imminent. For a discussion of this element of L.D.S. history and doctrine see B. H. Roberts, *op. cit.*

19. Parowan Stake, Cedar Ward Historical Record, No. 22183, 379 report of Sacrament Meeting in Cedar City Ward, Sunday, Oct. 19, 1879. I have taken the liberty of placing this statement in the first person to use as a quotation at the beginning of this chapter.

20. Kumen Jones, *op. cit.*, 23.

21. Letter on file in the L.D.S. Church Historian's Library.

22. Parowan Stake Historical Record, No. 22125, 185, report of quarterly conference held in Parowan.

23. Letter on file in the L.D.S. Church Historian's Library.

24. *Ibid.* Lyman received this letter August 29, according to his journal entry for that day.

CHAPTER II

THE EXPLORING EXPEDITION, 1879

From Moan Coppy the explorers looked to the northeast, over dry mesas and glistening sand hills where the lonely Navajo guarded his sheep and goats in a wilderness all his own.

— *Albert R. Lyman*

As noted in the previous chapter, many locations for the prospective southeastern settlement were under consideration; the San Juan River was only one of these. Since the settlement *was* ultimately made on the San Juan the fact is sometimes overlooked that this site was selected as a result of exploration and not merely because of a directive or command from church leaders.

The fact is that at the time of the mission call virtually nothing was known about the Four Corners area. It would have been foolhardy indeed to send an expedition of settlers including women and children with all their possessions into such an unknown region, with little chance of turning back in case no satisfactory place for a settlement could be located. It was therefore decided to send out an exploring party early in the spring of 1879 to pioneer a wagon road into the region and to determine the feasibility of future settlements. If appropriate locations were found, the men were to stake out claims, plow the land and plant crops, dig irrigation canals, build houses, and return home late in the summer to escort the main body of colonists to the new home site.

Under the leadership of Silas S. Smith this exploring party consisting of twenty-six men, two women, and eight children,[1] left Paragonah April 14, 1879. The women and children served as a sobering influence on the company and a constant reminder of the seriousness and the dangers of the whole undertaking. They did not expect to return to their old homes, but would stay on the San Juan, lending real permanence to the new colony. Although many of their neighbors and friends were planning to join them later in the year, others would not be among the expedition and would probably never be seen again. Records are meager concerning this subject, but there must have been some heart-breaking farewells as these people launched out into entirely unknown country to establish homes they knew not where — nor, indeed, did they know whether favorable locations could be found at all.

This company of explorers was well equipped for a six-months expedition, if that much time should be required. They had a dozen wagons, approximately eighty horses, and a herd of cattle estimated by George B. Hobbs at about two hundred head, although others seem to think this figure somewhat high.[2] Their course took the company up Little Creek, northeast of Paragonah, through Bear Valley and over into the Sevier Valley, following a well-established wagon road. At Orton's (about nine miles north of Panguitch) the expedition was formally organized for the trip. The complete list of officers is not known, but Silas S. Smith was sustained as captain with Robert Bullock as assistant captain and sergeant of the guard and James B. Decker as chorister. An unidentified chaplain was also appointed and regular religious services were held, including prayers, sermons, and the singing of hymns. Nielson B. Dalley,[3] who was placed in charge of the loose stock, reports that the horses were hobbled for the first few nights to prevent them from returning to the settlements, after which they were allowed to forage at night unshackled. As the company would experience considerable difficulty in keeping track of its livestock in wild, unknown, Indian-infested country, seventeen-year-old Dalley had an important assignment.

At his ranch four miles south of Panguitch John Butler joined the company and has the distinction of being the only member of the party to have a geographical landmark (Butler Wash) named in his honor.

The old wagon road crossed the Sevier River a short distance southeast of Panguitch and followed up the east rather than the west bank, as U.S. Highway 89 does today. The company traveled this road upstream (southward) through Hillsdale and on to the summit (the rim of the Great Basin) at the head of the west fork of Sevier River. Today this spot is known as Long Valley Junction, where U.S. Highway 89 meets Utah State Highway 14. A short distance beyond the summit the road turned left (following the approximate route of Utah State Highway 136) toward Upper Kanab, the site of the present-day Alton. From here the party continued down Johnson Creek to the Johnson Settlement, then turned east, following a wagon road toward Lee's Ferry. The route took the company to the Navajo Well, then southeastward over Buckskin Mountain and thence down House Rock Valley to House Rock Spring. This road presented obstacles, especially in one section of the Buckskin Mountain where wagons had to be lowered with ropes.[4] Skirting the Vermilion Cliffs, they camped at Jacob's Pool, Soap Creek, and Badger Creek before arriving on April 30 at the Colorado River ferry[5] six miles upstream from the present Navajo Bridge at Marble Canyon.

At Soap Creek "George Urie and John Gower broke an axle out of their wagon. [The] company laid over and made an axle out of an old cottonwood tree."[6] This repaired wagon was probably taken to Lee's Ferry where it was abandoned, to be picked up in the fall by its owners.

May 1, 1879, found the company busily engaged in ferrying their wagons across the Colorado. "Silas S. Smith having a small bunch of horses did not want to pay $1.00 a head for their being ferried over, so drove them into the river to swim them across. The river was one-fourth mile across and the horses struck below the landing and had to swim back nearly losing one over the rapids."[7]

Once across the Colorado there was a difficult climb out of the river gorge and up over "Lee's Backbone." This led to the plateau south of the river and along the west base of Echo Cliffs, paralleling present Highway 89 for many miles. Here was one of the most difficult stretches of the whole trek, as water was very scarce and of poor quality. Distances between waterholes seemed endless; there was always apprehension lest the known watering places (Navajo Spring, Bitter Spring, Limestone Tank) would be dry when the thirsty train arrived. Here the company was first introduced to the hazards and hardships of desert travel and gained an inkling of what lay ahead. Men, women, children, and livestock learned what it meant to make dry camp, then travel all the next day without a drink.[8] There was one stretch of some thirty-five miles with no water at all — just loose drifting sand, thick choking dust, deep gullies, and the blazing Arizona sun. George Hobbs has left us a vivid description of this part of the trek:[9]

From the river we started on an almost impassable road to take our wagons over the so-called Lee's Backbone, and after this arduous labor was accomplished, we continued our journey and thence to Bitter Springs. On the Bitter Springs desert we traveled 50 [thirty-five] miles without water and at least one fourth of our cattle died of thirst. One of the first teams that arrived at Willow Creek was unloaded and packed with water and sent back to relieve the straggling train and thirsty cattle that were choking along the way. After a short rest at Willow Springs we moved on to Moan Coppy.[10]

At the old Indian village of Moenkopi John W. Young was engaged in the construction of a mill for processing wool from the Navajo flocks. Finding some members of the company anxious to earn money in order to augment diminishing food supplies, Young hired several men to work for a few days quarrying rock and helping in other ways in the building of the mill.[11] Most of the pay was in the form of Indian corn.

While recuperating for about a week at Moenkopi the opportunity was taken to repair wagons, harnesses, and other gear, and to shoe horses and otherwise prepare for the difficult journey ahead. Thus far the trip, even over a reasonably well-established wagon road, had been difficult enough. But "From Moan Coppy the explorers looked to the northeast, over dry mesas and glistening sand hills where the lonely Navajo guarded his sheep and goats in a wilderness all his own."[12] The route lay across unknown country where wagons had not been taken before — a road would have to be built almost every foot of the way. Settlers at Moenkopi discouraged the explorers, claiming that it would be utterly impossible to take wagons through the Navajo country to the San Juan; the Indians would not welcome this trespass through their domain.

At Moenkopi leaders of the expedition made the acquaintance of Seth Tanner[13] and hired him and an unidentified Navajo to guide the company to the San Juan. Thales Haskell also joined the expedition at this time.[14] In addition to these three men, members of the expedition were also named as scouts to precede the main company of wagons. Most accounts mention the fact that four scouts went ahead to locate the possible route. Kumen Jones is usually mentioned as head scout, with Robert Bullock, George B. Hobbs, James B. Decker, and John C. Duncan helping at times.[15]

Because the young cattle and calves had sore and bleeding feet (having already traveled some 275 miles over very rough trails) and because of the obvious risk involved in driving them through unfriendly Indian country, Captain Smith ordered all loose stock to be left at Moenkopi until a road could be pushed through to the San Juan. James L. Davis and his family decided to follow the advice of John W. Young and Wilford Woodruff (who happened to be at Moenkopi at that time) and remained there also. Harrison H. Harriman and his family chose to go ahead with the main company.

Water is the most precious commodity in the desert, and the scant supply must be guarded carefully if life is to be sustained. The Navajos

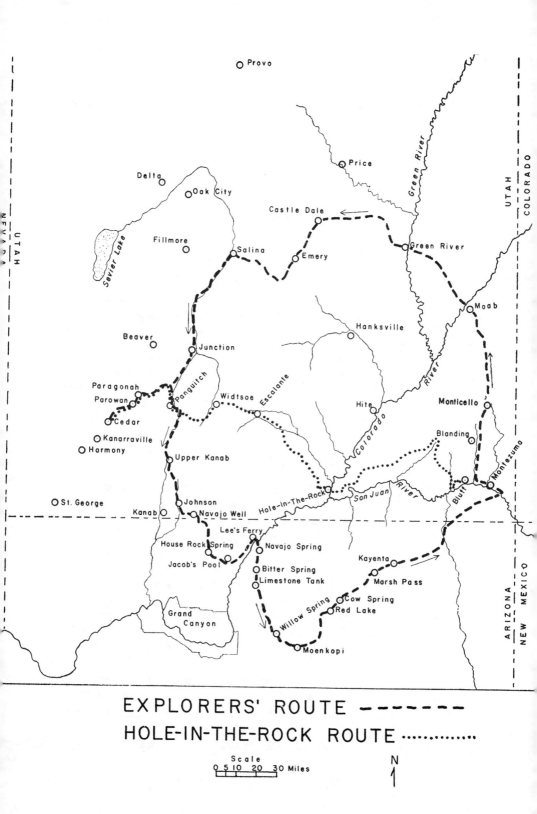

EXPLORERS' ROUTE — — — —

HOLE-IN-THE-ROCK ROUTE ....

Scale

0 5 10 20   30 Miles

N

were at times reluctant to let the company water stock at the infrequent springs along the way. All accounts of the expedition emphasize the seriousness of the water situation, as in the following statement from the San Juan Stake History:

On the journey they dug wells and made roads; in some places the roads had to be cut through the solid rock and water was obtained in many dry places, not by striking it with a cane, as Moses did, but by laboring diligently with picks and shovels. Usually when water was obtained in this manner, it was bad, but it sufficed to quench thirst and save the lives of both man and beast. Two or more of the brethren always went ahead of the main company to look out roads, water and camping places.

Kumen Jones, writing many years later, had this to say:[16]

It soon became apparent that water was going to be the source of our greatest anxiety, and wherever a damp place was found, shovels, spades and picks were soon brought out and digging for water commenced, and as a rule, plenty of water was soon secured, which fact was easily used to our advantage with the quick witted Navajos, as they were told that the watering places would be theirs as soon as we passed on, this news was soon spread, and the Indians ahead were all anxious and gave us a hearty welcome, occasionally bringing a mutton out to show their appreciation. It may be added here that some of the watering places developed by the company . . . have been used up to the present as permanent waterholes.

Although other accounts disagree with Jones regarding the friendliness of the Indians, all agree that the new wells dug by the expedition constituted a major factor in purchasing safe passage and preventing serious Indian hostility. Even so, there was considerable friction. The first major encounter with the Indians was possibly the most trying. Albert R. Lyman's account of it is very interesting:[17]

At one place in the desert the only water was claimed by an Indian Chief who insisted that there was barely enough water for his own herds. He refused the jaded teams a drink, and when some of the boys insisted, he struck savagely at one of them with a club. Twenty young men, full of fire, were hardly the combination to endure it tamely, and a strained situation was relieved when the president suggested they dig a well in the sand. They dug several wells, found water at an easy depth, supplied their animals, and next morning presented these new sources of drink to the Indian.

This generous grant of water evidently did not permanently sweeten the disposition of Chief Peokan for when those who had remained at Moenkopi resumed the journey a few weeks later they found him even more disagreeable.

Without extensive field work it is impossible to determine the exact route and actual camp sites of the expedition between Moenkopi and the San Juan River. In my research in preparing a map of the route (p. 21) and to supplement my own field work, I made use of a series of United States Geological Survey maps[18] on file in the L.D.S. Church Historian's Library, on which the entire route from Paragonah to Montezuma has been marked in pencil. This marking was done several years ago, probably under the direction of Andrew Jenson with the aid of one or more members of the original exploring company. Partial "Camp Records" of the expedition are also on file in the church library as part of the San Juan Stake History. Since this history furnishes the most detailed and without doubt the most reliable information available on the subject, it is here quoted verbatim:[19]

Tuesday, May 13, 1879. The explorers left Moan Coppy at 11 o'clock a.m., drove five miles, going as far as the road had been broken by the brethren who were hauling wood for some ox teams which had been promised to the brethren to help break the road through the grease wood which in some places grew as high as eight feet. Some of the brethren went back to Moan Coppy, but returned to camp at 9 p.m.[20]

Wednesday, May 14. The explorers started at 11 a.m., drove 10 miles through heavy greasewood, 3 yoke of cattle being used to break the road with a forked tree. Two men from Moan Coppy helped the explorers with this work.

Thursday, May. 15. Silas S. Smith found his band of loose horses gone in the morning and one other animal. The company moved on while Isaac Allen and Bro. Smith's boys went out hunting the horses, but they returned to camp at 2 p.m. without them. Bro. Silas S. Smith himself then took the trail and after following it three miles he met Wm. Gardner, an Indian interpreter, driving in the horses. It was now so late in the day that the brethren remained in camp the rest of the day.

Friday, May 16. The company started at 9:30 a.m., drove 5 miles to the farm of Peokan (a Navajo Indian).[21] Here they dug out some good springs and then traveled 7 miles to a dry lake (Red Lake) at the lower end of which the brethren obtained water by digging wells.

Saturday, May 17. The Company resumed the journey at 8:30 a.m., drove 9 miles to Cattle water (as the Indian name signifies), dug out the springs and got plenty of water. Here was also good grass; the roads were nearly level, and there was not much sand. The course traveled was north by east.[22]

Sunday, May 18. The company traveled 20 miles and made a dry camp in the cedars, where grass was plentiful, but no water. The brethren dug out a spring and obtained a very little water.[23]

Monday, May 19. The company traveled 10 miles, did some work on the road and met Robt. Bullock and Seth Tanner who reported an open way for 75 miles ahead; plenty of water was found on a sandstone tank or lake.[24]

Tuesday, May 20. In the morning the brethren found that some of their stock was lost. They were not recovered until late in the day, after which the company traveled 6 miles and found plenty of water; some Indians came in with mutton to sell.[25]

Wednesday, May 21. The company resumed the journey at 9 a.m., passed a spring two miles from camp, and saw another watering place to the left. They then drove 12 miles to another sandstone tank where thousands of Indian sheep are watered. The water here was nasty, but the brethren had to drink it in order to quench their thirst. The color of the water was almost the same as that found in a corral.[26]

Thursday, May 22. The company resumed the journey at 8 a.m. and traveled over a heavy and sandy road about 15 miles. They made a dry camp and burned sage brush for fuel.[27]

Friday, May 23. The company traveled 6 miles to water and found a camp of Piutes and also a camp of Navajoes.[28]

It was probably at this point that the following episode occurred, reported by Kumen Jones:[29]

An incident occurred before reaching the Chinalee showing the tact of our captain. Upon passing a large camp or village of Pahutes, one of their number (later known as Peeagament), came blustering out and demanded $500.00 before the train would be allowed to proceed through his country. The Captain's being the first team, a short stop was made to try and passify the old fellow. A few mild explanations were attempted, the only effect being to cause the old man to press his demands in a higher key. Noting this, Smith ordered him out of the way, and proceeding some distance, struck camp for dinner. The captain quietly passed the word around camp that it would be the right thing to give the Indians a little something to eat, or other small gifts such as tobacco, etc. Especially the small children were to have something to eat, but no one was to give the noisy old fellow anything or notice him in any way. The result soon made the wisdom of this course apparent as the Indians old and young were all jolly and friendly, and the old man was a psychological study, thoroughly whipped and the lesson seemed to last him all his life.

Barring the above, our travels through the reservation was agreeable and pleasant on both sides, and reaching the San Juan on the last day of May we crossed the next day.

Let us again continue the "Camp Records."

Saturday, May 24. The brethren remained in camp waiting to hear from the explorers. Bro. Robert Bullock and others had gone ahead again to look out the road. Explorers were kept ahead all the time.

Sunday, May 25. The brethren remained in camp. The exploring party started out again,[30] those who remained in camp held two meetings, one at 2 p.m. and another in the evening.

Monday, May 26. Bro. James B. Decker returned from the exploring party and the brethren in the camp hitched up their teams at 5 o'clock p.m. and drove three miles down the wash.[31] Soon after turning out for the night Bro. Dalley's mare kicked Silas S. Smith's horse, breaking his leg. Bro. Smith seeing the crippled condition of his animal, shot him.[32]

Tuesday, May 27. The company traveled 12 miles over deep sand and bare naked rock.[33] They did more work on the road than on any previous day on the journey, and at last came up a steep rock where it would seem impossible for wagons to travel. They camped for the night at Lost Spring and dug wells for water.[34] In their travels the explorers usually brought enough water along with them to suffice for one camp.

Wednesday, May 28. The brethren remained in their camp at Lost Springs. Silas S. Smith ascended a point[35] three miles off with a glass to look out the way. Bro. Bullock and his party of advance explorers returned from the San Juan river in the evening.

Thursday, May 29. The company traveled 8 miles to Chimney Wash where they found water. They then traveled five miles to Cave Springs, where water was very scarce; not sufficient to water their stock.

Friday, May 30. The company traveled 8 miles through heavy sands to Alkali Gulch where they found plenty of water though of a poor quality. Resuming the journey, they traveled 10 miles further over a terribly rough, sandy road and camped at 9 p.m.[36] They drove the stock to the San Juan River, and the herders remained out with the stock all night, bringing them back to camp in the morning. Explorers were still kept ahead of the company to find the way.

Saturday, May 31. The company traveled 3 miles and camped on the San Juan River.[37] Here they found six men who were making farms; they were camped about two miles above them on the San Juan River.[38] The explorers found that these men who were making farms were having trouble with getting the water out of the river. The place of their location was immediately below the so-called McElmo Wash.

Sunday, June 1. The brethren remained in camp. Silas S. Smith and one or two others went over to the houses which had been erected by the farmers already mentioned just below where McElmo wash puts into the river. Bro. Smith and those with him hunted for fords to cross the river.

Monday, June 2. The camp crossed the river safely by raising the wagon boxes on the bolsters; they found the current very swift.[39] Later in the day Silas S. Smith went four miles to the camp of Peter Shirts[40] who lived in a cabin at the mouth of the Montezuma Wash, 5½ miles below Mitchell's camp at the McElmo wash.

Tuesday, June 3. Silas S. Smith went up to examine the Mitchell ditch; he found the men discouraged. They had decided to give up their crops, unless the explorers who had come with Bro. Smith would help them to get out the water. Peter Shirts was laboring in conjunction with the Mitchells.

Wednesday, June 4. The exploring party remained in camp.

Thursday, June 5. The advance explorers returned to camp and reported a small body of land on the river some distance below.[41]

Friday, June 6. The brethren of the exploring company looked for land for making farms near the Mitchell settlement. Mr. Mitchell and those with him had arrived on the river the previous fall.

Saturday, June 7. The explorers under Silas S. Smith moved their camp about three miles up the river to a place in the immediate vicinity of where the dam had to be built in the river.[42]

Sunday, June 8. A meeting was held in the camp. Most of the settlers below came up and Bro. Silas S. Smith spoke on the first principles of the Gospel. In the evening H. H. Harriman was by vote of all present appointed foreman on the dam, the explorers having concluded to help the settlers who had preceded them on the river. These first settlers had promised to share their crops with the new comers. In the forenoon of this day the brethren organized a Sabbath school in their camp with John C. Duncan as superintendent and Kumen Jones as clerk. Three classes with teachers for each were organized. The following week was spent by some of the brethren working on the dam, while others explored the valley up and down the river and located lands.

Sunday, June 15. Meetings and Sunday School were held in the camp.

Monday, June 16. The brethren continued work on the dam. The closing length of the dam went out towards night.

Tuesday, June 17. The brethren continued work on the dam in the forenoon. In the evening they went to Mr. Mitchell's place to attend a wedding. Miss Clara M. Mitchell and a Mr. Willians were married by a Presbyterian minister from Mancos, Colo. This is supposed to have been the first marriage of white people on the lower San Juan River.

Wednesday, June 18. The brethren organized a party to go for supplies and explore the country up the river; another party was organized to explore the country near the Blue Mountains, and still another party was organized to return to Moan Coppy in Arizona after the loose stock which had been left there by the explorers on their trip out. The brethren drew lots for the land which had been located and agreed to work on the cooperative principle through the season, explorers and farmers to share alike.

The important task of returning to Moenkopi to guide the rest of the company and the loose livestock was entrusted to James B. Decker, Hamilton Wallace, Parley Butt, and Nielson B. Dalley.[43] Traveling on horseback with one pack animal they arrived at Moenkopi in four days and prepared for the return trip to the San Juan. Dalley gives a brief but interesting account of this trip.[44]

We gathered all our cattle ready to go. The night before we were ready to leave we lost one of my horses & one of Parley Butts. We had turned them out. We hunted them 3 or 4 days but couldn't find them. Parley B. & [James B. Decker] went on with the cattle, while we stayed to hunt. On the 4th day we got word that Parley Butt [and] James Decker had found our horses.

The Navajos were parading & were riding our horses . . . [Decker and Butt] had to pay . . . $5.00 to get them. We never knew whether . . . [the Indians] took them from Mioncopy or found them on the road back. Ham & I left immediately & overtook them 40 miles [from Moenkopi] in a swampy country. The cattle watered in a muddy pond. We only had to dig 2 or 3 ft. to get water to drink. Old Peogon appeared again he was peaved at us staying on his lands.

There were 2 boys from S.L.C.[45] stayed with us one night. The old Indian was peaved & began pushing the smallest of the SL around but . . . [the Indian] was too much for him, pushed him into one of the water holes. At this the S. Lers mother dog jumped out of the wagon & grabbed the Indian. The S Ler took his raw hide whip to the dog but the Indian grabbed the ax & was going after the dog. The owner stopped him but the Indian started on him; the other S L grabbed a shovel to interfer. But we finally pacified the Indian. We wrote to the Indian Agent & explained the trouble & we went on.

James L. Davis also found occasion to record the events of this day.[46]

They advised us with familys to stay there [in Moankopi] on account of the dangers ahead of us. And let the young men go and find a suitable country to locate. We did so and in two months five of the boys returned and reported finding a place. We started again on our journey. We traveled peacefully until we nooned the third day, then we were in some very bad Indian country. One by the name of Peascon, came to our camp and caused a great deal of trouble. (He was the one that caused the killing of Apostle George A. Smith Sr., the first L.D.S. to be killed by the Indians, and we were close to the place where he was killed.)[47] This Indian would kick the dirt on our food, and struck our knife blades on the rocks. He would draw his knife across his throat to show my wife and children what he would do to them when he got help. Our boys acted like the time had come for them to kill or be killed. I begged them not to fire the first shot. The Indians left for help and did not return by night-fall. We expected them to return before sunrise as those Indians were sun worshipers and believed that the sun can see and tell the great spirit all they do, but if the sun didn't see the spirit doesn't know. So when daylight came and the sun came up and they had not returned we felt very much relieved, and had decided to cook our breakfast. I saw at a distance an old Indian coming toward us. He came and told us to hitch up our horses as quickly as possible and travel fast. We did so but was a little doubtful as to the Indians plans. We feared he might be leading us into a trap. The roads were thru deep sand so the horses had to stop often. This seemed to anoy the Indian. He would stand upon the spring seat and look far and wide, then he would urge us to hurry faster. After a time he told us we could stop as long as we liked then travel as slow as we wished. He asked me if I did not know him. He told me my name and where I had come from, and said he had been to my place many times, and we had always given him something to eat, and was good to him. He knew I was there with my family he had watched us on our journey and we did not know it.

He said the Indians were planning to kill and rob us soon as they could find enough volunteers and he had come to save us by hurrying us out of their territory. In two weeks time we arrived at the San Juan River at a point called Montezuma Fort. I very much liked the look of the country, but my wife felt that we were isolated from all civilization and she was very down hearted.

This was July 17. Mrs. Davis had a right to be downhearted: the birth of her baby was expected at any time — the child was actually born two weeks later. One might well marvel that the rigors of this most strenuous trip had not brought about a premature birth.

One more entry from the "Camp Records" will complete the account of the journey of the explorers to the San Juan:

On the 17th of July Silas S. Smith returned to the camp from a visit to Colorado. He had left on the 18th of June, together with his son Stephen, George Urie and Adelbert McGregor,[48] and traveled up the river for some distance. Leaving the river they turned to the left and arrived on the 21st of June at Mancos, Colo. . . . After securing supplies at Alamosa, the brethren returned to the San Juan river, arriving in the camp of the brethren there as stated, on the 17th of July. On the same day some of the boys arrived with some of the cattle from Moan Coppy. The crops on the San Juan had failed and during the absence of Bro. Smith and companions, the brethren had moved down two miles below their first encampment or onto the grounds on which Fort Montezuma afterwards was built. . . . The explorers who came under Silas S. Smith put in no crops that season (1879) except a little corn near the McElmo Wash which burned up for lack of water.

Having arrived safely at the San Juan the company spent the next several weeks exploring the whole river bottom from well above McElmo Wash to Butler Wash. Every piece of possible farmland was discovered and claimed and a few houses were built, some just a mile upstream from the present site of Bluff.[49] Scouts were sent to explore the adjacent country, some going as far north as Blue Mountain, where excellent range land was located and noted carefully for future use. Work crews finished the dam across the San Juan at McElmo Creek and dug ditches to convey water to the parching land, to no avail. This dam, constructed of logs, stones, sticks, and mud was a structure some two hundred feet long which raised the river water three feet.[50] But the irrigation project was doomed to failure; the water level fell off too rapidly as the season advanced. Crops came up, but withered and died for lack of water. This experience might have served as a portent of things to come. Future settlers at Bluff and Montezuma would have a constant struggle with the turbulent San Juan.

In the meantime regular church services were held — Sunday School classes every Sunday morning and Sacrament meetings in the evening.

An interesting and important event was the celebration of the Fourth of July. As the day approached, there was deep concern over the lack of a flag and Elizabeth Harriman assigned herself the role of flag-maker. The blue came from her little girl's dress; for the red, Zechariah B. Decker donated his underwear. Who is to say that this was not the prettiest flag ever to fly over Montezuma? It was at least the first. Pioneer Day was appropriately commemorated on July 24 and the same flag probably saw service again. Non-Mormons and Indians joined in this gala event; the Indians were especially interested in the display of guns and shooting.

On August 2 another memorable event occurred; a baby girl was born to James L. and Elizabeth Davis. The baby, christened Ethel, has the distinction of being the first white child born in the San Juan Mission.

After some two and a half busy months of exploration, house building, etc., the time arrived for the men to return to the settlements. Some of the company had found the new land very pleasing and satisfactory; they would soon return with their families and possessions. Others were going home to stay; the San Juan Valley did not offer what they sought. Harvey Dunton elected to remain at Montezuma with the Harriman and Davis families while the rest of the company made preparations for the homeward trip. By the middle of August plans for the return were set in motion.

Since the long, dry, hazardous trek from Moenkopi had presented such difficulties the explorers decided that route would not be feasible for the larger company, and the decision was therefore reached to return to the settlements by a northern route which might prove more practicable for future use.[51] Preceded by a few scouts and road builders the major part of the company left Montezuma August 19, 1879. Their route lay westward along the north bank of the San Juan to Recapture Creek, then north up that stream to the foot of the Blue Mountains. Passing through the future site of Monticello they continued north, striking the Old Spanish Trail west of the southern end of the LaSal Mountains. After crossing the Colorado River at Moab they followed this trail through Green River, Castle Valley, and down Salina Canyon to Sevier Valley. It was mid-September when they again reached Paragonah, via Bear Valley. They had made a circuit of almost a thousand miles and had built several hundred miles of road through desolate desert country. Most important of all, they had located a site for the San Juan Mission settlement.

Footnotes

1. Most accounts state that there were 26 men, 2 women and several children; one mentions 29 men but does not list them (Charles Redd, "Short Cut to San Juan," 5). In attempting to compile an accurate list from all available sources, I have arrived at 26 men in the original company as it left Paragonah. However, John Butler joined the party at Panguitch, Hamilton Thornton joined somewhere along the way, and Seth Tanner and Thales Haskell were engaged as guides at Moenkopi, making a total of 30 men, 2 women, and 8 children. The complete list, as nearly as I have been able to determine it, is found in Appendix I of this volume.

2. San Juan Stake History. Nielson B. Dalley states that there were six wagons, ten head of loose horses and thirty head of cattle (Dalley's Diary, Appendix II).

3. We are indebted to Dalley's San Juan Exploring Company and his Diary for the identification of some of these officers.

4. E. Lenora Jones, Life of Parley Butt, 3.

5. Lee's Ferry, established in 1872 by John D. Lee at the mouth of Paria River, had by 1879 become a major link in the highway from Utah into Arizona. The ferry provided the only known wagon crossing of the Colorado between Moab and that point. The old buildings are still standing (1957), although some of them are rapidly deteriorating.

6. Dalley's Diary, 2.

7. *Ibid.*

8. In his Diary, Dalley adds a rather unpleasant detail: "Went to gather horses and found one of James Davis's mules down with its hind foot through its halter and had dug both eyes out so we had to kill it."

9. San Juan Stake History.

10. In the accounts Moenkopi is variously spelled as: Moincopy, Moan Coppy, Moen Coppi, Moyincoppy, etc.

11. Dalley specifically mentions rock quarrying in both his accounts of this expedition.

12. This description is from the pen of Albert R. Lyman as cited in San Juan Stake History.

13. Seth Tanner was an old settler in that part of Arizona, probably as well informed as any man regarding the nature of the country to be traversed and the character of the natives inhabiting it. "Tanner's Crossing of the Little Colorado was named for him. This crossing is about a mile above the present bridge at Cameron, Arizona." (Elden Beck, "Mormon Trails to Bluff," *Utah Magazine,* October 1940, 29.)

14. According to Dalley's Diary. Haskell probably did not accompany the expedition all the way to the San Juan.

15. In published accounts, Kumen Jones is usually listed as the main scout, which may very well be true. However, the "Camp Record" mentions Robert Bullock more often than any other.

16. Kumen Jones, Preface to the Writings of Kumen Jones, 3.

17. San Juan Stake History.

18. Titles of these maps are: Arizona: Marsh Pass Sheet, 1901 reprint; Arizona-New Mexico: Canyon De Chelly Sheet, 1901 reprint; Arizona: Kaibab Sheet, 1903 reprint; Arizona: Echo Cliff Sheet, 1901 reprint.

Andrew Jenson, as Assistant Church Historian, did a great deal of work to help clarify the records regarding this expedition and the subsequent Hole-in-the-Rock trek.

19. The author of the account is not known, although part of it is believed to be written by Silas S. Smith. As far as I have been able to determine, this record has never before been *accurately* copied for publication. I find it unique and interesting enough to merit this complete reproduction. I have taken the liberty of placing the headings for each day in italics and have added a few punctuation marks. Needless to say, the original wording has been retained.

20. Travel this day was in an easterly direction up Moenkopi Wash. This is not the route followed by the present highway, which runs northwest from Moenkopi to Tuba City and thence strikes a northeasterly course toward Kayenta. In his Diary, Dalley states that the expedition followed Moenkopi Wash for 20 miles. Upon leaving the wash the company turned to the north and came into line with the route of the present highway. They pioneered this road as far as Kayenta.

Dalley's Diary also adds this interesting bit of information: "Our first night from Moencopi was at the head of a wash or near where young George A. Smith was killed while doing missionary work among the Indians some years ago." See n. 47 below for further reference to the murder of George A. Smith.

21. There are various spellings of the name of this Indian Chief: Pearcon, Peokon, Peogon, Peascon, Pealon, Peaquan, etc. In his Diary, Dalley states that Peokon "claimed he [had] killed Brother [George A.] Smith."

22. This day's travel took the company past the "Elephant's Feet" and on to Cow Spring — "Cattle Water."

23. The location of this camp was probably about the center of Klethla Valley.

24. This camp would be a few miles south and west of Marsh Pass.

25. The party went through Marsh Pass this day and camped in the vicinity of Tsegi. Concerning the presence of Indians and their reception, George Hobbs said: "Occasionally several hundred Indians surrounded the explorers who sometimes would allow these natives to herd their animals at night for which service the brethren would give the Indians a shirt, or some provisions in the morning." (San Juan Stake History.)

26. The company had now arrived at Kayenta, an important Navajo center.

Desert travelers are usually happy to find any water at all and have to become accustomed to its condition. More often than not the supply in the natural rock tanks is replenished only by very infrequent rains and becomes stagnant or is roiled by large flocks of sheep coming daily to drink.

27. Leaving the route of the present highway, the explorers turned to the east, following Laguna Wash. This day's travel took them well beyond Church Rock.

28. This camp must have been in the vicinity of Dennehotso.

29. Jones, *op. cit.*, 4.

30. The advance exploring party had evidently returned to camp with unfavorable reports and now left to try again.

31. Continuing down Laguna Wash, the explorers would now be approaching Chinle Wash.

32. One account states that: "Twenty minutes after the shot was fired the waiting Navajos had the carcass sliced up and on the fire to roast." (Ellen Atkin, The Story of the Hole-in-the-Rock, 2.) The Indians evidently did not stop the feast until the whole animal had been consumed. Commenting on the loss of Captain Smith's horse, Dalley (in his Diary) adds: "But it caused no delay as Brother Smith had a bunch of eight or ten loose horses."

33. Dalley's Diary account is more detailed: "After we had crossed the wash, we traveled down a canyon for a number of miles and we came against solid rock hill. We had to take picks and axes and make notches in the rock so the horses could get footing and then we put eight horses on each outfit it was so steep. We then traveled some five or six miles without a bit of dirt — solid rock, but it was rather smooth, some up and down."

34. Having learned from the Indians that there had formerly been a spring in the area, Smith and his camp dug for and located the water. George Hobbs reported: "On one occasion the company came near famishing for the want of water as they dug wells in vain. By accident one of the brethren struck a vein under a rock and at once a large stream of good water gushed forth. This spring the brethren named Lost Springs because the Indians had previously spoken of the existence of such a spring in that particular neighborhood, but it had been lost for a long time." (San Juan Stake History.)

35. Probably Boundary Butte.

36. This long day's march brought the company to the bluffs only 3 miles from the San Juan.

37. The San Juan was reached at a point usually called Allan's Bottom, about midway between Montezuma and McElmo creeks, but sometimes called Brewer Bottom (Jones, op. cit., 3).

Nielson B. Dalley insists that the company reached the San Juan on May 18; however, it seems to me that Dalley is in error concerning this matter. Although in some places his Diary appears to have been written at the time, close examination will disclose the fact that it was written some time later — how much later is not known. An example of this evidence is contained in his entry for May 19, which contains an account of crossing the San Juan, exploring the region, returning to Moenkopi to escort the rest of the party, etc.: it seems that this account does not allow enough time for all these activities. Regardless of the possible error in time, however, his entry for May 18 is interesting and adds additional detail:

Camped five or six miles from the San Juan River at a small spring. After breakfast George Urie and myself took our fishlines and walked on ahead of the teams and wagons and had a mess of fish for dinner. We pitched our camp on the south side of the river for two days. The same evening we arrived Robert Bullock went up the river about a mile to where Peter Schurtz [sic.] was camped, being an old acquaintance of his and borrowed a canoe which Peter had made to cross the river back and forth, the river being quite high. We wanted to locate a place where we could ford the river to locate a permanent camp for summer. Brother Bullock had some rough experience coming down, not paying much attention to where he was going, the current took him under some fallen trees and skinned his face.

38. Concerning these early settlers the San Juan Stake History has this to say: "In the fall of 1878 two families by the name of Mitchell moved down from Montezuma Valley, in Colorado, and located at the mouth of McElmo Wash, about six miles above Montezuma. Later the same year John Brewer, and Geo. Clay from Colorado settled near the Mitchell ranch. All these were non-Mormon. The Mitchells were real anti-Mormons."

39. June 2 would find the San Juan near its highest point for the season. Fording the stream at this flood stage would be very difficult and hazardous.

40. Peter Shirts had formerly been a pioneer in southern Utah and was acquainted with some of the explorers. He had gone to the San Juan area during 1877, had built a cabin at the mouth of Montezuma Creek, and was employed in hunting, trapping, fishing, and farming. He was the only Mormon living along the lower San Juan when the scouts arrived. He is said to have been much interested in the history of the conquest of Mexico and to have given the name "Montezuma" to the stream on which he chose to settle. (San Juan Stake History.)

41. Advance scouts had evidently explored as far downstream as Butler Wash, having located the future site of Bluff in the course of these explorations.

42. This would be just below the junction of McElmo Creek with the San Juan.

43. Dalley's Diary, 4.

44. Nielson B. Dalley, San Juan Exploring Company, 3, 4. In quoting from this account I have taken the liberty to include one or two periods and capital letters to clarify the text. Any other additions are enclosed in brackets. The original is a penciled manuscript probably written several years after the events had taken place.

45. There is no hint as to the identity of these boys. Notice that Dalley uses a unique system of abbreviation: "S.Lers" for Salt Lakers.

46. James L. Davis, History of the Life of James Davis (Appendix III).

47. Apostle George A. Smith, Sr., was not killed by the Indians; this reference is to his son, George A. Smith, Jr., who was killed by Indians November 2, 1860. Young Smith had gone into the region as one of a small missionary company headed by Jacob Hamblin; the destination was to have been the Hopi village of Oraibi. After the fatal encounter with hostile Navajos the remainder of the party was forced to return to Santa Clara. Jacob Hamblin's fascinating account of this incident, as well as that of his return trip to gather up the victim's bones, is found in Paul Bailey's biography of that famous Mormon missionary to the Indians: *Jacob Hamblin, Buckskin Apostle* (Los Angeles, 1948), 226–242. Hamblin's report to L.D.S. church officials is found in the *Deseret News Weekly,* December 5, 1860. His account does not mention the name of Peoken in connection with the death of Smith, but he does relate a later encounter with his "fiery war chief" in which the latter's tempestuous character is very well demonstrated (Bailey, *op. cit.*, 358–365).

These accounts of Smith's death are very vague as to geographic location; however, the accounts given by members of the San Juan exploring expedition tend to give us the approximate place of this tragic event. In addition to the previously quoted reference by James L. Davis, Nielson B. Dalley, in describing the trek of the explorers from Moenkopi to the San Juan (that is the original group), states: "We camped within two-hundred yards of where young Geo. A. Smith was shot. Thales Haskell helped to show us the road. The old Indian was in camp that night. We went 20 miles to Peoquans ranch the one who shot Geo. A. . ." Since Thales Haskell had been a member of Hamblin's party at the time young Smith was killed, he could supply accurate information about the location and probably identify the murderer. The killing apparently occurred some 20 miles south of Red Lake, not far from Moenkopi Wash; possibly in the Wash or one of the tributaries.

48. Dalley states that John C. Dalton possibly also made this trip. (Exploring Company.)

49. Dalley's account states: "We made our camp about 20 miles above Bluff. Niels. D., James J. Adams & the Decker boy built their [cabins] about 1 mile above Bluff." (Exploring Company, 4.)

50. San Juan Stake History.

51. John Gower and George Urie returned via Moenkopi and Lee's Ferry to pick up their broken wagon (Dalley, Exploring Company, 5).

CHAPTER III

THE ESCALANTE SHORT CUT: BACK DOOR TO SAN JUAN

> It was on the strength of this [Andrew P. Schow and Reuben Collett] report that this route had been chosen.
>
> *— San Juan Stake History*

Silas S. Smith had reported the finding of suitable land for two or three settlements on the San Juan. But how would the colonists get to the proposed sites? The exploring expedition had not found a satisfactory route to the San Juan! The long, hot difficult road they had blazed via Moenkopi and through the Navajo reservation was not deemed practical for the large party of colonists that would soon be on the move. The explorers had experienced great difficulty in locating and developing sufficient water for themselves and the few cattle and horses they had taken with them; to take a large company of more than two hundred people, with eighty or more wagons and hundreds of horses and cattle, was unthinkable. Besides the difficulties offered by nature, there were also the Indians. Although not downright hostile, they had shown themselves to be anything but friendly to the idea of this migration through their grazing lands. Everything considered, the southern route was out of the question.

The northern route, however, would have been practical; and in view of their experiences on the Hole-in-the-Rock road, expedition leaders probably should have decided to go that way. By retracing their steps over the Old Spanish Trail, the company could have arrived at the site of Moab on a fairly well established trail. South of Moab the recently returned explorers had pioneered a road all the way to the San Juan. Wagons could easily have been taken that way again. But the distance was considered too great, necessitating a trek of some four hundred fifty miles to get to a point only two hundred miles almost due east.

As a result there was a general demand for a short cut to the San Juan. Surely a wagon road could be blazed nearly straight through, and hundreds of miles and many weeks of unnecessary labor could be avoided. The settlers wanted to get to their new homes before the dead of winter; they *must* be there before spring in order to prepare for the season's planting. The farthest flung Mormon settlement east of Iron County — and almost in a direct line between Parowan and the site of Montezuma — was the frontier town of Escalante, established in Potato Valley just a few years earlier (1875–76), where several families now lived. Perhaps a new road could be cut by way of this remote outpost.

The region southeast of Escalante was not entirely unknown to those who lived in that isolated little town. Cattlemen had been operating in the area for several years and some of them were ranging their cattle southward toward the Colorado. Prospectors had also examined the region, but found little encouragement in their quest for gold. But neither cattlemen nor miners were particularly interested in wagon roads, and although they had ridden horseback over the whole country, they had not done so with the idea of locating wagon routes. Furthermore, the deep, almost perpendicular walls of the Colorado River gorge effectively blocked further penetration in that direction. Absolutely no thought had been given to building a wagon road through that country — certainly not across the river and into the maze of sandstone buttes and box canyons beyond. Yet wagons of the San Juan Mission would soon be rolling through.

Just why the mission leaders decided on the Escalante "short cut" through the Hole-in-the-Rock has never been fully explained. That the new route was chosen as a result of some exploration and favorable reports by Charles Hall, Andrew P. Schow, and Reuben Collett of Escalante is well known and definitely established, but the exact nature of those explorations and reports has become confused and somewhat controversial during the passing years. There are two basic theories regarding this problem: the first centers attention on Hall's explorations; the second on the reconnaissance of Schow and Collett. The latter two men are known to have been working together in this pioneer undertaking, while Hall is usually depicted as having been exploring alone. It is very likely that the three were engaged in the enterprise together and that the confusion has resulted because of inadequate records and faulty reporting through the years.

Charles Hall was born in Maine, where he spent his youth and early manhood. During that time he became a skilled cooper and also acquired considerable experience as fisherman, boatbuilder, brickmaker and carpenter. Shortly after his migration to Utah he was named one of the colonists selected by the church to establish the settlement of Parowan, where he lived from 1851–1876. That year a few hardy pioneers moved into Potato Valley to found the village of Escalante; Hall was among them. Equipped with tools of his trade this skilled craftsman was a major asset to the new outpost, where he not only helped with the construction of houses, but soon found employment supplying barrels for the budding sorghum industry. In 1879 when it became known that the leaders of the San Juan Mission were desirous of finding a short cut to the Four Corners area and that such a route would necessitate the crossing of the Colorado River, it was quite natural that Hall with his knowledge of boats should have been selected among those who were to conduct preliminary explorations in search of such a route.

Indeed most accounts, both published and unpublished, give Hall the sole credit and/or blame for having discovered the Hole-in-the-Rock and for having reported favorably to church authorities regarding the feasibility of building a road through that rough country.[1] It seems that most of the actual members of the Hole-in-the-Rock expedition who wrote anything at all about the subject, and also other persons who have written after having interviewed some of the original pioneers, emphasize Hall's role in this respect. In view of the many accounts that stress his part in those original explorations it must be concluded that he did conduct a reconnaissance and did make a report. However, the date of his trip, just where he went, what he saw, the exact nature of the report he made, remain obscure.

How well acquainted with the area Hall was before making his exploration is not known. However, as one of the early settlers of Escalante he had probably gained considerable firsthand information concerning the desert land to the southeast. At any rate, according to the accounts he was authorized by George A. Smith in behalf of the church to scout the country for the San Juan Mission.[2] Hall seems to have gone southeastward as "directed" along the base of the straight cliffs of Fifty-mile Mountain[3] to the brink of the Colorado River gorge. Exploring along the rim of Glen Canyon he came to that narrow cleft in the canyon wall soon to become famous as the Hole-in-the-Rock, peeked down through the slit to the river almost two thousand feet below, observed the apparently slow river current (there were no rapids visible), glanced eastward toward the barren sandstone knobs that mark the head of Cottonwood Canyon and hurried back to Escalante with this report: "It would be something of a problem to get wagons down to the river, but once down and across, it would be a simple matter to move on to the San Juan, about sixty miles away."[4]

Most narratives of the San Juan colonization agree in giving Hall credit for having discovered the Hole-in-the-Rock and for deciding that wagons could be taken that way, and many have been very critical of his favorable report in view of the hasty and inadequate exploration he had completed. The supposed fact that his wife was expecting a baby is sometimes cited in explanation of his hurried return to Escalante; but this story is not based on fact.[5] Perhaps after examining the Hole-in-the-Rock he should have declared it too difficult for a road. But we must remember that when the main body of pioneers eventually reached the "Hole" they did not consider *it* an impassable barrier. Nowhere in the records do I find any real doubt expressed that a road could be blasted down through that cleft in the canyon wall. *It was the country to the east, beyond the river, that seemed too rugged!* Hall's report would have been of little value there. Although he had not been on the eastern side of the stream, he had had an excellent view of the country from the canyon rim above the Hole-in-the-Rock, and from that observation point it looked passable.

Directly across from the Hole the small open valley of Cottonwood Creek extends four or five miles almost straight away toward the east. From the river rim the valley doesn't appear too rough for wagons; and indeed it is not. This section eventually proved to be one of the few pleasant sections of the whole undertaking. Today a hike up Cottonwood Creek is one of the easiest and most enjoyable of the whole road, after one gets over to the Cottonwood to begin such a hike. Hall might easily have reasoned that once across the river the going would be quite easy for at least a few miles. Surely there would be some way to get up and over those sandstone buttes at the head of the small open canyon lying clearly in view. This as we shall see, proved to be a grave mistake. But almost anyone might have made the same error. It is easy to criticize today, with three quarters of a century of hindsight to help draw conclusions.

In spite of the frequency with which a report of Hall's reconnaissance is repeated in the various accounts of the Hole-in-the-Rock trek, rather extensive study and research have led me to the conclusion that he was not the person most responsible for directing the San Juan pioneers to take the supposed short cut. Indeed Andrew P. Schow and Reuben Collett seem to have been much more responsible than he for the choice of that route, if church and family records have any validity. These two men had made a much more thorough exploration than had Hall before the San Juan expedition got under way. Exactly when they conducted their reconnaissance is not known, but it was certainly during the summer or early fall of 1879. A few basic facts regarding their exploring activities might now be examined.

According to Collett family records Bp. Schow and Reuben Collett had been specifically called by church authorities to explore the country southeast of Escalante for the expressed purpose of locating a route to the San Juan — the same claim others have made for Charles Hall. Furthermore, "Bishop Andrew P. Schow, Reuben Collett and Silas S. Smith were very close friends. They were all veteran scouts."[6] In view of this friendship, it seems very likely that Smith had contacted these men, had kept them appraised of the proposed expedition to the San Juan and encouraged them to examine the region southeast of Escalante for a possible route. Their exploration was likely to be undertaken while Smith was leading the exploring expedition by way of Lee's Ferry, Moenkopi, and the Navajo reservation. Such instructions from Smith might very well be considered as "church authorization" since he had been appointed to head the whole San Juan Mission. One searches in vain for any other record of such a "call" — either for Hall or the two men under study here.

Melvina Duke Collett, long active in assembling Collett family history, makes the following contribution regarding this matter:[7]

It has been a definite idea [in the Collett family] that Schow and Collett had been asked by Church authorities to explore all the country pertaining to the future roadway to the San Juan Valley. They explored for a great length of time, from early spring and on through the summer, up and down the Colorado Canyon walls for a distance of 75 miles south and for many miles up stream. They covered all the vicinity surrounding the place where the Hole-in-the-Rock is now located. When the high water went down, then the effort was made to cross the river. They were trying to find the best descent to the river. Definite evidence of their effort is shown. Silas S. Smith had agreed to their making these efforts.

This record definitely claims for Collett and Schow the honor of having discovered the Hole-in-the-Rock; no mention is made of Charles Hall.

Schow and Collett had been among the early settlers of Escalante and had helped develop that outpost into a thriving community. Schow became first bishop of the new town and as such had occasion to become well acquainted with the welfare of his small flock by scouting for better range land, new sources of water, timber, and farmland. Having had previous experience as a lawman, Collett was appointed as constable, a position which necessitated his gaining a knowledge of the settlers, cattlemen, and prospectors of the area.[8]

During his years as constable, farmer, cattleman, and store keeper, Collett had gained considerable knowledge of the surrounding country by the time of the San Juan Mission call. He had, in fact, headed several exploring trips into the Colorado River country and had possibly explored the west rim of Glen Canyon for several miles, including that portion where the Hole-in-the-Rock is located.[9] Since Collett and Schow were "good friends" of Silas S. Smith he doubtless knew of their activities in the Escalante region. It was quite natural, therefore, that Collett and his bishop should have been selected to make a more thorough reconnaissance to determine whether or not wagons could reach the San Juan that way.

Sometime during the summer of 1879 these two men took "an improvised two-wheeled cart" carrying a wagon box boat all the way to the canyon rim — this being the first wheeled vehicle to pass that way. After examining the narrow notch at Hole-in-the-Rock, they continued upstream a couple of miles, seeking a possible approach to the river below. There are two original accounts of this exploration: the one compiled by Mrs. Collett; the other (taken from interviews with original Hole-in-the-Rock participants such as Kumen Jones and George B. Hobbs) is located in the files of the L.D.S. Church Historian's Library as part of the San Juan Stake History. The church account is quoted here; it is brief but significant.

These two brethren [Collett and Schow], after traveling up the river about two miles from the Hole-in-the-Rock, had reached a point near the place where Escalante Creek empties into the Colorado river. There they took this wagon box (which measured about 7 ft. in length, 3 ft. in width and about one foot in depth) off the running gears and slid it over the face of the rock to the levels below — first to a narrow bench where there was considerable grass and then over another precipice to the river. They had succeeded in crossing the river in their box and from the other side, by climbing a short distance, they could see in the distance the San Juan River. The two brethren then recrossed the river, and the report of their explorations and the crossing of the Colorado was to the effect that a good road could be made by way of the Escalante desert to the Colorado river, and thence through the country beyond to the San Juan River. *On the strength of this report it was that this route had been chosen.*[10]

The Collett family account is substantially the same, but adds an additional detail or two, especially regarding the country beyond the Colorado.[11]

These meager descriptions leave one wondering just how far eastward the two men explored. In order to have reached a point from which the actual waters of the San Juan could have been seen they would have had to hike much farther than a "short distance." Having been in that region a few times, it is my conclusion that they reached a point from which they could see the San Juan River gorge, but not the water.[12] They did probably reach Cottonwood Creek and no doubt ascended that stream two or three miles. However, they evidently did not go beyond the bald sandstone cliffs at the head of that canyon — else their report must surely have been a negative one.

But they made a favorable report and carried it in person to Parowan and other Iron County settlements.[13] At Parowan they met the San Juan missionaries preparing for the trek. Members of the exploring expedition, recently returned, had spread accounts of the almost endless desert miles through the Navajo country, hostile Indians, shortage of water, miles of drifting sand, deep straight-walled gulches and canyons, limited grazing for livestock, and other hardships encountered. Silas S. Smith, reporting the activities of the explorers at a session of the Parowan Stake conference September 28, 1879, advised the company not to attempt the southern route, "saying that it was almost impossible."[14] Since the northern route was deemed much too long to be practical, news of a possible short cut to the San Juan by way of Escalante and Hole-in-the-Rock found the company in a very receptive mood, ready and willing to try the new route. Smith, eager as anyone else to avoid the long southern or northern haul, seems to have accepted the Schow-Collett report without reservation and decided to take (or send) his company to the San Juan via Escalante. Let us repeat, by way of emphasis, that according to L.D.S. Church records: "It was on the strength of this [the Schow-Collett] report that this route had been chosen." By taking their wheeled vehicle all the way to the canyon rim, lowering a "boat" into the water, actually crossing the river and exploring briefly in the country to the east, then making a favorable report, they seem to have been more responsible than Charles Hall for having pointed out the way for the pioneers of the San Juan Mission. They had actually blazed the trail!

This narration is in no way an attempt to detract from the contributions of Charles Hall or to upset long-standing tradition. It is merely an honest attempt to present an accurate, historical account of this whole episode. At the time of the incidents here portrayed, Hall was employed at least part time as a cooper to supply barrels for Reuben Collett's sorghum plant. He also built a small boat to be used by Schow, Collett and members of the Hole-in-the-Rock party for further exploration of the Colorado River. It was he who later engineered and directed the construction of a ferry to transport the wagons across the stream. Yet there seems to be no tradition or historical information in the Hall family to the effect that he had been directed by the church to explore the country in question for the purpose of locating a wagon road — in spite of the numerous accounts which make that claim for him. What he was "called" to do, according to his own family records, was to build a ferry or raft to be used in the river crossing.[15] This task he performed in a most admirable way as we shall see in a future chapter. All three of these Escalante trail blazers would provide additional guide service and material aid as the Hole-in-the-Rock expedition eventually pushed into the desert.

It may seem incredible that church leaders would send a large company of more than two hundred men, women, and children to build a road through this rugged and unknown region on the strength of such inadequate exploration. But at least sixty-five miles had been fairly well explored and found passable, and it was believed that the Colorado could be reached via the Hole-in-the-Rock and either ferried or forded. Once that major obstacle had been overcome, could there possibly be anything worse ahead — anything that could be called an effective obstruction to pioneer road builders? The explorers had found no such barrier!

The Escalante "short cut" would soon prove to be anything but short. A trip that was expected to take six weeks would stretch out into almost as many months. In fact, either of the rejected routes (north via Salina Canyon, Green River and Moab, or south via Lee's ferry, Moenkopi and the Navajo reservation) would have been much shorter in time and immensely shorter in terms of hard work and energy expended under most trying circumstances. By either of these "front door" approaches, the expedition could have arrived at its destination — Montezuma or Bluff — in the same amount of time it actually took to reach the rim of the Colorado River gorge at Hole-in-the-Rock, with the major obstacles of road building still before them. Perhaps this "back door" to the San Juan should have been left closed, as suggested by Morgan Amasa Barton.[16] But then we would have no story! And who is to say that any other course would have actually been a better one in the long run, in spite of our opinions today?

FOOTNOTES

1. In "General Move to the San Juan Mission," Appendix V this volume, Kumen Jones states that Charles Hall *and* Bp. Schow were sent to make this original reconnaissance. A few writers have followed this lead, but most have failed to recognize the role of Schow (and Collett) in this respect.

2. Not all accounts mention Apostle George A. Smith, but many of them do. Of course some of these accounts are merely copied from earlier ones. L.D.S. church records throw no light on this subject.

3. Fifty-mile Mountain extends from about twenty miles south of Escalante to the Colorado River — approximately fifty miles to the southeast. Its "straight cliffs" mark the eastern wall of the Kaiparowits Plateau.

4. Charles Redd, "Short Cut to San Juan," *Brand Book*, Denver, 1950, 7.

5. *Ibid.* Hall family records disprove this assertion.

6. Melvina Duke Collett, The San Juan Mission, 1.

7. *Ibid.*, 2.

8. Several years earlier, while living in Cache Valley and after having lost an arm in a threshing machine accident, Collett had been deputized to arrest an outlaw. He gained a reputation by apprehending the criminal, relieving him of his two guns and marching the subdued man to the local jail. With this sort of background it is not surprising to find Collett acting as constable in the recently established village of Escalante. And he had work to do as peace officer in his newly selected home site.

As already stated, the country southeast of Escalante (and especially down along the Escalante River) had been found to be good range land and was soon occupied by various cattlemen. Two of these, Washington Phipps and a Mr. Boyington, had developed rather large spreads there, but eventually got into a quarrel over grazing and water rights. The friction grew steadily worse, finally resulting in the murder of Phipps at the hand of Boyington, November 30, 1878. This meant work for Constable Collett, who played a major role in securing the killer for trial.

9. Collett, *op. cit.*, 2.

10. Italics supplied.

11. After tracing the journey to the river's edge, this account continues:
They removed the seat from the box, and using two boards as paddles, Schow and Collett finally succeeded in crossing the river in their wagon box. After climbing the mountains a short distance on the east side of the Colorado, the San Juan River could be seen. The country, being rugged on the San Juan side, made it necessary to blaze a trail by marking anything that would retain a mark. By using this precaution, they easily found their way back to the Colorado and safely to camp.

12. On the other hand, they may have traveled southward instead of eastward after crossing the Colorado. In that case they could have reached the rim of the San Juan River gorge two or three miles above its junction with the Colorado. But certainly they would have found no route for a wagon road there! Of course, this is all speculation; it is not even known how much time these men spent in the region.

13. Collett, *op. cit.*, 3. This account adds: "Pres. Smith took Reuben to Cedar City with him to tell the Saints about the condition of the road and country."

14. Parowan Stake Historical Record No. 22125, 189.

15. Letter from Lillie Hall Denny, February 1955. See also Chapter VIII, this work.

16. Morgan Amasa Barton, Back Door to San Juan.

CHAPTER IV

THE TREK BEGINS

> . . . with boundless faith in God, the emigrants moved forward
> in fine enthusiasm and splendid form.
>
> *— Anonymous*

During the summer of 1879, while the exploring expedition was accomplishing the task of locating a desirable site for a settlement, those planning to move were busily engaged in making necessary preparations for the migration. Since this was expected to be a permanent move for most of the missionaries, adequate preparations involved considerable work and planning. Homes and farms, much machinery, furniture, and other bulky items must be sold or otherwise disposed of. The trip would require good wagons and harnesses, with adequate horses and oxen to pull the heavy loads. Riding horses, saddles and other gear must be in top condition.

Herds of cattle and horses that were to be taken along with the expedition were normally grazed on the various ranges of southern Utah and must be located and rounded up in preparation for the migration. This alone was a major undertaking. George W. Decker and many other young men spent most of the summer in this capacity. Livestock not located by the time the expedition got under way would have to be left behind.

Clothing, cooking gear, food supplies, tents, and innumerable items associated with a large migration must all be provided for before the trek could begin. The hustle and bustle of these activities as the summer advanced and the time for the move approached must indeed have been something to behold. All these necessary arrangements had been pretty well completed by the middle of October and the migration could get under way. As we have already noted, Reuben Collett, and Andrew P. Schow arrived at Parowan and the other settlements right at this time, bearing the welcome tidings that a short cut by way of Potato Valley and the desert southeast of Escalante had been located. There was no need for longer delay; the San Juan missionaries were instructed to begin the trek.

There was no intention that the expedition should travel as one large body on the first leg of the journey. In fact, that would have been very inconvenient or even impossible since settlers were coming from many different parts of Utah and would not all reach Escalante at the same time or over the same route. Not all would be ready to start at any specified date. Silas S. Smith was not ready to start as soon as some outfits from Cedar City, Parowan and other points. Platte D. Lyman was living at Oak City (then known as Oak Creek) in Millard County and would arrive at Escalante by an almost entirely different route. So instructions were sent out for the colonists to get under way — to travel in small groups if necessary; the general rendezvous point would be somewhere in the desert beyond Escalante. As it turned out, Forty-mile Spring became that place of general meeting, not because of previous planning but because the rugged, unexplored country to the south presented obstacles too great for individual or small group action. But the emigrants could not know these things in advance. The immediate objective was to get the wagons rolling. The season was rapidly advancing; it was already October and the new home site — Montezuma on the San Juan — should be reached before the severest winter weather set in.

Sufficient provisions for a six weeks trek, in addition to seed grain and breeding stock, were to be taken by each family. Some of them loaded in supplies to last twice that long.

All livestock, wagons, food, grains and other necessaries were carefully itemized and approved by the authorities; most of the wagons and harnesses were new and the horses young and strong. Nearly every wagon carried at least one woman, and many of them carried one or more small children, also numbers of chickens were stowed away in the wagons.[1]

Of course these hardy pioneers could not know that this "six weeks" trek would stretch out into as many laborious months before the travel weary train would reach the site of Bluff, during the first week of April, 1880.

Definite and detailed information is almost completely lacking concerning the organization, beginning, and early phases of the Hole-in-the-Rock expedition. It seems that later experiences at the "Hole" and in the rugged country east of the Colorado — Cottonwood Hill, the Chute, Slick Rocks, Clay Hill Pass, San Juan Hill — left such an indelible impression on the minds of the participants that the earlier part of the trek (from Cedar City, Parowan, Paragonah, and other settlements to Forty-mile Spring by way of Escalante) seemed quite commonplace and unimportant by comparison. Furthermore, since there was no "complete" Hole-in-the-Rock expedition during this early portion of the migration, an account of any one segment would hardly be considered as the account of the whole expedition.

Jens Nielson of Cedar City, more or less by common consent assumed leadership of a large group of approximately twenty-five wagons from Cedar and vicinity, and the first major contingent of the Hole-in-the-Rock expedition got under way October 22, 1879. This Cedar City group soon merged with contingents from Parowan and Paragonah, and the combined band, still under the direction of Nielson, became the advance guard, and was no doubt the largest single group to push over the rim of the Great Basin to Escalante and into the desert southeast of that frontier hamlet and on to Forty-mile Spring. Smaller groups continued to struggle over the mountain and into Escalante for a couple of months or more, but most of them overtook the main vanguard at the Forty-mile Spring by the latter part of November.

The route to Escalante, although not well known by many, if any, members of this company, was over a well-established wagon road. It differed somewhat from the present highway in spots, but paralleled it in many places. A short distance north of Paragonah (called Red Creek in some of the early accounts) the road turned eastward up Little Creek to Bear Valley instead of following Bone Hollow as does present Highway 20. Adequate grazing and a reasonably good road made the going relatively easy, so the expedition got off to an excellent start. As higher elevations were reached, early morning ice was found on water buckets and along the edge of streams, but no one gave it a second thought. Passing through Bear Valley, the road took the settlers into Sevier Valley at a point known as Orton's (sometimes called LeFevere's) approximately nine miles north of Panguitch. At the beginning on good roads this great jointed train of white tops, with a drove of cattle for a caboose, is said to have been almost two miles long.[2] It must have been an impressive sight.

Since this early stretch of the route held little danger from Indians or other sources, the expedition had a chance to organize and develop a camp routine. Under Nielson's direction the expedition was formally organized at Holyoak Spring in Bear Valley. Little is known about the details of this organization; however, since most of the emigrants had crossed the plains to Utah in wagon or handcart companies, this new wagon train would have been organized on a similar basis, with definite leaders appointed and every person made responsible for the completion of specific tasks. Designated scouts were always out in front to explore the country, examine the road, prepare for road work where needed, locate favorable camp sites, springs, and grazing areas. Others were placed in charge of the livestock; still others were commissioned to provide firewood and help organize the camps.

Campfire meetings were also well planned and conducted, with instrumental as well as vocal music, readings, speeches, and gospel sermons. Musical and other talent no doubt emerged during this early part of the trek. Singing, violin, accordion, trumpet, and jew's harp are all mentioned as part of the music furnished. Dancing was thoroughly enjoyed by most members. At least three violins were in the company: Samuel Cox, Charles E. Walton, and Peter A. Mortensen each had one. These men furnished music for the dances where level ground or smooth rocks afforded facilities for such recreation. Samuel Cox had his trumpet along and Charles Walton had brought a cornet. These horns were used not only for musical selections but also to call the camp together for morning and evening prayers and to signal the beginning of the day's march. The ability to provide necessary recreation was to prove an important function as the pioneers prayed, sang, and blasted their way to the San Juan.

The San Juan Mission had been thoroughly publicized; it was the most important event in southern Utah that season. There is reason to believe that most of those not going on the trek turned out to bid the travelers God's speed and good luck in their important undertaking. Likewise, when the company arrived at Panguitch a lively celebration was held in its honor. This afforded a chance to display the fine wagons, new harnesses, and excellent teams of horses of this magnificent train. Also, and more important, the stop at Panguitch afforded opportunity to obtain additional equipment found lacking on the first leg of the journey.

Pleasant as the Panguitch reception was, not much time could be lost and "with boundless faith in God, the emigrants moved forward in fine enthusiasm and splendid form."[3] A few miles south of Panguitch the road turned eastward, taking the colonists up Red Canyon, in many places paralleling present Utah State Highway 12. These pioneers must have noticed the fantastic formations and beautiful colors found in such profusion in Red Canyon, but as far as I have been able to determine, they failed to mention this scenery in any of their writings. Near the site of present Bryce Canyon Junction the company turned to the left, following the wagon road into the valley of the east fork of Sevier River and approximating the route of present Highway 22. At or near the site of Widtsoe a brief stop was made at the Riddle Ranch.[4] From this point the expedition turned east, following Sweetwater Canyon toward the base of Escalante Mountain.

Travel was relatively easy for the first few miles, or to the location of Sweetwater Spring situated some three and a half miles below the summit. However, beyond the spring the road was steep and rough all the way to the top and for an equal distance down the other side. Snow blanketed the ground; travel was difficult. Later in life Henry John Holyoak remembered: "While crossing the mountain snow fell until it was up to the axles of the wagons. I drove the loose stock, and got my feet frozen. While crossing the divide my mother drove one of the wagons, with a team of horses, while my father drove the wagon drawn by an ox team."[5] Here was the first real test of equipment and nerves.

If previously there had been any tendency to regard the enterprise lightly, this steep, rough climb, with several breakdowns and near tipovers, acted as a sobering agent; it indicated that much difficult work lay ahead. From the summit the trekkers had a seventy-five mile view ahead — to the southeast along the face of Fifty-mile Mountain all the way to the Colorado, and even beyond. And what they saw was not heartening. Although it was a beautiful and awe-inspiring sight, the country appeared enormously rugged to that band of pioneer road builders — who were not there to take pictures and admire the scenery.

Once over the summit, a relatively easy twenty miles brought the company into the sprawling little hamlet of Escalante. Here was literally the last chance to obtain fresh supplies of flour, potatoes, sorghum, and other necessities, to repair worn equipment, and to trade jaded expedition teams for better stock. Some of the colonists complained that the local citizens took unfair advantage of the situation by jacking up the prices as the supply of desirable commodities became scarce. In his autobiography Samuel Rowley states: "The People of Escalante, on hearing of our coming, held a convention and raised the prices of everything we would be likely to need, almost double what it was before."[6] The biographer of Parley Butt asserts that: "Word had come [that] they [the emigrants] could buy provisions far below the going prices at Escalante, but the Escalante people raised their prices so the money only went one-fourth as far as expected."[7]

Descendants of those early residents of Escalante resent these claims that their forebears took undue advantage of the Hole-in-the-Rock pioneers. At least one chronicler points out that the Escalante people were more than generous, giving freely of goods, time, and hard work to insure the success of the expedition.[8] Although the emigrants couldn't realize it at the time, they would soon be very thankful for every pound of foodstuff obtained, regardless of price, and would keep pack and wagon outfits busy obtaining more supplies from this last frontier settlement as the company pushed on toward the Colorado.

Among the San Juan missionaries were some expectant mothers who began the trek confidently believing that the journey would be completed and that they would be comfortably situated in their new homes long before the time when the babies were expected. However, three babies were born before the company reached the site of Bluff. Although several published accounts of the trek mention this fact, none of them indentifies more than one of the infants. Careful research and inquiry have produced details regarding the arrival of the second and third of these (Lena Deseret Decker and John Rio Larson), accounts of which are contained in later chapters of the present work.[9] But there is still very little known concerning the first birth, not even the date or identity of the parents or child. Only this much is known: The first baby of the expedition was born at Escalante. The child was either stillborn or died shortly after birth; it is probable that it was a stillbirth. The baby was likely prematurely born, for no woman would have started on that kind of journey expecting to give birth to a baby within two or three weeks from the time of leaving home. A premature birth would lessen the baby's chances of survival. Had it been alive there would probably have been a christening and the child would have been identified, and had it lived any appreciable length of time there would also have been a funeral, with records of the event. A stillborn infant would not be counted as a death, and most writers have stressed the fact that no death occurred among expedition personnel en route. Burial was probably in the Escalante cemetery, where some unmarked baby graves are found today.

The account of this incident comes through the family of Mary Alice Barker Shurtz who was living in Escalante at the time of the Hole-in-the-Rock trek and also expecting a baby. Mrs. Shurtz remembered the incident well because she had not been able to prepare a layette and was becoming concerned about the matter. Upon hearing of the birth and loss of the baby to a member of the wagon train, she immediately contacted the mother and traded "some butter, eggs, bacon and other things" for a supply of baby clothes.[10]

Having neither intention nor desire to spend any more time than was absolutely necessary at Escalante, the company plunged into the desert to the southeast. For a few miles, and possibly as far as Forty-mile Spring, the trail was well broken, for cattlemen had been using that range during the past several years. How far a wagon road extended into the area is not known; probably no farther than Ten-mile Spring. However, as noted in the previous chapter, a two-wheeled cart driven by Andrew P. Schow and Reuben Collett had carried a wagon-box boat all the way to the Colorado. Regardless, however, of how far wagons had gone before, the trail was found to be completely inadequate for this large caravan, and considerable road work was necessary beyond Ten-mile Spring.[11]

From Escalante the road struck across the relatively flat region immediately south of town and dropped into Harris Wash (or False Creek). Following down this sand-swept wash the pioneers arrived at the first major watering place, Ten-mile Spring. George W. Decker's account states that the water in Harris Wash was high but the feed scarce. However, when the Lyman party arrived there a few days later, they found insufficient water for their animals. More often than not, the spring was, and still is, more of a name than a reality, being merely a seepage where limited water may be obtained for man and beast. But this was only a temporary camp site and the expedition pushed on to the southeast.

Road conditions through this part of the desert varied from good hard surface to loose drifting sand; from fairly level plain to steep-walled gulches and canyons. There is no written evidence that any of these pioneers saw the spectacular little valley now known as the "Devil's Garden," which is located approximately seventeen miles south of Escalante and about half a mile west of the old road. The course was approximately parallel to the Straight Cliffs that mark the east side of Kaiparowits Plateau; sometimes the wagons rolled almost in the shadows of the cliffs as the winding road took them westward to the base of the mountains in search of sites where gulches could be headed or crossed. Water and forage continued to be the primary problems. Fortunately, however, springs or seepages were located in the major gulches or washes, and these were conveniently placed about ten miles apart — a good day's wagon travel.

The second temporary camp was at Twenty-mile Spring, located in what is now known as Collett Wash. Although scarce, water could be found by digging in the sand, and enough was obtained to supply meager quantities for livestock as well as for the personnel. Approximately another ten miles to the south the company wheeled into Coyote Wash (sometimes called the Coyote Holes), where water was also obtained by digging. The expedition had now penetrated some thirty miles into the desert southeast of Escalante. The next stop — and first major camp site and general point of rendezvous — was Forty-mile Spring. Wagons began assembling at that spot about the middle of November.

The account that most nearly approximates what might be called original source material covering this early phase of the trek, from Parowan to Forty-mile, is that compiled by Margaret Nielson and based primarily on information supplied by George W. Decker, some of it apparently written by him. Because this narrative supplies some interesting details and episodes not recounted elsewhere, it is partially quoted here:

Oct. 22, 1879. The Cedar City contingent of the San Juan Mission called by John Taylor, Pres. of the Mormon Church to locate in Southern Utah, to curry favor and win the friendship of the Indians, mostly Navajos. The Cedar City contingent was the first to move, started the trek Oct. 22, 1879. They moved 12 miles that day and camped at Summit Fields. On the 23rd they moved on to Paragonah fields, and just missed mixing with the Parowan contingent as they left Parowan the same time of day that Cedar City contingent was gathering their stock at Summit Fields. The Cedar City contingent camped at Paragonah and Parowan camped 1½ miles up Little Creek Canyon. On the 24th of Oct., Parowan moved to the head of Little Creek Canyon and Cedar City contingent caught up with them that night at sunset. Geo. Decker was left at Parowan to bring on 150 head of horses that they didn't dare risk in the canyon. They expected him to catch up with them when the Cedar City contingent did, but he was detained and din't catch up until just as the day was breaking in the east. He was riding and driving horses at a brisk speed, when the horses began to call and was answered by the camp horses. The men in camp came running with guns to head him off, thinking Indians had come. The morning was just breaking over the eastern horizon as these Mormon missionaries stood with rifles ready to shoot. They yelled, "Halt, or we shoot." They were answered by Mr. Geo. Decker, "You . . . fools, I am just bringing up your loose horses . . . it's George! Quiet down!"

Oct. 25, 1879. Got fried bacon and potatoes and moved over into upper Bear Valley and spent two days and three nights in this beautiful valley getting our drinking water from Holyoak Springs, which we thought was the best water in the world. At this place, Jens Nielson, Danishman, recognized as leading Elder, proceeded to organize his flock and lay down some simple regulations for the conduct of his charges, the people of the San Juan mission. . . .

Oct. 28, 1879. Moved to the head of Bear Valley creek just out of Bear Valley.

Oct. 29, 1879. Moved to Beaver Dam in Bear Valley canyon.

Oct. 30, 1879. Moved to the Lefevere Ranch mouth of Bear Creek canyon.

Oct. 31, 1879. Moved to the south up Sevier Valley to Big Sandy town.

Nov. 1, 1879. Moved through Panguitch to Flour Mill, 3 miles east of town.

Nov. 2, 1879. Foraged stock in Panguitch fields.

Nov. 3, 1879. Moved up river past Butler Ranch into Red Canyon.

Nov. 4, 1879. Moved through Red Canyon to west edge of East Fork where they had plenty of grass and wood.

Nov. 5, 1879. Moved north on west side of East Fork to Riddle Ranch.

Nov. 7, 1879. On to Sweetwater.

Nov. 9, 1879. Into Escalante Field. . . .

Nov. 12, 1879. Moved 5 miles south of Escalante Town.

Nov. 13, 1879. Moved to 10 Miles Gulch, feed scarce, water up. . . .

Nov. 15, 1879. Up to 20 mile Gulch, feed good, water bad. We tarried here a few days looking over the route farther down toward 40 mile Gulch. From here we moved in sections. The loose stock tender had to keep loose stock three miles ahead of the caravan, and laid out the route clear to Fifty mile.

Nov. 16, 1879. A few of the wagons moved out toward 30 Mile Hollow.

Nov. 17–20, 1879. Camps assembled around 20 miles and the 30 miles Hollows. Work out road toward 50 Mile Point.

Nov. 21–24, 1879. Camping at above center sending men out all the time to explore route and locate roads by which we might reach the banks of the Colorado.

Nov. 30, 1879. Road was opened to Coyote Wash a little each day. Some worked road. Leaders reached 40 Mile Hollow.

It is obvious that this account supplies some interesting details, especially regarding the more or less daily movements of the company.

The accuracy of the dates is subject to question. There is little doubt about the starting date, but serious question regarding the progress of the camp between Bear Valley and Forty-mile Spring, where (according to this account) leaders of the expedition first arrived on November 30. These dates are in conflict with the daily journal entries of Platte D. Lyman, who arrived at the Forty-mile camp on November 27 and found the main body of the expedition already there.[12] In fact they had apparently been camped there at that spot for several days, long enough to allow four men sufficient time to reach the Colorado and cross that stream for a six-day exploration of the country to the east. These scouts had already returned when Lyman arrived on November 27. Although it is possible that these four scouts may have left the expedition before the vanguard arrived at Forty-mile Spring, most accounts seem to be in agreement that this reconnaissance was conducted after the camp had been established at that point.[13]

Regardless of some discrepancies in the various records we can say that probably the advance company established a major camp at Forty-mile Spring about the middle of November, almost a month after having left the settlements. Nearly four weeks of the expected six-weeks' trek had slipped away, and the major obstacles still lay ahead.

In the meantime other units of the expedition were wheeling their way toward Forty-mile Spring. Platte D. Lyman and a small party had left Oak City on October 20 and as we have noted, arrived at the Forty-mile camp November 27, just a few days after the advance company had reached that point. Lyman's journal charts the daily progress of his contingent and supplies many details regarding road conditions, water supply, forage, etc. His company had followed a route from Oak City south about twelve miles and then east to Scipio, thence south and east, following the approximate route of Utah State Highway 63 to a point just south of Salina. From here they turned south through Sevier Valley, Monroe, Marysvale and Junction to the East Fork of Sevier River. Following the East Fork up past the present sites of Kingston and Antimony, the contingent arrived in Sweetwater Canyon November 3. From this point they followed the route of Jens Nielson and company, who had preceded them by a few days.

Lyman found the road rough and steep from Sweetwater Spring to the summit. His party spent several days traveling and camping between the summit and Escalante, plagued by heavy snowfall, straying stock, and bad roads, arriving in Escalante November 15. After laying in additional supplies there, the party pushed into the desert, not far behind the advance company. When they reached Ten-mile Spring and found insufficient water and forage for their animals, two of their members were sent eastward down Harris Wash in search of better grazing land. These men drove the Lyman herd to the Harris Ranch located at the confluence of Harris Wash and the Escalante River, where they remained while the wagons pushed forward along the already deep wagon tracks. Lyman's journal entries for these days indicate the nature of the country as it appeared to the man who would soon be actual captain of the expedition.[14]

From time to time other small groups passed through Escalante and pushed on to the point of rendezvous. One of these was led by Silas S. Smith, who, with his contingent of a "few wagons from Red Creek," reached Escalante November 16, according to Lyman's account, and followed the tracks of the advance company into the desert. He arrived at Forty-mile Spring on November 24 to take temporary command of the Mission.

Forty-mile Spring is located approximately a mile and a half southeast of Dance Hall Rock; it is not to be confused with Willow Tank, about four miles north of the Dance Hall. Although this spring afforded the best water supply between Escalante and the Colorado River, it was very sparse, indeed, not much more than a mere seepage, when the advance vanguard of emigrants arrived there. However, they were able to develop it into an adequate supply, if used very sparingly.[15] Today the spring is still a major source of water in that part of the desert. It has been piped into nearby troughs where it supplies the needs of cattle on the surrounding range.

The camp at Forty-mile was the major expedition headquarters for more than three weeks, from approximately November 15 to December 5. Various contingents of San Juan missionaries kept drifting into that location, swelling the population of the camp to well over two hundred persons. Here many of the expedition personnel, assembled from various southern Utah settlements, met for the first time and became acquainted.

The routine business of supplying the needs of this large group halted at one spot for the first time, required considerable planning and organization. Vegetation was, and is, as scarce as water in that desert country. The problem of finding forage for more than a thousand head of loose cattle and several hundred horses was a major task assigned primarily to the young men of the company. Every possible acre of grazing land between Escalante and the Colorado and from the base of the Straight Cliffs of the Kaiparowits Plateau to the Escalante River gorge was sought out and put to use.

It should be noted here that during the passing years — more than three quarters of a century — since the Hole-in-the-Rock expedition, considerable confusion has developed in the minds of some persons interested in the history of that trek regarding the cattle herd belonging to the company. The belief has been expressed that this herd did not accompany the wagon train through Hole-in-the-Rock, but rather was sent over the southern route via Lee's ferry, Moenkopi and the Navajo reservation. This contention is definitely not true.

One of the primary reasons for seeking a "short cut" by way of Escalante was the hostile nature of the Indians encountered by the exploring expedition of 1879; another was the extreme shortage of water and forage in Navajo country. It will be remembered that the explorers had experienced considerable difficulty in securing safe passage for even their small herd between Moenkopi and the San Juan; under these circumstances it would have been foolhardy indeed to have entrusted this large herd[16] to a few young men in that unfriendly Navajo domain.

Proof that the cattle went along with the main wagon train does not rest entirely on logic or circumstantial evidence, but is bolstered by actual written testimony of one of the chief cowhands, George W. Decker. To this young man, one of the highlights of the whole expedition was his task of helping drive the herd across the Colorado at Hole-in-the-Rock during the latter part of January and early February, 1880. He states that this undertaking necessitated his fording the river on horseback at least twenty times before the feat was accomplished. The fact that most of the livestock reached the San Juan in fairly good condition speaks well for the efficiency of the expedition's cowboys.

As has been pointed out, Forty-mile Spring and camp are located a short distance down the wash from Dance Hall Rock. This huge sandstone formation is so constructed as to constitute a large amphitheater with a relatively smooth floor. Pioneers of the Forty-mile camp held dances at the "Hall" and thus gave it its name. With three fiddlers in the company to supply music, several pleasant evenings must have been spent in this way. Modern-day ventures, following in the wake of the Hole-in-the-Rock wagons, often stop there to enjoy a Virginia reel on the rocks.

At Forty-mile camp, expedition leaders were faced with serious and urgent problems, the solution of which was absolutely necessary if the migration was to succeed. Thus far the going had been fairly easy, over a well-established road most of the way. Even so, a month had already elapsed, a couple of inches of fresh snow covered the ground; winter was literally upon them. More important, rumors spread through the camp that the country ahead was so cut by deep gulches and canyons that no road could possibly be built that way. Cattle herders and others who had scouted ahead had nothing but negative reports to make. In his Autobiography, Samuel Rowley explained the situation plainly: "Before we left our homes we were told that the country had been explored, and that the road was feasible. But now we found that someone had been mistaken."[17] A spirit of gloom spread through the whole camp. Had the San Juan Mission been led into impassable country? After coming this far, would the expedition have to turn back in failure? These questions demanded immediate answers. There was only one way to get those answers, and that was to send scouts into the unknown country ahead.

FOOTNOTES

1. Trail of the San Juan Mission, 1. (Unsigned, typewritten article located in the files of the Utah Historical Society.)

2. *Ibid.*

3. *Ibid.*

4. Margaret Nielson, San Juan Expedition, n. p. Account based on information supplied by Geo. W. Decker.

5. Henry John Holyoak, History of Henry John Holyoak (Appendix XIV). William N. Eyre reported snow two feet deep on the summit (see his Brief History of William Naylor Eyre Appendix XII).

6. Samuel Rowley, Autobiography of Samuel Rowley (Appendix VI).

7. E. Leonora Jones, Life of Parley Butt, 6.

8. Melvina Duke Collett, The San Juan Mission, 3, 4.

9. See pp. 81, 129–132 below.

10. Alice Bailey of Escalante, daughter of Mrs. Schurtz, supplied this information by letter April 24, 1956.

11. All distances in this region are expressed in terms of miles from Escalante.

12. Kumen Jones, Preface to Writings of Kumen Jones, 9, says that the company arrived at Forty-mile Spring early in November.

13. For an account of this exploration see Chapter V below. It should be noted that Samuel Rowley, in his Autobiography, infers that groups of explorers were sent out from Ten-mile Spring and that he was among them. However, Rowley as a member of the thirteen-man exploring party, left Forty-mile Spring November 28 (as recorded by Lyman's Journal). It is unlikely that he and/or other members made extensive explorations before the Hole-in-the-Rock expedition reached that spot. Rowley wrote his account many years after the events and could not be expected to remember details as well as one who was recording his daily journal on the spot.

14. Platte D. Lyman's Journal (Appendix IV).

15. Henry John Holyoak remembered having melted snow for drinking water at Forty-mile and Fifty-mile springs. (Henry John Holyoak, *op. cit.*)

16. Decker estimates that the total herd of cattle and loose horses numbered approximately 1,800 (see his Reminiscences, Appendix IX). Belt Dailey, son of Wilson Dailey, told me in 1954 that the Robbs drove a herd of some 500 head. This evidence should be considered as adequate proof that the large herd was actually taken across the Colorado at the Hole crossing.

17. Rowley, *op. cit.*

CHAPTER V

EXPLORATIONS FROM THE
FORTY-MILE SPRING

It is certainly the worst country I ever saw . . . most of us
are satisfied that there is no use of this company undertaking
to get through to the San Juan this way.

— Platte D. Lyman

Having arrived at the Forty-mile Spring, the company was literally
at the end of the road. Ahead of them lay almost unknown country —
entirely unknown, in fact, to any member of the expedition. On the
strength of the earlier favorable reports of Charles Hall, Andrew P.
Schow, and Reuben Collett, the expedition now found itself trapped in the
heart of this almost trackless wilderness. Even before Silas S. Smith arrived at the Forty-mile camp, Jens Nielson realized the necessity of obtaining more knowledge of the country ahead and authorized further
exploration of the desert to the south.

Four men were chosen for this important task: William W. Hutchings of Beaver, George B. Hobbs of Parowan, Kumen Jones of Cedar City,
and George Lewis of Kanab. They were instructed to push forward and
explore the country for the specific purpose of locating a spot where the
Colorado could be reached and crossed and also to explore beyond that
stream for a possible road out of the river gorge to the east. Equipped with
saddle horses and pack animals these men followed the track of the cart
used earlier by Schow and Collett. The trail took them by way of Fifty-
mile Spring to the Hole-in-the-Rock. They were evidently the first members of the San Juan Mission to obtain a breath-taking glimpse of that
famous cleft, soon to require so much of the company's time and energy.
Unable to descend to the river at that point, the four explorers continued
upstream. When they

. . . arrived at the point where Bro. Schow and Collett had descended to the
river they, in absence of ropes, tied their blankets together, by means of which
they lowered themselves over the two rocky ledges, and on reaching the west

bank of the river they found the wagon box with the seat lying across it and two boards which had been used for paddles on the river bank. Steps were immediately taken to cross the stream which was done by two men getting in the box at a time. On landing on the opposite shore one man was left there while the other returned with the box after another man. Thus three trips had to be made across the stream to get the four men over safely, by bailing water out all the way.[1] After crossing the river, the brethren now spent six days exploring eastward, but they found the country so broken up and cut into box canyons and draws that they only succeeded in getting about 10 miles away from the river. They then concluded that they were too far down in the draws of the Grand Canyon of the Colorado for their purpose and after recrossing the river and returning to Forty-Mile Spring Camp they made a report to that effect.[2]

The exact dates of this exploration are not known, but the four men evidently returned to Forty-mile Spring at about the same time Silas S. Smith reached that point. Allowing ten days for the reconnaissance we can safely estimate that it must have been conducted between November 15 and 24.[3]

The brief account of this exploration leaves us somewhat in doubt regarding the actual area covered and especially the extent of their travels east of the Colorado. It seems fair to assume, however, that the four men, after crossing the river, traveled eastward up Cottonwood Creek to a point near its head, then climbed the steep sandstone buttes in the vicinity of the spot that was eventually to become known as Cottonwood Hill. They probably journeyed eastward as far as the "Chute." It seems unlikely that they reached Grey Mesa. But they at least traveled far enough to become convinced that this was no region for a wagon road and concluded that they were too far down "in the draws of the Grand Canyon." This merely means that they felt that no feasible route for a wagon road could be found in that area and that the whole undertaking must be directed to some point farther upstream. From what they could see, there was no possibility of a route farther downstream — and they were certainly correct in this judgment.

A short distance of five or six miles to the southwest was the junction of the San Juan and Colorado rivers. Each of these streams flows through deep, straight-walled gorges that are still virtually unapproachable in anything but river boats or helicopters. A half-dozen miles west of the Hole-in-the-Rock the sheer cliffs of the Kaiparowits Plateau provide an almost impenetrable wall. To the south, rising out of a maze of deep gulches, canyons and barren slick rock buttes, majestic Navajo Mountain towers more than ten thousand feet into the sky. This is indeed some of the wildest, least known, least explored, and at the same time most colorful and spectacular country in America. Here the rumored rich veins of silver and no doubt fabulous uranium deposits remain undefiled by any but Navajo hands.

The four scouts sent out to locate a possible wagon road were not unimpressed with the indescribable grandeur of the region, but they saw the multicolored, straight-walled canyons as impassable barriers to their progress. It was this problem that led Lyman to describe the region as "the worst country I ever saw" when he arrived there a few days later. Back at Forty-mile Spring some two hundred men, women, and children were anxiously awaiting the explorers' report. It was already past mid-November; the new homes on the San Juan must be reached before winter set in — but not through this wild country, in the opinion of the scouts. Somewhere between the Colorado and Forty-mile camp the explorers encountered two California prospectors who had evidently spent considerable time in the area. Amazed at the thought of attempting to build a wagon road through such inhospitable country, the miners declared: "If every rag or other property owned by the people of the Territory were sold for cash, it would not pay for the making of a burro trail across the river."[4] A wagon road was simply unthinkable!

The negative report of the four explorers had a very sobering effect on the whole camp. Work crews had been busy, slowly pushing the road south from Forty-mile camp; but with the return of the scouts and their accounts all work came to a virtual standstill. The San Juan Mission faced a real crisis.

Just at this time Silas S. Smith and Platte D. Lyman with their respective contingents pulled into the Forty-mile camp. The stimulation of the arrival of the appointed leaders, plus the fact that Andrew P. Schow, Reuben Collett, and Charles Hall of Escalante had also arrived bringing a small boat for use in further exploration, injected new life into the company and road work was again begun.

Schow and Collett both insisted that a suitable route could be found and expressed the belief that the four scouts had merely failed to locate the most favorable site. It was therefore decided to send another expedition to the south, while most of the company, with headquarters at Forty-mile Spring, continued road work southward toward the Colorado. Considerable confusion has developed regarding the equipment, personnel and actual activities of this new exploring party. Since a primary objective of the present study is to clarify accounts wherever possible, major sources covering this scouting expedition will be examined and evaluated. The brief account contained in the L.D.S. Church records is as follows:

In the meantime Bishop Andrew P. Schow and Reuben Collett arrived in camp, bringing a boat with them to be used in crossing the Colorado river. Elders Schow and Collett thought the four explorers had failed in finding the best place to descend to and cross the river, and hence they led the way on another visit to the river, accompanied by Wm. W. Hutchings, Geo. B. Hobbs, Kumen Jones, and Joseph Nielson. These six men soon reached the river at the same point as the former expedition, launched the boat and started down the river with the intention of going down the Colorado to the mouth of the San Juan and then paddle up that stream to Ft. Montezuma,[5] but after paddling down the river about 2 miles they came to some rapids where the water roared like thunder and the brethren dared not go over these rapids in their boat. They consequently returned to their former camp on the west side of the river where they were joined by Platte D. Lyman, Chas. E. Walton and three others, which increased the company to 11 men altogether. This enlarged company now crossed the river and spent several days on the east side, exploring, but with all their efforts they did not succeed in getting as far to the east as the first explorers.

Platte D. Lyman provides us with a different account of this exploring company, as follows (quoted in full in Appendix IV):

Friday, Nov. 28th, 1879. By direction of bro Smith I started with 12 others to look out a way for a road across the Colorado and beyond, we have a boat on one wagon and our luggage on another.[6] We drove 10 miles over the roughest country I ever saw a wagon go over and camped at the 50 mile spring. The company is as follows: A. P. Schow, Reuben Collett, Wm Hutchings, Kumen Jones, Saml Rowley, Cornelious Decker, Geo. Hobbs, John Robinson, Jos Barton, Joseph Nielsen, Saml. Bryson, James Riley and myself.

Saturday, Nov. 29th, 1879. Drove 6 miles over rough sandstone hills and sand to the "Hole in the rock"[7] a cleft in the solid rock wall of the Grand Kanyon of the Colorado, which runs about a mile below us, the walls of the Kanyon rise 2000 feet from the water and are in many places perpendicular. We took our wagons 2 miles farther up the river to where the banks are not so abrupt but are still solid sandstone, and took the front wheels from under the boat and lowered it down about 1 mile onto a sandy bench from where we dragged it 1 mile to the river and slid it 200 feet over a rock into the river about 1 mile above the mouth of "Hole in the rock." After supper and a little rest we loaded our luggage into the boat and about midnight rowed it down [to] the mouth of the "Hole" where we tied up and camped. The river is about

350 feet wide, the current sluggish and the water milky but of good taste, the willows on the bank are still leaved in green.[8]

It will be noted that there are obvious discrepancies between these two accounts. The first one, quoted from the San Juan Stake History, indicates that Schow, Collett, Hutchings, Hobbs, Jones, and Nielson left the Forty-mile camp with the boat and were later joined on the Colorado by Lyman and others. Most published accounts of this important exploration have followed this general pattern — sometimes quoting verbatim from the church account. At least one narrative treats this six-man group as a separate and independent exploration, indicating that its members went to the Colorado, lowered and launched the boat, floated down the river to the rapids, explored several days east of the river, and eventually returned (bringing the boat with them) to Forty-mile Spring before Smith or Lyman arrived there.[9]

It is my belief, based on a careful study of all available accounts and documents, that there was no such special six-man expedition. It seems that the passage of time has tended to confuse the facts; and once confused there has been a perpetuation of the garbled story, down to the present day. Lyman provided the only contemporary record of this expedition — that is the only one that has been preserved and is still available. His journal, written on the spot and at the time, supplies dates and other details entirely lacking in all other accounts written many years later. It should be noted in passing that this journal, now deposited in the L.D.S. Church Historian's Library, was not on deposit there when the San Juan Stake History account of this expedition was being assembled during the second decade of the twentieth century. Compilers of that history seem to have relied almost entirely on the memory of participants in the San Juan Mission approximately three decades after the events had taken place. In cases of this kind, with the natural conflicts that arise because of the fallibility of human memory, a journal of the caliber of Lyman's must be considered the most reliable source of information.

As already indicated, Lyman points out that he, Schow, and Collett reached Forty-mile Spring together on November 27. The very next day, under instructions from President Smith, he and the twelve others started with two wagons, one carrying the boat which had been brought from Escalante. Since Schow and Collett had not reached the Forty-mile camp until November 27, then had started out as part of this thirteen-man company the next day, they could not possibly have had time to complete this questionable six-man exploration. Furthermore, according to Lyman's journal the thirteen men with two wagons and the boat seem to have been *part of the same group*. Details contained in the journal concerning the lowering of the boat over the canyon rim, launching it, loading camp gear, then floating downstream, etc., seem to indicate that Lyman was actually one of the participants at the time. He must have been. He certainly did not join the company after they had reached the river, as indicated by the first account. It is entirely possible (although this is merely speculation) that the company of thirteen did not travel all the way from Forty-mile to the river in one unit, but rather in two groups, some in wagons and some on horseback, until they reached the river rim. This could have been responsible for the later confusion about two separate companies. Lyman, at least, considered them all part of the same party. It would have required all of them to lower the boat over the cliff in the manner he describes.

Thus, in view of the facts available, there seems to be no possible place for this alleged special six-man expedition; the misunderstanding and confusion that have evolved through the years are now entirely clarified by the Lyman journal and closer examination of other documents. A bit of interesting and supporting information is the fact that Cornelius Decker, owner and no doubt driver of one of the wagons, is not even listed as a member of the "six-man" expedition.[10]

It seems quite obvious now that only the one formally organized and commissioned expedition — the Hutchings, Hobbs, Jones, Lewis group — consisting of Hole-in-the-Rock personnel had explored the region south of Forty-mile before Silas S. Smith and Platte D. Lyman arrived there. This does not rule out the likelihood that cattle herders and possibly others of the expedition had done some unofficial exploring in the region. The second and only other official exploration (that is, the thirteen-man expedition) conducted from that point set out on November 28 equipped with two wagons and the boat, as already indicated.

Now, having followed this second expedition to the river and thence downstream to the Hole-in-the-Rock, let us continue with Lyman's account of that exploration.

Sunday, Nov. 30th, 1879. One of the boys caught a fine fish called white Salmon large enough for our breakfast & dinner.[11]

We loaded our luggage into the boat and 7 of us got in and started down to find the mouth of the San Juan, but after going 1½ miles we ran aground in a rapid and were compelled to turn back to our starting point, from where 11 of us with our provisions and blankets on our backs started up over the bluffs to the east which were at first very rough and precipitous but soon we found a smooth open Kanyon with water wood and grass in it which we followed up for 3 miles and then began to ascend the bluffs which are at first sandy and afterwards steep solid sandstone hills[12] which continue as far as the summit 6 miles from the river, went one mile farther and camped in the rocks where we found plenty of water in the rocks.[13]

Monday, Dec. 1st, 1879. Started out to the east and after going a mile or two we found the country so rough and broken and so badly cut in two by deep gorges all in solid rock that we gave up all idea of a road being made there,[14] we then went back nearly to our camp and struck a Kanyon on a line with the one we followed yesterday which we followed down 4 miles right to the San Juan river,[15] which is about 250 ft wide, with a rapid current, its color is slightly milky but the water tastes good. The banks are nearly as high as those of the Colorado but not so steep nor solid. The little Kanyon we have followed down is a curiosity in its way. For 2 miles more or less, its width is from 15 to 30 [feet] while the walls of bare rock rise perpendicularly 200 or 300 feet and the bottom is much of the way smooth and level as a floor and is covered with a little stream of water seeping from the crevices in the rock which spreads over the surface so evenly that one can walk for rods at a time without wetting the uppers of their boots although in running water all the time. The grass and willows which grow in small bunches here are very rank and still very green. There are deep holes in places in the bed of the creek where we caught several mud turtles about as large as a mans hand.[16] The country here is almost entirely solid sand rock, high hills and mountains cut all to pieces by deep gulches which are in many places altogether impassable. It is certainly the worst country I ever saw, some of our party are of the opinion that a road could be made if plenty of money was furnished but most of us are satisfied that there is no us[e] of this company undertaking to get through to San Juan this way. We returned to our last nights camp after dark.

Tuesday, Dec. 2d, 1879. Walked back to the Colorado, crossed over and hauled our cart back to the top of the bank which was half a days hard work, and then camped.[17]

Wednesday, Dec. 3d, 1879. Drove back to [Forty-Mile] camp much of the way in the rain which wet me to the skin. In the evening an informal meeting was held in bro Smiths tent when those who had been out reported the result of their explorations, after which on motion of bro Jens Nielsen sen it was resolved unanimously to sustain bro Smith in whatever course he thought best for us to pursue. Bro Smith then said he thought we ought to go ahead and all present expressed themselves willing to spend 3 or 4 months if necessary working on the road in order to get through, as it is almost impossible to go back the way we came because of the condition of the road and the scarcity of grass.

Thursday, December 4th, 1879. Bro. Smith called a meeting of the whole camp to take an expression of their feelings in order that bros Sckow and Collet may know what to report to those behind, when it was unanimously resolved to go to work on the road.

Having quoted Lyman's journal covering this thirteen-man exploring expedition and its return to Forty-mile camp, let us now examine the account given by Andrew Jenson as contained in the San Juan Stake History. After stating that the second group of explorers had failed to penetrate eastward as far as the earlier four-man company, this account continues:

They, however, took another course, traveling in a southeasterly direction over a number of breaks and box canyons and at length succeeded in reaching the San Juan River, about 6 miles above its junction with the Colorado. Here they found a number of turtles and the scenery grand beyond description;[18] but they found the river itself hemmed in with perpendicular cliffs on either side rising in some places several thousand feet high, thus forming a complete box canyon through which the river wound its way. Finding it impossible to ascend the river, they returned to their camp on the Colorado to prepare a report to the effect that a road could not be made to the San Juan Country that way. In this opinion, however, there was one dissenting vote, namely that of Geo. B. Hobbs who believed that a road could be made, though with considerable labor. The company then returned to Forty-Mile Spring Camp, two days being spent between the river and the camp.

While this expedition was gone the brethren of the main camp had been busy making a wagon road from the Forty Mile Spring to the so-called Fifty Mile Springs, which road they had almost completed, though it led over the broken country intervening — a country cut up by numerous draws which all opened into the Escalante Creek. As the explorers returned they told the men who were working on the road that their labors were all in vain as they could not go through that way to their destination. On hearing this the brethren picked up their spades, picks, and shovels and returned to the camp on the Forty-Mile Spring.

In the meantime Silas S. Smith, the president of the company, and others who came along with him, arrived at the Forty Mile Spring Camp,[19] where the explorers immediately after their return were called to report at a regular prayer meeting. This happened to be on a Saturday night. The majority report made by the returned explorers on this occasion was to the effect that the mission must necessarily prove a failure so far as getting through that way to the San Juan Country. It was then decided to hold the regular Sabbath meeting the following day and then break up camp, some of the brethren deciding to return to their former homes, while others contemplated locating in Bull Valley, or on the Fremont River, or at some other point on the east side of the Wasatch range (or Rim of the Basin).

But at the meeting held on Sunday Bro. Geo. B. Hobbs was induced by
Pres. Silas S. Smith to make a minority report. This he did reluctantly, as he
did not desire to place himself in arbitrary opposition to the judgment of the
rest of his brethren, but being urged to express his opinion he reported to the
effect that under the condition the company was in he thought it was possible
to make a road through the broken country between the Colorado and the San
Juan rivers and reach Fort Montezuma on the San Juan. He described the
country so far as he had seen it and based his judgment on what he had observed. Bishop Schow and Bro. Collett indorsed the report made by Elder
Hobbs and intimated that if the rest of the company had as much backbone as
Elder Hobbs had the company would undoubtedly get through. This seemed
to change the sentiment of the whole camp, and when a vote finally was taken
it was to the effect that another attempt should be made to reach the place
of destination, as previously contemplated.

Kumen Jones, one of the participants in this exploration, recorded
the following results:[20]

After about one weeks tramping, the boys returned and gave their reports,
and there were about as many different kinds of reports as men. As a sample,
the four that were out farthest toward San Juan reported as follows: 1. It
would be out of the question for the company to attempt to get through on this
route. 2. With some assistance from the Legislature (that was about to convene) and by all the camp uniting in the undertaking, we could get the wagons
and stock through, but no permanent road could be made. 3. A good road may
be made over the proposed route in a few weeks without much trouble. (One
did not report).

Several meetings were called by the men at the head and it was finally the
almost unanimous decision to go to work and make a way to get through. One
thing or condition that made for this decision, was the fact that on account of
deep snow on the mountains over which we had just passed, it would be almost
impossible to return for several months; accordingly, preparations were soon
under way to commence work.

As far as I have been able to determine, virtually every printed account that is complete enough to treat the details of these explorations,
the reports that grew out of them, and the ensuing decision to push ahead,
has relied largely on the account carried in the San Juan Stake History,
which has, of course, been available for many years. Yet to the extent that
this account, compiled so long after the events had occurred, disagrees
with Lyman's record, written at the time and on the spot, his journal
must be considered more reliable.

One point of interest is the day of the week on which the explorers
returned and gave their reports. Every published account that mentions

the incident states that the first reports were made on Saturday night and that the decision was then reached to abandon the undertaking; but that the next day at the regular Sabbath services, George B. Hobbs' minority opinion proved effective enough to turn the negative vote into what is reported to have been an almost unanimous decision to push ahead. The compilers of this record seem to have forgotten that it was customary during the 1870's and 1880's to hold regular L.D.S. religious services on Thursday evenings, and to have taken for granted that the regular church meetings would have been held on Sunday. Yet this was not true at that time; regular Thursday services were held throughout the Hole-in-the-Rock trek. Lyman's journal points out clearly that it was on Wednesday evening rather than Saturday that the explorers' reports were made. It will be noticed that he states positively that the definite decision was made at this Wednesday meeting — at least among the leaders of the enterprise — to continue forward rather than attempt to retrace their steps. The meeting next day was called by Smith to get an expression of sentiment, or more than likely to obtain sort of a vote of confidence, from the mass of the membership and to impress Bishop Schow and Reuben Collett with the unanimity prevailing in the camp as well as to give them a positive message for other colonists who might still be on the road between Escalante and the settlements to the west.

Most accounts agree that George B. Hobbs, with encouragement from Collett and Schow, was responsible for changing the negative report, although there continues to be considerable disagreement as to exactly when and where this minority report was given. Several narratives state or imply that on the evening of the first reports the leaders accepted a motion by Jens Nielson that the decision be left to "President Smith and the Lord."

My conclusion, after having examined all these various accounts, is as follows: The thirteen explorers returned from their reconnaissance Wednesday, December 3. While traveling together from the Colorado River during the major part of two days they had ample time to discuss the nature of the report they would make — a negative one. But there were at least three men among them (Hobbs, Schow and Collett) who felt that a road could be built through that tangle of slick rock canyons and buttes east of the river, even though the scouts had been unable actually to locate a possible route.

As soon as the party arrived at Forty-mile camp President Smith called them to his tent to report their findings. At that time all reports, both favorable and unfavorable, were probably heard and discussed. A definite influence on the decision of those practical men was the fact that heavy snows in the Escalante Mountains had virtually blocked the return road and covered the very sparse forage for the already weakening animals. Jens Nielson, an important and influential leader of the company, although not a member of the exploring expedition, then moved that the final decision be left to "the president and the Lord." Not a man among them doubted for a moment that God would inspire Smith to make the proper choice. The vote to sustain their leader was unanimous, according to the Lyman journal.

But President Smith surely did not take it upon himself to make such an important decision alone — the leading men of the company must all have been called in for counsel. The lives of the whole expedition as well as the future of the San Juan Mission were at stake. Smith was not the sort of man to determine such important matters without the consent of those who would be most vitally affected. It is very likely that these deliberations consumed several hours and that there were numerous adjournments and reassemblings before the final decision was made. Kumen Jones speaks of several meetings. It is logical to suppose that earnest and sincere prayer was a major part of the deliberations; since this was the Lord's work, He should be called on to inspire the leaders to make the proper choice. All of this must have been accomplished during the evening of December 3 for Lyman recorded the results and decision in his journal before retiring for the night. Commenting on the significance of this decision, with a half-century of hindsight to guide him Kumen Jones had this to say: "Here is where a decision was made that has affected the San Juan Mission for all time. The country would have been settled, but it would have been under a different lineup, for that same bunch could not have been gotten together again."[21]

By the following day (Thursday, December 4) news of the decision had certainly spread through the whole camp and had, no doubt, been debated and discussed in every wagon and tent. A general meeting was then called by Smith in order that the whole camp might be given a chance to express opinions. This doubtless was turned into a "testimony" meeting where many people voiced their approval of what the leaders had decided. The whole camp was strengthened and unified at this session; with God's help they would now go forward and complete the task to which they had been called.

John R. Robinson later recalled having heard Jens Nielson declare that the company must "go on whether we can or not";[22] if the Saints had plenty of "stickie-ta-tudy" they could not fail. When a count was finally made, there were few, if any, dissenting voices. One courageous soul broke forth in song[23] and the stillness of the desert was soon broken by the well-known strains:

> The spirit of God like a fire is burning
> The latter-day glory begins to come forth.
> The visions and blessings of old are returning
> And Angels are coming to visit the earth.
> We'll sing and we'll shout with the armies of Heaven
> Hence forth and forever, Amen and Amen!

Bp. Schow and Reuben Collett were instructed to carry the "good" word back to Escalante and to encourage those who might still be somewhere along the road to make haste; the Hole-in-the-Rock Expedition was moving forward!

FOOTNOTES

1. The fact that the wagon box had lain in the sun long enough to have dried out considerably, requiring constant bailing to keep it afloat, would indicate that it had been left there several days or weeks before. This is a partial clue as to the time of the original Schow-Collett exploration — probably late in the summer, 1879.

2. Cited from San Juan Stake History.

3. Silas S. Smith's journal entry for Nov. 24 is very brief: "drove 5 miles to camp [at the Forty-mile]. Very unfavorable report from exploring party."

We do not know exactly when Jens Nielson's company had arrived at Forty-mile. Hence there is no way of definitely dating the beginning of this four-man expedition. We do know that they spent six days exploring the country east of the Colorado and at least three or four days on the trail, traveling both ways between the main camp and the river rim. The whole exploration must have consumed at least ten days. They had definitely returned with their negative report by the time Smith arrived and before Lyman, in company with Schow and Collett, who were bringing a better boat from Escalante to conduct further explorations in behalf of the company, reached Forty-mile Spring on November 27.

4. Kumen Jones, General Move to the San Juan Mission (Appendix V).

5. The fact that these men intended to row a boat from the mouth of the San Juan upstream to Montezuma demonstrates their total ignorance of the nature of that stream and the country through which it flows.

6. One of the wagons was that of Cornelius I. Decker, who had recently arrived at the Forty-mile camp (see his own account, Appendix VII).

7. This is the earliest contemporary account I have found which actually names the Hole-in-the-Rock.

8. It would seem from this description that the explorers left the boat on the back-wheel assembly of the wagon running gears and using the reach as a tongue managed to guide the outfit down the slope to the east end of Jackass Bench. The boat was then removed from the running gears and dragged to the river-edge of the bench, then lowered some two hundred feet to the water. (Compare this with Lyman's entry of Dec. 2.) A fine spring of water flowing from the base of the Hole-in-the-Rock cleft makes this a desirable campsite today.

9. Melvina Duke Collett, The San Juan Mission, 4.

10. Another minor item that needs examination at this time regards the nature of the boat used on this expedition. Mrs. Collett's family record speaks of a raft constructed of railroad ties: "Andrew P. Schow and Reuben Collett came to camp bringing a boat with them to be used in crossing the river. Charley Hall was an old boatsman. He had built this boat or raft by lashing railroad ties together." It seems to me that through the years this item has become confused with the ferry or raft that was ultimately constructed by Hall for use in crossing the Colorado with wagons. That a raft of railroad ties (wherever they might have been obtained) should have been hauled all the way from Escalante to the Colorado gorge, lowered over the canyon wall to the river below, launched, floated downstream for a couple of miles, *then paddled back upstream* to the point of beginning, and finally dragged up over that cliff to the canyon rim and carried back to the camp at Forty-mile Spring, seems beyond the point of probability. Such a craft could have been taken down to the river and launched, but how could it have been rowed back upstream for two miles with six men aboard? The heavy Colorado River water would make the task virtually impossible. Would they, or could they, have then hauled that craft of water-soaked railroad ties up the nearly perpendicular canyon wall and back to Forty-mile Spring?

The very circumstances suggested here seem effectively to rule out both the idea of the special six-man expedition as well as the idea that a raft instead of a boat was used for this exploration of thirteen men. Lyman and others speak of this craft as a *boat into* which they piled their gear before floating down the Colorado. The whole description is that of a boat, not a raft. Kumen Jones refers to it as a rowboat; Cornelius Decker calls it a small boat.

11. Cornelius Decker was the fisherman. Says he: "I set a couple of fish hooks that night and caught two large fish, one about 12 lbs. and one about 7 lbs. We ate the large one for breakfast; the other I took back to camp with me." The fish were, no doubt, channel catfish, still plentiful in the Colorado. (See the Decker account Appendix VII.)

12. The explorers had followed Cottonwood Creek as far as Cottonwood Hill.

13. This camp was at or near the top of Cottonwood Hill.

14. This exploration had probably taken the explorers as far east as the "Chute." A hike over that country today is almost necessary to understand what Lyman really meant by his descriptions of this region.

15. I have made no attempt to identify or explore this canyon.

16. Hoffman Birney in his *Zealots of Zion* (Philadelphia, 1931), 257, scoffs at this report of turtles: "The 'Turtles' is probably a stenographer's error in transcription of the notes of the veteran's recollections. Not until the *Chelonidae* develop wings will one be found on the summit of sandstone cliffs that gird the San Juan for the last fifty miles of its course." But Birney's account is loaded with inaccuracies.

17. This camp was on the canyon rim a short distance upstream from the Hole-in-the-Rock.

18. Yet Hoffman Birney (*op. cit.*, 254) had the audacity to assert concerning these pioneers: "Beauty and color, as purely aesthetic abstractions, were nothing in their lives."

19. We have already noted that Smith had arrived at Forty-mile before this exploring expedition started on its reconnaissance.

20. Kumen Jones, Preface to the Writings of Kumen Jones, 10.

21. Kumen Jones, Journal of Kumen Jones, part 2, 95–98.

22. Quoted from Lula R. Bastian, History of John R. Robinson, n.p.

23. Beatrice Perkins Nielson, Hole in the Wall, mentions this singing; it is referred to by other writers also.

CHAPTER VI

FROM FORTY-MILE TO THE
HOLE-IN-THE-ROCK

We drove 10 miles over the roughest country I ever
saw a wagon go over and camped at 50 Mile spring.

— *Platte D. Lyman*

The momentous decision had been made: The company would push
on to its destination over the new route. With God's help they would
build a road to the San Juan via Hole-in-the-Rock and go on to complete
their mission. Gloom and despondency, which had pervaded the camp,
were now replaced with optimism and good will. Road work that had
come to a standstill with the return of the scouts was recommenced. The
company pitched in with a united will and for the first time began to feel
and realize the full power it possessed. There would be no more talk of
turning back; nothing could stop the expedition now! "Come, Come, Ye
Saints" was sung with real spirit and meaning as this pioneer band struck
into the desert south from Forty-mile Spring.

As noted earlier, a cart and two wagons had already traversed the
country between Forty-mile and the "Hole." It was now necessary to
improve the trail thus blazed and construct a road that would accommodate the whole party. Platte D. Lyman, as he accompanied the scouts,
had described the region as "the roughest country I ever saw a wagon go
over." But it probably didn't look so bad now, for he and several others
had had a good look at one of the wildest regions of the West — the triangle formed by the junction of the Colorado and San Juan. They knew
that there was much very rough country ahead.

From a road builder's point of view, the sixty-five mile region between the town of Escalante and the Colorado River at Hole-in-the-Rock
grows progressively worse as one proceeds southward into the desert.
The San Juan pioneers had experienced considerable difficulty on the first
forty miles of the road, but the remaining fifteen miles they found several

times more difficult. This country is very deceptive: What appears to be a fairly level plain, lying between the Straight Cliffs of Fifty-mile Mountain and the Escalante River, is literally cut through and through with numerous gulches and almost straight-walled gorges and canyons which head in the Kaiparowits and cut deeper and deeper as they extend eastward toward the Escalante River gorge. Most of these gulches are not apparent to the traveler until he suddenly finds himself on the very brink of a chasm several hundred feet deep. Straight ahead, probably a quarter of a mile away through clear air, the "flat level" plain continues. The effect is the same, regardless of the mode of travel — horseback, jeep, or touring car.

If these gulches are to be crossed at all, it must be up toward the Straight Cliffs. The nearer they approach the Escalante gorge the deeper they become, and the more nearly perpendicular their walls. In their lower reaches these gulches and canyons contain some of the most beautiful and spectacular natural arches and bridges to be found anywhere in the West.[1] It is to be regretted that these scenic wonders are not approachable in any sort of wheeled vehicle.

From Forty-mile Spring southward the washes, gulches, and canyons not only become progressively more numerous, but also much more difficult to cross. If the San Juan pioneers had merely succeeded in building a wagon road through that part of the country — to Fifty-mile Spring — and then returned to the settlements, their achievement would have been outstanding. But this was really easy terrain to cross compared to what lay ahead.

During the 1940's and 1950's a truck and automobile road of sorts was constructed through this same region, following very closely the one built by the pioneers of 1879. The major improvement is the manner in which gulches and draws are now approached and crossed. Today a series of diagonals and zig-zag dugways have been built into and out of these numerous washes and gorges. The grade on the new road is such that cars and trucks can make it without too much difficulty if weather and road conditions are at their best. The old pioneer tracks are clearly visible in many places where that expedition knifed down into these gulches and out up the other side on grades that are too steep for a modern jeep.

The area between Fifty-mile Spring and the Hole probably offered the pioneers fewer difficulties than the previous ten miles. After dipping down into the upper reaches of Davis Gulch, the road winds for several miles among countless barren sandstone knobs and cliffs. There are a few very sharp pitches here, so steep that it taxes my imagination to conceive of enough horses being hitched to wagons to pull the heavy, loaded vehicles up the steep slick-rock slopes, especially if the rocks happened to be wet or frosty. But the San Juan missionaries seem to have negotiated those inclines without much difficulty.

Today the chief obstacle here is the fine, deep red sand which in a windstorm drifts around like snow. However, the sand that makes this part of the road so treacherous now did not affect the original wagon drivers three-quarters of a century ago, who were there during the winter when the sand was damp and at its best for traveling purposes. Although modern equipment has been employed to open the road from Fifty-mile to the Hole, the effort at present (1957) has not been very successful, primarily because of the sand.

This is definitely the worst country through which I have ever driven a touring car, and most people who have tried it will agree. It's still strictly a jeep and truck road — and for four-wheel drive vehicles at that. A person must actually traverse this region to appreciate the problems encountered in attempting to build roads through it.

There is still a question regarding the exact location of Fifty-mile Spring, where the Hole-in-the-Rock pioneers established a camp early in December, 1879. Today there are three springs that are sometimes referred to as the Fifty-mile Springs where the camp was supposedly located. The first of these, in a geographical line running southward along the base of the Straight Cliffs, is the Soda Spring in Soda Gulch — about ten miles from the Hole-in-the-Rock. This is a fair-sized flow of water that cattlemen have piped into nearby watering troughs to supply the needs of livestock. The Soda Spring contains some mineral but can be used for human consumption. There are reports extant of remnants of old dugouts located a short distance up the gulch above this spring. Perhaps these are remains of shelters constructed by pioneers of the San Juan expedition, for in the writings of one member of that pioneer band is the reference to the possible use of such shelters. Milton Dailey recorded this statement: "In order to make it as comfortable as possible for our families my brother [Wilson] and I made a dugout near a small stream to live in."[2]

About a mile and a half south of Soda Spring is another small seepage which currently supplies water for the Bailey ranch cabin. This ranch and spring are also quite commonly called "the Sodie." Here is an ideal camp site with plenty of level ground and nearby sandstone cliffs that would supply considerable protection from severe winter storms. Although of excellent quality, the spring is very small and would certainly not supply water for a very large camp. It is quite possible, of course, that this spring may have been much larger during the winter of 1879–80.

A mile or more south of the spring at the ranch cabin is a third spring, large enough to supply water for quite a large camp. Some of the local Escalante citizens maintain that this is the spring used by the pioneers. Platte D. Lyman and others of the original company estimated the distance between Fifty-mile and the Hole to be five or six miles; these calculations would tend to favor this third or southernmost spring. However, since the exact location of the Fifty-mile Spring is never clearly given and there is so much confusion regarding it, it is obviously impossible to state with any degree of certainty which of the three was really the one used by the San Juan pioneers. Very likely all of them were used.

Because there was no water between Fifty-mile Springs and the Hole-in-the-Rock or at the top of the Hole, expedition leaders decided to divide the company until a road could be completed down through the Hole and out of the river gorge to the east. Probably about half of the wagons and personnel settled down at the Fifty-mile while the remainder moved on to the Colorado River rim immediately above the Hole-in-the-Rock.

As it turned out, lack of water was not the most difficult problem, since numerous rain and snow storms kept replenishing the supply stored in the natural rock tanks found in abundance. This natural supply was the primary source for those camped on the canyon rim; it also supplemented the meager supply furnished by the springs at Fifty-mile camp.

The exact number of persons located at either camp is not known. Cornelius I. Decker supplies the only positive statement yet uncovered regarding the general division of the company into two groups. He points out that the Parowan and Paragonah outfits stayed at the Fifty-mile, whereas those of the Cedar City contingent established themselves at the top of the Hole.[3] Obviously, this division leaves out those from several communities not mentioned in the Decker account. However, by inference and incidental references the location of other members of the company can be determined. The Lymans and supposedly the Stevens outfits from Holden were camped at the Hole. The Redds from New Harmony were also there, as was George W. Sevy of Panguitch and probably George Morrell of Junction. Wilson Dailey of Harrisburg is known to have camped at the Fifty-mile;[4] the Milton Dailey family and Henry Wilson from St. George no doubt camped at the same spot. No attempt has been made to actually determine the location of each family, as this would be well-nigh impossible.

More important than the identification of the personnel at each of the two camps is the division of work allotted to each group. This information is also supplied by Cornelius I. Decker.[5] He states that the men from Fifty-mile camp were responsible for building the road out of the Colorado gorge to the east while those camped at the top of the Hole were engaged in blasting out the fissure and making the necessary fills in the chasm below in order that wagons might be driven to the river. Those from the Fifty-mile camp would walk the half-dozen or so miles to the construction site on Monday morning, work there all week, and return Saturday evening.

The people from both camps faced about the same type of problems and "enjoyed" about the same kind of camp life. Scarcity of fuel was one major problem, as there was virtually no timber available in that country — nor is there today. Obtaining a sufficient supply for cooking fuel was a constant worry, and when a larger campfire was needed for light and warmth for a camp meeting or dance, the problem was even more difficult. The commonest shrub in the vicinity, a scrubby bush known as shadscale, was unsatisfactory for anything but the smallest fires. When larger fires were needed, men were sent out with lasso ropes to gather up huge bundles of this small bush. The biggest bundle that could thus be obtained would usually be consumed in less than a half hour. Some wood was doubtless hauled from the timbered regions back along the trail toward Escalante.

Food supply was an ever-growing problem. Although most of the company had come well supplied for a trek of some two months, it soon became apparent that the trip would be at least twice that long. Flour supplies ran dangerously low long before the Colorado had been ferried. As a result people in the pioneer camps soon found themselves reduced to the necessity of grinding seed wheat and other grain in their small coffee mills. At Fifty-mile camp Wilson Dailey, who had brought his forge and other blacksmithing equipment along, rigged up a long handle for a coffee mill, fastened the machine securely to a plank, and thus enabled expedition personnel to come to the mill and grind with less effort.[6] This make-shift mill was reportedly kept busy most of the daylight hours; Belt

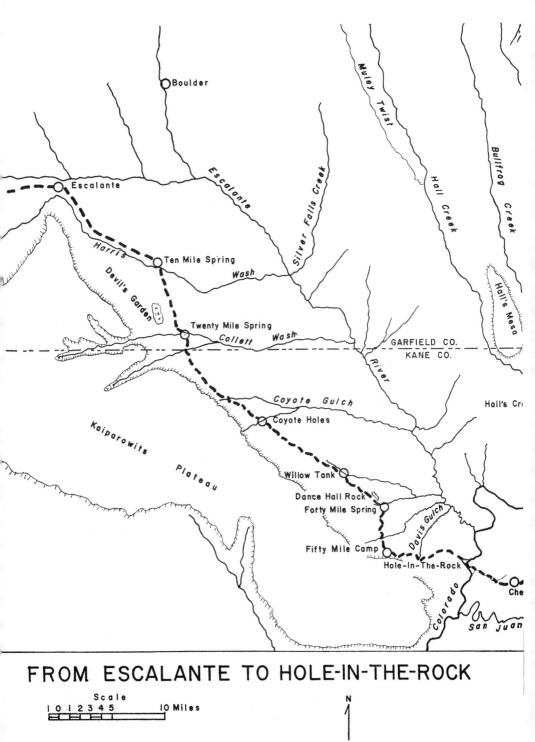

FROM ESCALANTE TO HOLE-IN-THE-ROCK

Scale

1 0 1 2 3 4 5   10 Miles

N

David E. Miller

Dailey remembered that it was often running as late as midnight. Parched corn became a regular and common article of diet. Although the small community of Escalante could help out to a limited extent especially in supplying flour until the mill froze, the longer the trek lasted and the farther the company pushed into the desert, the more difficult it became to replenish food supplies.

Escalante folk helped supply more than flour for the expedition; limited quantities of beans, corn, and other produce could be had there for a price. Reuben Collett had established a sorghum plant at Escalante and was producing a satisfactory quality of molasses by the summer of 1879. Most of his production that season went south toward the Hole-in-the-Rock.

Reuben Samuel (or R. S. Collett) the eldest son of Reuben, was almost sixteen years old at that time. He said he knew of his father rolling out eleven barrels of Sorghum and of his driving as many as five beef at one time to the Saints, as his cattle were fat. . . . R. S. said that Platte D. Lyman came with a wagon and a driver. Brother Lyman, R. S., and his father, Reuben, loaded the wagon with the barrels of Sorghum, which Reuben had made. He raised his own sugar cane, and sent to the states for the mill. Charley Hall . . . made the barrels which were large at the bottom and small at the top. The family never knew what father [Reuben Collett] contributed, as he was a very selfless man who never talked of his good deeds.[7]

On January 19, 1880, Elizabeth M. Decker wrote: "We have just sent our last five dollars to Escalante to get some pork and Molasses."[8]

Since the country afforded virtually nothing in the way of wild game, the expedition was forced to rely on its own resources for meat. The pioneers were reluctant to slaughter cattle that must be saved to form a nucleus for future herds in the new location; nevertheless, slaughter of a beef is mentioned occasionally. For example, Platte D. Lyman in his journal entry for December 11 says: "Killed our beef in the morning and loaned most of it to the camp." As other food supplies ran low, the expedition was eventually reduced to a diet consisting mostly of beef, the quality of which grew steadily worse as the trek continued. Slaughter time was always of interest to the boys of the expedition, especially if something out of the ordinary occurred. Such an incident was remembered by Nathaniel Z. Decker, young son of Z. B. Decker, Jr., as he later recorded the following:

. . . about the first that I remember after we located a camp in a secluded spot [at Fifty-mile] where we were located over a month near enough to [the Hole-in-the-Rock] where the day to day grind of the labors continued, was a big steer was shot in the forehead and dropped. When the man with the long butcher knife jabbed it into his throat or neck he got to his feet and gave the man on foot [a merry chase] . . . finally after he had nearly bled to death they got him down to stay dead.[9]

Another serious problem continued to be the lack of sufficient forage for the livestock. The large herd soon picked off all available grass and other edible vegetation. At the Hole-in-the-Rock camp forage was extremely scarce. Shortly after arriving there, expedition leaders decided to risk driving their horses over the precarious trail, used by earlier explorers and by company personnel down onto Jackass Bench, which afforded an estimated hundred acres of tolerable grazing. But the venture proved to be costly; nine of the animals slipped from the narrow trail and were dashed to death on the rocks below.[10] The Jackass Bench supply of grass and other edible growth was soon consumed and most of the loose stock had to be driven north beyond Fifty-mile Spring in search of forage. "Warren Taylor, Albert Nelson and Caleb Haight were given the job of herding the horses. They took them back 10 miles to Sooner Spring."[11] So desperate had the forage problem become at the Hole camp that Lyman was forced to enter this record in his journal: "Found one of my mules in a ditch and so weak that it could not stand so I killed it." This brief journal entry (January 12, 1880) speaks volumes concerning the deplorable condition of the livestock.

Most of the loose stock pastured back along the trail toward Escalante remained there until the expedition could send men back to round up the cattle. Needless to say, some stock was lost during this winter operation. Cattlemen and herders responsible for the welfare of the herd spent many perilous days and nights in the course of this endeavor. Young George Westover, herding for L. H. Redd and James Monroe Redd, for whom he expressed the highest regard, had one of those difficult experiences: ". . . he and another boy got lost . . . in a snow storm and to keep from freezing they wrestled all night . . . long. They were so tired and sleepy, but kept on until daylight when they were able to get back to camp."[12]

In the camps shelter from the severe winter winds and snow was supplied primarily by the covered wagons and some tents. As suggested above, there is some evidence that crude dugouts may have been used at Soda Spring. But these would be very crude indeed and only temporary, as the company hoped to be on the move before long. On occasion, wagon boxes were lifted from the running gears and placed on the ground in order to make them more accessible and more comfortable. Blankets and pieces of canvas were hung here and there to serve as windbreaks.

In most accounts of the Hole-in-the-Rock expedition, the winter weather is described as the most severe that part of Utah had experienced up to that time. Concerning this point Mrs. Henry James Riley had the following to say:

We did not expect our journey to be so long and hard, but cold weather set in early. Work was very hard with the few tools that were on hand. I carried my baby for many hours with his little feet in the front of my dress against my body to keep them from freezing. Water was taken from the deep holes in the rocks left from the rain and snow for all purposes. Our faith was surely tested, but we put our trust in the Lord. Lots of sickness was indured, but all of our lives were spared.[13]

It is known definitely that the company experienced some snowstorms of blizzard proportions before spring arrived. One of these storms engulfed the four scouts on Christmas Eve at the base of Elk Ridge (see Chapter VII) and a short time later struck with all its fury at the river camp, depositing six inches of new snow. During the last part of February the company traveled across Grey Mesa in a foot of snow; a howling blizzard paralyzed the camp at the foot of Clay Hill Pass, March 13; George Hobbs tells of spending several days in deep snow while traveling through the cedar forest between Elk Ridge and Snow Flat.[14] But between storms the weather was often relatively mild, and the pioneers seem to have been more interested in the replenishment of their supply of water by the winter storms than in their inconveniences. At times, of course, the weather was bitter cold, slowing work and rendering camp life almost unbearable. On Christmas day Platte Lyman recorded: "The weather has been so cold and windy with some snow that we have been unable to do much work so far this week." By December 30 crews were just getting back to work in full strength. But the coldest weather was yet to be experienced — after the river crossing.

Under the existing circumstances of the camp (inadequate food and water supply and extended camp life, much of it during severe winter weather) it is not surprising to read of sickness in the company. But most accounts stress that *no serious sickness* occurred; there were no deaths. The pioneers were indeed a hardy lot.

Both camps, at Fifty-mile and at the top of the Hole, were established about December 10, 1879, and remained intact until wagons rolled again — through the Hole-in-the-Rock during the last week in January, 1880. Christmas and New Year's Day came and were appropriately celebrated. On Christmas Eve the children, sure that Santa would be able to find them in even this remote desert, tied their stockings to wagon wheels, sang a carol or two, and snuggled into bed. The next morning they were not disappointed to find some parched corn and cookies in their stockings.

The grown-ups gathered huge piles of shadscale and danced on the not-too-smooth sandstone rocks to the tune of the company's violins. It must have been a strange new sound that wafted over the desert country: violin music, singing, joyful voices, laughter. Members of the two camps were actually enjoying the Christmas season while the four scouts sent ahead to locate a possible route were wandering in a blinding snowstorm on the south slopes of Elk Ridge.

Concerning this Christmas celebration, a biographer of Joseph Stanford Smith has this to say:[15]

The company had brought quite a herd of cattle with them. One man owned a fine two year old beef steer which he offered to sell chances on at one dollar per chance. Twenty men of the party took chances on the first choice of cuts of the beef, which was killed and quartered for the contest. Each man paid a dollar for three shots at a target, and according to their scoring they had the privilege of selecting the piece of beef for their family. This contest was one of the highlights of that Christmas day, and furnished quite a diversion from the constant drilling, blasting and shoveling in filling up the hole. Jumping, racing, and wrestling matches, were also part of the day's fun. "As good luck would have it," said Mr. Smith, "I had a little forty-four Ballard rifle. I was top marksman, and we did have a great time."

Only meager first-hand descriptions of camp life have been preserved. Although the company was in more or less constant communication with relatives and friends in the settlements, by way of the Escalante Post Office, few of their letters seem still to be in existence. However, some letters of Elizabeth (Lizzie) Morris Decker have been preserved. One of these dated January 19, 1880, at Fifty-mile camp is here quoted at length because of the light it casts on some aspects of life in the pioneer camp:[16]

Dear Father and Mother,

We received yours of the 26 on 17. and was glad to hear from you. I Bawled three hours the other night because Em[17] got a letter and I didn't but I got one the next day so I quit squaking. The letter that you wrote New Years beat the one that you wrote Christmas. . . . Father said for us to tell you how we are gitting along for grub and things. I just more than wish I had some of that Sausage and pork, for ours is all gone. We (me and Em) had to board George[18] all the way till his father came: I do their baking and washing and mending. The old man has had a notion two or three times to go back. George wants to go home but his father won't let him. George Hobbs came back and is making pack saddles to take grub to Harrimans: he is going to take five mules.[19] The men think they will begin taking wagons down through the Hole in the Rock the last of this week or the first of next and then we will soon be across the river. I have never seen the river yet. About half of the Company are camped two Miles from the river and the rest of us about five. They will have to let the wagons down with ropes it is so steep that the brakes won't hold a wagon back. If the boys had plenty of powder they would soon make a good road, but the powder has not got here and the boys are getting tired of waiting. They want to be going so they can put a crop in. It is just like spring here, we have only had about two weeks of winter here. We have just sent our last five dollars to Escalante to get some pork and Molasses. We are living on bread and beef now; all our grub that we brought from home is gone. Cornelius has got plenty of shoes but his boots are wore out with working in the rock so much. They have just gone down again this morning to work across the river. We are all well except me. I have got a cold, the first I have had this winter. Genie and Willie[20] are as fat as little pigs and just as full of fun as they can be. I don't believe you would know Genie if you was to see him now, he is just setting it up with a slate and pencil, writing. He has just been playing horse out to the woodpile. . . . Willie is out there with Rowly's Children making a dugway and playing he is blasting the Hole in the rock down. We have got the stove in the wagon and it is quite comfortable. We had a rumpus the other night between Nell Hobbs and Mrs. Rowly; you bet it was fun.[21]

> Your loving daughter,
>
> Lizzie Decker.

Religious services, held Thursday evenings as well as Sundays, were a regular and important part of the life of the camp. Reports of such meetings are very brief. On occasion the names of speakers are mentioned; but more often than not the typical Mormon expressions, "had a good time," or "a good spirit prevailed," are the only descriptions given. In addition to gospel sermons, the meetings gave the members a chance for expression in song, readings, and dramatizations.

The contingents were favored with a flock of good singers among them were the Perkins men and wives, Miss Sarah Williams, Mrs. Dave Hunter . . . Kumen and Mary Jones, all the Deckers and wives, Joe and Harriet Ann [Barton], Hyrum Fielding and wife, and Geo. Hobbs, all the bachelors: Am. Barton, Jesse Smith, Ross Mickleson, Geo. Decker. All the Robbs and Dick

Butt were great lovers of dancing, and some of the evenings were indulged in dancing. When prayers were to be said the bachelors formed a squad in the background. The bachelors were indespensible in building fires, carrying water, and finding feed for the stock. All the spring water down the Colorado Plateau called the Escalante Desert was terrible alkaline. At the top of the Hole in the Rock was a sand rock surface 60 x 80 ft, where all the public services were held.[22]

Among those who loved to dance was Benjamin Perkins. His snappy Welsh jigs furnished no end to entertainment and enjoyment for the company. Virginia reels, Scotch reels, polkas, minuets, Schottisches — all were enjoyed by this fine band of pioneers. The songs most often sung are still popular in the L.D.S. Church: "Oh My Father," "Come, Come Ye Saints," "High on the Mountain Top," "Come Let us Anew our Journey Pursue," "God Moves in a Mysterious Way His Wonders to Perform," "The Spirit of God Like a Fire is Burning." Their strains echoed over the chasm of the Colorado gorge and reverberated from the Straight Cliffs of Fifty-mile Mountain.

January 3, 1880, was an important day at the Fifty-mile camp. On that day Mrs. James B. Decker gave birth to a baby girl. Here was the family, fifty miles from the nearest settlement and a hundred more miles from the nearest doctor — and, it might be added, a hundred and fifty miles from the proposed settlement on the San Juan. There was not even a midwife in camp. But as the time approached, the expectant mother was made as comfortable as possible. Her wagon box home was lifted from the running gears and placed on the ground. Snow was then banked two or three feet deep around it to keep out the drafts and to act as insulation. Ellen Hobbs Fielding offered her services to assist in any way she could. The result: a perfectly normal birth. They named the baby Lena Deseret Decker. There would be another birth in this company before Bluff was reached.

FOOTNOTES

1. A recent article dealing with these arches and bridges is entitled "Escalante: Utah's River of Arches," by W. Robert Moore; *National Geographic Magazine,* September, 1955.

2. Cited in a letter from Birt Gardner, July 21, 1954.

3. Cornelius I. Decker, Sketch of the Life of Cornelius I Decker (Appendix VII).

4. Belt Dailey, son of Wilson Dailey, supplied this information in a conversation with the author during the summer of 1954.

5. Decker, *op. cit.*

6. Belt Dailey supplied this information.

7. Melvina Duke Collett, The San Juan Mission, 3, 4.

8. See footnote 16, below.

9. Letter from N. Z. Decker, April 7, 1954.

10. San Juan Stake History.

11. According to Warren Taylor as quoted by Lillie Hall Denny in a letter of Sept. 4, 1955.

12. Quoted from a card written by Lina Walker, daughter of George Westover. Card written to Mrs. Lucretia Ranney.

13. Cited in a letter from Mrs. M. Riley, July 2, 1954.

14. His account is contained in Appendix IX.

15. Lydia Hammond Fielding, Biography of Joseph Stanford Smith.

16. Letter lent the author by Edgar T. Decker, son of Cornelius I. and Elizabeth Morris Decker, summer, 1955.

17. Em: Emma Morris Decker, wife of Nathaniel Alvin Decker, and sister of Elizabeth, the writer of the letter.

18. George W. Decker, son of Z. B. Decker, Sr.

19. Hobbs and three companions had explored the route all the way to Montezuma and returned. See Chapter VII for Hobbs' account of this exploration and Appendix IX for his account of his return to Montezuma with supplies.

20. Genie and Willie: sons of Cornelius and Elizabeth Decker.

21. Nell Hobbs: Probably Ellen Hobbs Fielding. This is one of the very few references to friction in the pioneer camp, and was evidently nothing of much importance.

22. Margaret (Maggie) Nielson, The San Juan Expedition.

CHAPTER VII

FOUR SCOUTS EXPLORE:
GEORGE B. HOBBS' ACCOUNT

It was Christmas day, 1879, which found us on the side of
Elk Mountain without food, in the midst of a piercing
cold, and not a mountain in sight that I could recognize.

— George B. Hobbs

Silas S. Smith, the expedition president, got his first breath-taking
look at the Hole-in-the-Rock on December 11, 1879, when he and Platte
D. Lyman rode horseback from Fifty-mile Spring to the camp on the
Colorado River rim where fifteen wagons had already assembled. The
two men returned to camp that evening. It is safe to assume that Smith
could not have had a clear understanding of the magnitude of the undertaking to which his company had committed itself until he stood at that
spot and examined the situation himself.

Three days later Smith returned to the Hole, where a meeting of the
leaders was called to consider what steps should now be taken to promote
the general welfare of the company. New contingents of wagons caught
up with the pioneer train from time to time, swelling the total company
to approximately two hundred fifty persons and some eighty-three wagons.
All agreed that blasting powder and additional tools were urgently needed
if their project was to succeed. There was also unanimous agreement that
the man most likely to obtain these supplies was Silas S. Smith, their president. The legislature of the territory was about to convene, and Smith, a
prominent past member of that body, agreed to petition the lawmakers
for an appropriation to help supply the necessary equipment.

So it was that Smith returned at once to the settlements on what was
expected to be a three weeks' fund and supply-raising campaign. The
men could not know then that their appointed leader would be absent
approximately five months and would not overtake his company until it
had reached the destination of Bluff and Montezuma and had spent a

month trying to conquer the treacherous San Juan River. Smith's departure left Lyman in actual charge of the expedition from December 15 until mid-May, when Smith finally arrived at Bluff.

Two days after Smith's departure an additional and very important decision was reached — to send another exploring party across the Colorado River for the purpose of charting a course all the way to Montezuma and to determine whether a road could actually be built through that rough and inhospitable country. Leaders of the expedition didn't doubt their ability to construct a passable wagon road down through the Hole; the river could also be crossed without too much trouble. But once across that stream, would it be possible to take wagons on to the San Juan? It was the region lying immediately east of the Colorado that earlier scouting parties had found impassable. Whether a route for a possible road could be charted through that wild country must now be definitely learned; if the company must turn back, better now than later. The only way to obtain this vital information was to send scouts all the way to Montezuma for that purpose. Platte D. Lyman, now field captain of the expedition, chose George W. Sevy, Lemuel H. Redd, Sr., George Morrell, and George B. Hobbs for this difficult and important task.

Many years after the events of this memorable trek, Hobbs told the story of that exploration and the experiences of the four men who made it. It is his account that is reproduced on the following pages. Hobbs dictated this account to Andrew Jenson, Assistant Church Historian of the L.D.S. Church, in October, 1917, almost forty years after the events related had taken place. It is, therefore, not surprising to find some minor items of confusion, some mistakes in fact, and a possible over-emphasis of the importance of the narrator.[1]

Even though Hobbs may tend to over-emphasize his own importance and undervalue the wisdom and actions of his fellows, his is the only detailed account of the actual events of that exploring expedition. That fact alone greatly enhances the value of the document. The account should be considered as not merely George Hobbs' story of his own exploits but as an account of the experiences of the four scouts as one of them remembered those experiences many years later. It is, indeed, regrettable that the other members of the party did not also record their versions, but we are fortunate that one of them did take the time and exert the effort necessary to do so.

The narrative is fascinating, full of human interest and humor, and, with the general exceptions noted, quite accurate. Many of the physical features described are well enough portrayed to enable ready location today. Since the account was dictated, not handwritten by its author, I have taken the liberty of making some corrections in punctuation, spelling, typographical errors, and paragraphing. Needless to say, the original wording has been retained. Andrew Jenson's brief preface to the Hobbs account is included here, just as it appears in the San Juan Stake History.

Andrew Jenson's Preface to Hobbs' Account

The company at the Hole-in-the-Rock decided to make a trail down the rocks, at the point where the boat had been taken down to a grass-covered bench of about 100 acres about half way down to the river, where grass and water seemed plentiful. The water was found in holes in the rocks. After spending about 500[2] days work on making this trail, it was still so dangerous that nine head of the horses that were taken down to the bench below slid off to the river bottom, about 1,800 feet, and were killed, nobody knowing where they landed and no one daring to go to the place where they had fallen. This trail was subsequently useful in getting pack animals of the next expedition down to the river.

About the time the trail was finished Geo. Sevy of Panguitch, and Lemuel H. Redd of Harmony, came up with a company of settlers, to the Hole-in-the-Rock.[3] These men were arranging to send an expedition through to locate farms for themselves and company on the San Juan river, and it was proposed by the company that Geo. B. Hobbs should accompany them. He, however, was loathe to go, as the former expeditions which he had accompanied were too weak hearted to go on through. But Bro. Sevy then made the assertion that if Brother Hobbs would consent to go with them, they would follow him as far as he dared to lead. Following is Bro. Hobbs' verbatim report:

George B. Hobbs' Account of Exploration from Hole-in-the-Rock to Montezuma and Return

I agreed to accompany these men and returned to my wagon at Fifty Mile Spring to get supplies for the journey. Geo. Morrell asked, if it was possible to take a burro to pack our bedding and food, for some of the former explorers had reported that it would take a thousand dollars to make a sufficient trail to get the burro out the first ten miles from the river. I laughed at this assertion, saying that I believed it was possible to get him out with very little labor. Bro. Redd said he had a mule that was not much larger than a burro, and if we could get a burro out, he thought we could get the mule out. Bro. Sevy said he had a horse not larger than the mule mentioned, and if we could get the mule and burro out, we could get the horse out also. Jos. Lillywhite furnished me a horse that was no larger than the Sevy horse. This gave us two packs and two riding animals. George Sevy, Lemuel Redd, Geo. Morrell and I started out the 17th of December, 1879, carrying sufficient food to last us 8 days, as a map which we carried with us showed that the distance was about 70 miles direct in an air line to Ft. Montezuma. Not wishing to be overloaded we took rations for eight days, thinking we could average about twenty miles a day.

The first day we got our packs ready and got down the trail previously made to the river.[4] The second day, having crossed the river, we made a little trail to get out,[5] and then traveled over a bench to what is called The Slick Rocks or Lookout Rocks.[6] Just before reaching these rocks a herd of Llamas 14 in number, came up and followed us for some distance. They were quite curious to know what kind of animals we were! While cooking breakfast the next morning at Lookout Rock one of these animals came within 15 ft. of our camp fire and stood watching us. I tried to catch it with a pack rope, but it was very active in dodging the lasso. I could have shot it, but I thought the animal was too pretty to kill. I followed it for some distance. It seemed to draw me off down in the rocks until I finally got to the bottom of the rocks, about a half a mile from camp; there the animal left me. I climbed back up the rocks and soon learned that Bro. Sevy and Morrell who had been trying to find a way to get down these rocks, but had returned to camp, reporting that we could go no farther. I told them that I had already been clear to the bottom. They then told me to swallow my breakfast and lead out and they would follow me. This seemed to be the only passage down these slick rocks.

Our route lay thence nearly due east, and while traveling along a ridge about 11 o'clock we first saw to our left what is now called Lake Parahrit.[8] Continuing our journey eastward we dropped into Castle Gulch [Castle Wash], after traveling about 15 miles to the so-called Green Water. Here three canyons centered, one leading northeast, one due east and one southeast. As we had been traveling to the northeast I suggested we take the southeast canyon but Bro. Sevy thought the east canyon would be the right one. Bro. Redd and Bro. Morrell suggested we take the northeast canyon, which seemed to be a little the largest. Each one explored his own canyon to suit himself. The southeast fork boxed up about a mile. The east canyon boxed up at about the same distance, while the other was an open canyon. Night coming on we camped at this point in the open canyon, all having now joined again.

The next morning we started up the northeast canyon and after traveling a short distance came upon a Cliff Dwellers' dwelling, in which there were 7 rooms, the bake oven being in such a perfect state of preservation that by cleaning out the dust it would be ready to bake bread in at this late day.[9] This certainly seemed good to us, as it looked like we were getting into God's country once more.[10] Time, however, had obliterated this [the Indian trail] trail for several miles, but we thought it must follow up this canyon.

We followed the canyon or wash for several miles when we came to a fork leading to the east. This fork did not look very encouraging to our party and they refused to go up this wash. Being still anxious to bear further south, I explored this canyon on my own account. After going about a mile, I discovered the old Cliff Dweller trail again and going about a mile farther I came to a break in the cliffs leading due east. Satisfied that this was our route, I ran back down hurriedly in order to catch up with my companions who had started up the left hand canyon. After going a short distance up that canyon I met them riding very fast coming back as they claimed a bear had interfered with their passage. After telling them what I had discovered, we immediately followed up the canyon which brought us to the top of Clay Hill.[11] In going down that hill on the east side, we followed the Cliff Dwellers' trail in many places, it being well defined and plain in most places.

We chose a route going almost due east, but had only gone a few miles when we were cut off by the Grand Gulch, which in many places was inclosed between perpendicular walls from one to two thousand feet high. We then undertook to find the old Cliff Dwellers' trail again, bearing to our left for that purpose. We, at length, found the trail and camped about three miles west of what is now called Cow Tank.[12] After discovering Cow Tank the next morning, we journeyed northeast, picking up the trail here and there where it was not obliterated. We camped that night at Dripping Spring.

The next day [December 23], traveling about the same direction, we came to Grand Flat, near the Elk Mountains. The snow fell about 8 inches that night upon our beds, obliterating the tracks of our animals, so that they were very hard to find. This compelled us to make a very late start the next day, as it was snowing very hard all the time. We could scarcely tell which way we were going, but late in the afternoon it cleared up and turned very cold. The Grand Gulch still to our right forced us up on to the side of the Elk Mountains, where night overtook us. That morning we had cooked the last food we had, consisting of a slap jack baked in a frying pan and about one inch thick. The man who cut the cake had to take the last choice.[13] This was about our eighth day out.

It was Christmas day, 1879, which found us on the side of the Elk Mountain without food, in the midst of a piercing cold, and not a mountain in sight that I could recognize. I was the only member of the party that had been to Ft. Montezuma on a previous trip. It surely looked like our bones would bleach not far from that point, as it was impossible for us to retrace our steps to our river camp, and not knowing which way to go to reach our destination on the San Juan. Bros. Sevy and Redd (who had large families at the river camp) and Bro. Morrell, who having a family at Junction, were feeling very much discouraged and were accusing one another of getting them in their present predicament. Not wishing to listen to them, I started for a ridge a short distance north from camp, where the snow had drifted off the ridge. But I could still see nothing that I could recognize, although I could see mountains to the east, as far as 150 miles away. I could see the needles called El Capitan, a hundred miles southeast in the Navajo nation.

Seeing a small mound to the south I climbed it to see if I could see any further. This was surely Salvation Knoll,[14] for on looking to the northeast across a spur of the Elk Mountain I discovered the Blue Mountains, about 10 miles away. This was the land mark we had been looking for for several days. I called to the boys who were still jangling among themselves, that the Blue Mountain was about 10 miles to the north of us. The brethren ran towards me as fast as they could come and were soon beside me. From this point we could locate ourselves, but knowing we were a long distance yet from Ft. Montezuma we lost no time in starting and following a canyon to the east. We camped that night in a cliff dwellers' dwelling,[15] and although hungered yet we were happy to know that there was yet a chance for us to get through. This was an eventful Christmas for us poor men; no food but yet hopeful.

Our traveling east the next day brought us to Comb Wash.[16] This wash derives its name from a perpendicular cliff about thirty miles long on its east side which is scalloped out resembling a comb to some extent and here we came face to face with that cliff. This cliff which runs almost due north and south we followed that day.

The next day we came to a break in this cliff where the cliff dwellers had previously done a vast amount of work in making a trail leading up the side to the top.[17] After repairing the trail in places and pushing and pulling our animals up jump offs that spanned the trail we arrived at the top towards night. Going but a short distance further east we encountered another gulch now known as Butler Gulch, paralleling Comb Wash. Bro. Sevy remarked that we might have to go up this wash 50 miles in order to get across, as the walls were perpendicular and obstructed our passage going to the east. Night overtaking us, we camped in this small canyon,[18] this being our third night without food. I cut my name in the rock with the date I was there, not knowing that I would survive the journey.[19]

That night snow fell and the next morning in going to look for our animals we discovered that a band of Navajo Indians had passed near our camp going south. Thinking that perhaps they had stolen our horses and were possibly ambushing themselves to kill us. But a better fate was in store for us. Finding our animals in a secluded box canyon, we cheered up our spirits and started up the Butler Gulch to try and find the crossing.

After going up on the west side for some distance we saw where we could get out on the east side of the wash, but could not get into the wash from the west. Going a short distance further we found where we could slide our animals in, which we did. I sure did hope one of them might have a leg broken or get hurt in this slide, as it would not have been long for us to have put some "jerkie" meat on the fire. No doubt this would have killed us, but our starving condition would have kept us from resisting such a feast. However, all got down safely, although the burro who lit on his back sounded like he had broken it. Climbing out of the wash, our road to the east was unobstructed, but the miles seemed to have no end. Our mode of travel was as follows: First two would ride one hour, while the other two walked, and so on. Bro. Sevy and Redd having watches, were time keepers, and they rode together. Bro. Morrell and myself thought our hour was somewhat lengthened out, but we were the youngest and the most able to take the heavy part.[20]

When nearing the place where Bluff City now stands we saw a calf standing in a valley. I drew my six shooter with the intention of killing it in order to have something to eat, but Bro. Sevy persuaded me not to, as he said there must be help near. Going about three quarters of a mile further, we discovered a camp occupied by white people. It proved to be a Bro. Harris, with his sons Geo. and Dan who had come from Colorado and settled just south of where Bluff City is now situated.[21] These were settlers that we had not looked for as they had come in since Silas Smith's company had left Montezuma the previous August. Expecting that a large company would show up soon they were surely pleased to see us, and we certainly were pleased to see them. Supper was about ready, and as this was our fourth day without food, and we were weary beyond description — the last part of the journey we had traveled through slush and mud nearly up to our knees. While Sister Becky Warren, a member of the Harris family was frying the meat for our supper I don't believe any torture in hell could have been worse to us.

Supper was soon ready, however, and we were told to eat. Food enough had been cooked for three families and set for us. After eating about 5 biscuits and the meat all being consumed, I thought I would quit, as it might injure me. But I couldn't resist the temptation of taking another biscuit, thinking that would be my last, when I would take another one. In all I believe I ate 22 biscuits. I thought this would be a happy death; but the others were doing the same.[22] This was the 28th day of December, 1879.

Taking breakfast with these good people the next morning,[23] (Dec. 29th) we continued our journey up the San Juan to Ft. Montezuma, and here we found H. H. Harriman and family, James Davis and family and Harvey Dunton. These people were eating their seed wheat ground in a coffee mill.[24] They having lived about two months on this kind of food with very little meat. Our first meal of chopped wheat would shame a dose of salts in its purging propensities.

As we were crossing Montezuma river just before reaching the fort proper we met two men coming from the east (Ernest Mitchell and James Merritt); they had three pack animals well loaded with provisions and bedding and two riding horses. As I had met these men on my previous trip I introduced them to my two companions while our horses were drinking nose to nose. They told us they were seeking a cattle ranch where they could drive cattle and no one interfere with them; some isolated watering place. They said they did not even mind blasting a way down to the San Juan or Colorado river if they could find sufficient grass to justify. As we had seen Lake Parahrit from a distance as we were coming out it looked good to us for a place as they wished to find. Seeing their packs were well filled and not knowing where we would get any supplies for our return trip, they looked like mighty good company for us. So we did all in our power to persuade them to wait for us while we made the trip up to the fort and returned. But this they refused to do. While we were talking, it started to rain, raining harder as we approached the fort. It rained all that night and the next day [Dec. 30, 1879] compelling us to stay at the fort.

What to do for supplies to return we did not know, as none could be bought and the nearest market was 125 miles further east. Flour was selling there $80 per hundred. While wondering what to do, we saw a trapper passing the fort. Going out and accosting him we found he was loaded with two burros with beaver skins, also a sack of flour. After arguing with him and persuading him, we finally got him to let us have a 48 pound sack of flour for $20. [According to James M. Redd, son of Lemuel H. Redd, the man who sold them the flour was Peter Shirts.][25] This was all the provisions that we were able to obtain.

We found the families had but little wheat left, but by economy they thought they could hold out for 60 days.[26] Bro. Sevy, Redd and Morrell promising them that they would get help through by that time. I was not a party to this agreement as I happened to be gone after the horses at the time.[27]

We now started our return Journey, Dec. 31, 1879, Harvey Dunton joining our party as he wished to meet his son[28] who was in the company and bringing provisions for him. Just after crossing the Montezuma Wash we discovered our friends Mitchell and Merritt who had been driven to shelter in a cabin that had been built on a piece of land close by. We still thought Providence was favoring us and that we could yet persuade these men to accompany us to Lake Parahrit. After my friends talked long and loud to them with no effect, Mr. Merritt dropped back to where I was driving the pack and I used my persuasive power. But Mr. Merritt informed me he was not hunting a cattle ranch at all; providing

I would keep the secret he would tell me what he was after. I promised I would, but as they met death later the secret is not now a secret at all.[29]

Mr. Merritt in passing from Ft. Wingate[30] to Lee's Ferry about a year before, through the Navajo Nation, had discovered three crude smelters, where the Indians had been smelting silver from silver ore which assayed at 90% silver. He was going to try and locate these mines and promised me, if I would leave my companions and accompany him, he would grubstake me and give me one-fourth interest in our discovery — the same as he was giving Mr. Mitchell. I thanked him kindly for his offer, but told him that I was a representative of a large company who were at the Colorado river and they were waiting for our return, so they could proceed on their journey. We traveled together until we came to the mouth of Comb Wash[31] when we separated, they crossed the river to the south going on the south side which was free from snow; we going up the Comb Wash, north into a snowy region. We separated about 4 o'clock in the afternoon, they going their way and we going ours.

Going up the wash a few miles we got out of it on the west side trying to make a new trail, but [the] canyon boxed up and we could go no farther forming camp. [According to James M. Redd, and confirmed by Kumen Jones, these men turned west from Comb Wash and were hemmed in for many miles working northward, and when they camped L. H. Redd dreamed that they would strike a trail the next day which would lead them out.[32] Next day at what is now known as Road Canyon, they found the trail up to the "Twist" and directly to Grand Flat. Making a big cut on the way they came out, and also found a place where the wagons could be taken through. James M. Redd also states that his father bought two mules of James Davis to take back with them from Montezuma because they had been short of horsepower on the trip out.][33]

Next morning (New Years Day, 1880) I tried to find a way out to the west, but I couldn't find one. It had been a cold bitter night, frost settling on our bedding about three inches deep. Returning to our camp, I found a flour slap jack and flour mush awaiting me. When eating the breakfast one of the brethren says: "O don't I wish I had some of Merritt's coffee." Another said "I wished I had some of his bacon," and all were wishing for something that we did not have, wondering how it was they couldn't persuade them to accompany us to Lake Parahrit. I said, "O shut up, they were not hunting a cattle ranch at all, Merritt told me what he was after, but I promised not to tell." But my companions would not leave me alone until I told them, and as we were miles apart I thought my promise was not particularly binding. My companions were then wild to follow them, using all my persuasive power not to do it. They started to follow them anyway.[34]

Going down this wash a short distance we discovered an old trail leading to the west. This was the other end of the trail we had discovered many days before in Castle Wash. It looked like Providence had had a hand in directing us, and I stated so. We decided to follow this trail which we did about ten miles.[35] Dan Harris caught up with us at this point and accompanied us.[36] I was leading when the snow got so deep we could follow the trail no longer and it was bitter cold; they murmured because I was keeping them too far to the north. I was making back for the Elk Mountains to take up our trail from there back. Harris asked, "Which way does your camp lay from here?" We told him almost due west. Harris says: "Follow me. I can go due west." I told him the Grand Gulch lay between us and our destination and that we would have to go up near the Elk Mountains to get across it, he sneered at this idea and said we could find a crossing lower down. Starting out I followed behind.

We travelled two days due west and it looked like we were within about 10 miles of the Clay Hills.[37] The morning of the third day we came to the Grand Gulch which we thought was about 2,000 ft. deep and impossible to cross. I asked which way they were going then to get across, up or down. They said, "Down." I says, "We part company right here. I am going up and go through and tell the tale. All I ask is my share of the flour that is left." We took the flour sack from the pack mule and measured it out. There was about one quart for each man. Putting mine in a seamless two bushel sack, it hardly dusted the sack to the bottom. Geo. Morrell then decided to follow me, as we were bed companions and I had most of the bedding. Lemuel Redd decided that he would also follow. This changed the attitude of all so they all decided to go up to get across.

This made us retrace our footsteps of the previous day and we traveled all the next day in a northeasterly direction. Then we got into the Grand Gulch, traveling up it until we found a place to get out on the west side.[38]

A snow storm now set in and not being able to take our bearings we crossed the backbone, got into the canyon where the natural bridges later were discovered. The snow storm letting up, we again got our bearings. But some of our party, seeing a break in the red cliff to the west of us thought it was the Clay Hill break, not being satisfied until they rode a number of miles till they discovered their error.[39]

A little later the Clay Hills loomed up about 30 miles ahead of us. We were now back on our old trail and making good time. It was at this time that our flour porridge gave out, and we were again facing starvation. We had been living on one pound of flour a day. We had never even seen any kind of game to kill, as the snow was so deep and bitter cold. The next day, passing the Clay Hills, we discovered the Clay Hill Spring.[40]

Our course lay down Castle Gulch to a point where we thought we should take out and reach the lakes that we had seen on our previous trip. We hunted some time to find the lakes.[41] But all gave up except myself, declaring the lakes were a phantom. The only way I convinced them was for myself to take a bucket and get water which I did, finding the lakes over the next ridge. The next morning we made an early start and watered our animals at the lake. We then continued the journey hoping to reach our camp at the Colorado River.

After traveling about 6 miles we came to the Slick Rock where the Llamas [Mt. Sheep] had been seen on our previous trip.[42] Snow covering the rocks changed the appearance of the face of the rock. We still believed that a better way could be found in getting up the rock, but after exploring to the right and the left we found it impossible as they turned into perpendicular cliffs. Our efforts were then made to try and climb the rocks at that point, which seemed to be without avail. All then gave up except Geo. Sevy and myself. We kept trying while the others lay and laughed at our futile efforts, as hunger at this time had made them almost maniacs.

Bro. Sevy and myself succeeded in getting about two-thirds of the way up. The sun came out, shining brightly on the snow which snow blinded me. Bro. Sevy said, "You'll fall!" But I fell as soon as the words were spoken, sliding nearly a quarter of a mile to near the bottom of the rocks. My companions at the bottom enjoyed this feat immensely, but I retraced my tracks to where Bro. Sevy was. The sun, coming out more brightly, melted the snow a little which enabled us to make a snow dugway up the face of the rock.[43] Fortunately this froze during the night sufficient that the next morning our efforts were successful in getting to the top.

Here nothing seemed to impede our way to reach camp that day. Some of our party then started out leaving myself and Geo. Morrell to drive our packs. I rode one of the horses which had worn its hoofs almost to the hide, leaving a circle of blood at every step. But we were so weak we had to do it. We were now on the backbone between the Colorado and San Juan River, and could see our companions miles ahead of us making every effort to reach camp. They followed this ridge when they should have taken off to the right into a draw that would lead them in the right direction.[44] I told my companion of this. He said, "You lead which way you think is right and I'll follow."

About noon we came to a place where the snow was melted off of the side hill. Stopping there, we took the packs off and let our animals eat the grass which was plentiful at this point. About one hour and a half later we had put the packs back on, when our companions came in on our tracks, the horses foaming with sweat. Apparently they had lost themselves, traced back, and had even missed our tracks where we turned into the draw and had been riding like demons to find us. The laugh now being on them, they immediately spurred past us keeping to the draw when they should have left a short distance below, bearing again to the right.[45] In about half an hour they again showed up from behind. Bro. Sevy says: "If we get to camp tonight we will have to follow Bro. Hobbs." This they did and in a short time we slid our animals into a box canyon which led directly to the Colorado river.[46]

Now I told them they could follow the trail as they could not get out, so they sent me ahead on the best horses with Lemuel Redd. Not knowing the object of this I asked Bro. Redd and he told me. They had figured that I would have to swim the river to get the boat, as they believed nobody would be waiting for us, as we had been gone 24 days instead of 8, and the people would believe Indians had killed us, and the Indians would possibly track back to see where we came from, and would kill anyone that would be looking for us. This idea I disbelieved. I knew I had friends who had not yet given me up as I had been in mighty hard places before. If it had been necessary for me to swim the river to get the boat, I believe I could have accomplished it, although the river was running thick with ice floes.

Upon reaching the river, however, we found four men on the lookout for us. These men had just got supper ready for themselves when we arrived. The odor of cooked food was sure a treat for us. We pushed them to one side without saying a word and went to devouring. Our friends looked from one to the other trying to figure out our emaciated appearance, finally asking: "Where are the other boys?" We said: "Coming Cook some more!" About the time we had devoured all the food in sight our companions arrived, they having to wait some time while the boys baked more bread and fried the meat. This surely was a torture to them.

These boys had a prearranged signal to the lookout on the opposite cliff on the other side of the river, 1½ miles away. They gave the signal that we had arrived. Bro. Sevy was so anxious to again meet his family that he, with one of the lookout party, crossed the river and climbed the cliff to the Hole-in-the-Rock the same night, myself and companions resting over night and crossed the river next day.[47] It was surely a joyous reunion; also the report we brought that we could get through was well received, and good news indeed to the waiting saints who were anxious to proceed.

Work was progressing slowly on the road at the Hole-in-the-Rock as they had to blast the cliff back (which was 45 ft. high). The country above the cliff sloped at about a 45 degree angle, which necessitated us blasting it back for about 300 ft. in order to make a passage through, which was just wide enough for our wagons to get through.[48] The sandstone made a footing underneath and we filled the larger holes with big rocks. This was the work that was going on by about 50 of the men when we returned, as was also the work of slowly lowering them by a rope over the cliff which was a tedious job and the rope was wearing through.

About 30 men also were working on the road below, making a dugway through the solid rock, in order to get out onto a sand slide. The way this dugway was made was by carrying small cottonwood poles from the Colorado river three quarters of a mile below, drilling holes in the face of the rock, putting in pins, then laying the poles against the pins to form a base for the dugway. We then blasted out the rock above and filled it up against these poles. This made the upper wheel of the wagons to run in a groove so that they would not tip over.[49]

While working at the cliff above I noticed a small seam in the sand stone just above our heads that seemed to reach along the face of the cliff for some distance. After exploring this seam I believed that a foot trail could be picked out at this point which would save lowering and raising the men with a rope morning and night.[50] Some laughed at my idea. But the second day they saw I was going to be successful so they started at the lower end, picking their way to meet me. We picked out a trail about two feet wide so that the men could crawl on their hands and knees up and down. This narrow trail was in places 60 feet from the bottom, 500 ft. from the top; but it was used successful until the Cliff was blasted sufficient for us to crawl up and down on the new wagon road.[51] I helped work on the road after that for about a month until it was completed to the river. My wagon was the first one taken down.[52]

FOOTNOTES

1. Although he states that he was asked to accompany Sevy and companions on this scouting venture, Hobbs tends to make himself the hero and central figure of the group — the one who actually saved the expedition from starvation and from becoming hopelessly lost; the one most instrumental in locating the route that was ultimately followed by the whole company.

While examining this account, the reader must realize that Hobbs was the only one of the four who had been to the San Juan on the earlier exploring expedition, during the spring and summer of 1879, and the only one who knew anything at all about the country into which they were heading. And *he* knew only the San Juan region east of Comb Ridge; the country between Hole-in-the-Rock and the point on the San Juan ten miles west of Bluff was completely unknown. However, with his background it would seem natural that the other members of the party should on occasion look to Hobbs for leadership. But was he as completely in command of the situation as his account would seem to indicate?

This account was published under the editorship of Dr. Elden Beck as part of his "Mormon Trails to Bluff," *Utah Magazine,* February through April, 1941. However, a comparison of this printed version with the original Hobbs account discloses the fact that the editor did not attempt to make a verbatim copy, but chose rather to make numerous interpolations. The account carries virtually no editorial comment.

Under the title: "First Exploration of the Forbidding San Juan County," George B. Hobbs published another and very similar account of his exploration in the *Deseret Semi-Weekly News,* December 29, 1919, 6. This account is cited in footnote references.

2. Five hundred days' work? Perhaps five days' work.

3. In his *Deseret News* account Hobbs implies that Sevy, Redd, and George Morrell (more or less independently of the main company) were preparing to go on to the San Juan and that he was chosen to represent the major portion of the "mission" company. Platte D. Lyman, in his journal, states very definitely that he, as leader of the whole expedition, requested Sevy to head this four-man exploring party.

4. This was the trail already referred to; not a trail down through the Hole-in-the-Rock.

5. Probably near the head of Cottonwood Creek at what later became known as Cottonwood Hill.

6. This bench was Grey Mesa. Details are lacking concerning the actual route followed in reaching the mesa, but it was probably not far from that ultimately taken by the wagons. After traveling over Grey Mesa the party arrived at the northeast rim where the mesa terminates abruptly. The name most commonly applied to this point is the "Slick Rocks."

7. Both of Hobbs' accounts refer to these as llamas. They were obviously mountain sheep, plentiful in the region at that early date but rather scarce now.

8. There are several spellings of this name, the most commonly accepted being Pagahrit. It is also known as Hermit Lake. The four scouts were traveling eastward

along the divide between the San Juan and Colorado drainage. The wagon road would ultimately be built several miles to the north, by way of the lake.

9. This is Castle Ruin, from which Castle Wash gets its name. The ruin, located in a large cave about a mile up the wash from Greenwater Spring, is in a remarkably fine state of preservation; stock men use it as a salt storage depository for their cattle.

10. At this point there seems to be an omission in the account; there is obviously something lacking. In the *Deseret News* account Hobbs states that he located an old Indian trail at this time.

11. By discovering Clay Hill Pass the explorers had found the only possible place where a road could have been built through that region. It became one of the major obstacles for the wagons soon to arrive there.

12. Cow tank is a large natural rock tank which still supplies water for stock when most other water holes have dried up.

13. Charles Redd, "Short Cut to San Juan," *Brand Book*, 16, says that Hobbs was about to cut the pancake when one of the others remarked that he hoped Hobbs knew how to cut it even, whereupon Hobbs handed the knife to the speaker and stated, "Be sure you take the last piece."

14. In his *Deseret News* account, Hobbs names this "Xmas Point." It is sometimes called "Christmas Knoll." The present highway from Blanding to Natural Bridges National Monument passes right at the base of this hill. From the top of it, the Blue Mountains are in clear view — my son and I checked this during the summer of 1954.

Charles Redd's "Short Cut to San Juan," *op. cit.*, states that all four men climbed the knoll and made the important observations, detracting somewhat from Hobbs' own personal contribution.

15. The *Deseret News* account states that the same Indian trail was located again and led the party past Kane Springs and on to this cave.

16. The party reached Comb Wash December 26 at a point several miles north of the route ultimately used by wagons. The wagon route was located by these same explorers on their return trip from Montezuma.

17. This is at Navajo Hill where the present highway from Bluff to Mexican Hat cuts through Comb Ridge. Remnants of the old Indian trail were still visible during the summer of 1957 on the south side of the draw. The modern highway has been cut on the north side, leaving the old trail undestroyed. Navajo Hill is some five miles north of the San Juan River. Contrary to some printed accounts wagons of the Hole-in-the-Rock expedition were not taken up Navajo Hill.

18. This does not mean in Butler Wash, but rather in one of the numerous small canyons or gulches running into Butler from Comb Ridge.

19. This inscription was located May 14, 1960, on the face of a cliff in one of the small draws draining into Butler Wash from the west. The discovery came as a result of a systematic search led by Wiley Redd who enlisted the aid of E. N. Porter and a troop of Explorer Scouts. Howard Shumway was the first of the group to sight the partially eroded inscription.

20. This is without doubt entirely imaginary on the part of Hobbs. He probably rode as much as either of the others.

21. In his *Deseret News* account Hobbs states that the Harris family had heard of the contemplated Mormon settlement on the San Juan and had moved in from Colorado during the summer of 1879. He lists the number of people in the camp at ten grown persons and five children.

22. Since there was a shortage of food, the Harris people had rationed themselves to two meals a day and were just preparing the evening meal when the four scouts made their appearance. So they ate the food prepared for 15 people. Although three days late, this was probably the best Christmas dinner Hobbs and his companions ever enjoyed.

23. *Deseret News* account: "Breakfast was served more sparing the next morning, as there would soon be a famine in camp."

24. Davis had hauled this wheat from Mancos, Colorado, a distance of about 125 miles, and even then had been able to obtain only six bushels at $11 a bushel, according to the *Deseret News* account. They were eating the wheat without any salt because the meager supply of that commodity had been exhausted, making the food even less palatable. See James Davis' account, Appendix III, this work.

25. This notation is in the original draft.

26. Before leaving Montezuma arrangements were made for the Davis and Harriman families to share supplies until the explorers could return.

27. Although Hobbs may not have considered himself a party to this promise, he was the one who eventually returned with loaded packs, arriving February 24, 1880, several weeks before the wagons.

28. James Dunton.

29. Both Mitchell and Merritt (or Merrick) were killed by the Indians in Monument Valley. For an account of their fate see Charles Kelly, "Chief Hoskaninni," *Utah Historical Quarterly,* July 1953, 223.

30. Immediately east of Gallup, New Mexico.

31. In returning, the party evidently followed a trail along the San Juan to the mouth of Comb Wash instead of taking the difficult route through Butler Wash and over Comb Ridge at Navajo Hill.

32. Hobbs later indicated that he was the one who had received divine aid.

33. This note in the original.

34. The *Deseret News* account is substantially the same. It seems entirely contrary to the character of these three scouts to suggest that they would desert families and friends as related by Hobbs while he, the only single man of the four, remained loyal and true to those who waited at the Colorado.

35. With Elk Ridge in sight, directly to the north, they had a good land mark to guide them.

36. This would increase the party to six — the four original scouts, Harvey Dunton, and Dan Harris.

37. Ten air miles — but the party was not air-borne.

38. This must not have been far from the head of Grand Gulch, judging by the time it took the party to wander over into the upper reaches of Armstrong Canyon, a branch of White Canyon.

39. This must have been Red Canyon.

40. Today the small spring known as Clay Hill Spring is located just northeast of the Clay Hill Pass, well off the old road. Hobbs' journal seems to indicate that the spring they located was west of the divide. It must have been the one known today as Irish Green Spring.

41. Anyone who has been in that region will not be surprised that these scouts had difficulty relocating the lake which they had seen from a distance some two weeks before. It does seem odd that Hobbs should use the plural "lakes" since there was only one.

42. They evidently had passed the north end of the lake on the natural dam and marked the route to be followed by wagons a few weeks later.

43. Hobbs estimates that they built three-fifths of a mile of snow dugway up the Slick Rocks (*Deseret News* account).

44. Traveling southwest along the top of Grey Mesa the men in front evidently continued to the extreme southwest instead of turning northward into a gulch.

45. This incident probably occurred in the vicinity of the "Chute." If one failed to keep to the right at this point, the small canyon leading to the location of "Cheese Camp" would be missed; this would lead far to the south of Cottonwood Canyon also.

46. This box canyon was no doubt Cottonwood Canyon.

47. Jan. 9, 1880. The men encountered by the four scouts were doubtless part of the road-building crew.

48. This means that the approach (from the west) up to the natural notch lay on an incline of about 45°. Then there was a 45-foot drop almost straight down. The 300 feet referred to is the approach or trench leading to the Hole itself, all of which had to be blasted from solid rock. This approach trench is not more than half as long as Hobbs indicates.

49. This is a good description of "Uncle Ben's Dugway." Evidences of it are still plainly visible.

50. Men were lowered over the cliff on ropes in order that they might work on the trail below the notch. Also, the men working on the actual notch were lowered in half-barrels and held in place while they drilled holes for the powder charges. All this was a very slow, tedious job, often carried on under the worst possible weather conditions.

51. I find no evidence of this ledge today. It was probably cut away as the road was being completed.

52. Information contained on later pages of the Hobbs account indicates that his wagon was still at Fifty-mile.

CHAPTER VIII

DOWN THROUGH THE HOLE

The way we did make dirt and rock fly was a caution.

— Cornelius I. Decker

On the river rim above the Hole-in-the-Rock, December 14, 1879, before Silas S. Smith returned to the settlements for supplies, the company was formally organized into traveling and working units. The following officers were selected and sustained:

Captain of the company, Silas S. Smith
Assistant Captain, Platte D. Lyman
Captain of the first ten, Jens Nielson
Captain of the second ten, George W. Sevy
Captain of the third ten, Benjamin Perkins
Captain of the fourth ten, Henry Holyoak
Captain of the fifth ten, Zechariah B. Decker, Jr.
Captain of the sixth ten, Samuel Bryson
Clerk, Charles E. Walton
Chaplain, Jens Nielson

It is assumed that every man and each family was placed under the immediate leadership of one of these captains of tens, that future camp sites were selected and prepared under this organization, and that the company traveled, more or less, in groups as organized. However, this was not a close-knit organization with harsh discipline, and modifications were doubtless made to meet situations as they arose.

The company now found itself face to face with the most difficult obstacle to be encountered on the whole trek — the Hole-in-the-Rock. Here was a narrow cleft in the solid wall of the Colorado River gorge, a cleft that was really not much more than a very narrow crack before the pioneers widened it into a wagon road.

The exact width of this crack cannot be definitely determined. Most accounts agree that it was too narrow to allow passage for man or beast. However, on December 16 Platte D. Lyman was able to conduct a "survey" of it with the aid of a square and level; he found that the new road would drop eight feet to the rod for the first third of the distance to the river and five and a half feet to the rod for the rest of the way. In order to have conducted such a survey, he must have been able to enter the slit and descend for some distance — at least so it would seem. Possibly he was lowered into the crevice by rope in the same manner that workmen were lowered shortly thereafter; Lyman's silence regarding this matter, however, leads one to doubt that he was dangled over the cliff in this manner.

At any rate, the notch was found to be too steep and narrow to allow men to pass up and down through it as they went to work on the wagon road toward the river. All accounts agree that during the early stages of the roadbuilding operations men were either lowered over the cliff on ropes or climbed down the trail, some two miles upstream, previously used by the scouts. Within a few days, however, a foot trail through the Hole was completed, after the ropes began to wear thin and men became more and more reluctant to trust their lives to the fraying strands.

The first and most difficult obstacle was at the very top of the Hole. By climbing about fifty feet up an incline of approximately 25 degrees, along the edge of the narrow slit, the men found themselves at the brink of a sheer drop of forty-five feet. It was now necessary to cut away that huge block of solid sandstone in order to approach the lower portion of the notch which the leaders considered feasible for a road. The existing narrow crack had to be widened and deepened on a grade that would not be too steep for wagons.

From the base of that forty-five foot drop the crevice broadened somewhat, being wide enough for wagons in most places. But it was exceedingly steep, with a grade of approximately 45 degrees, full of pits and strewn with huge boulders. There were some places that would have to be widened and many that would need to be filled in order to pass over the huge blocks of stone that had fallen into the notch from the sheer walls towering above. This condition continued for approximately a quarter of a mile, or about one-third of the distance to the river. From that point the notch fans out still more into a sort of canyon. The upper part of this canyon, but still below the notch itself, the pioneers found to consist mostly of solid rock, but the grade was not quite so difficult, and by comparison a road could quite easily be built there. The bottom third of the descent was mostly through deep sand, which was probably a welcome change for wagonmasters going down because the sand would act as a sort of brake. Today the sandy soil supports a thriving patch of poison ivy and other shrubs.

Once the Colorado had been reached and crossed, there still remained the difficult problem of getting out on the other side. Since several of the men had already explored the east river bank, they understood the immensity of the problem facing the company. In order for wagons to roll eastward a road would have to be hewn from the face of a solid sandstone wall some two hundred fifty feet high. Even when completed, of course, the road would merely take the company out of the Colorado River gorge; there still remained ahead approximately a hundred and fifty miles of almost impassable country.

There were thus three major road-building tasks to be accomplished: First of all the notch itself (the real Hole-in-the-Rock) must be put in order; secondly, a road through the region lying between the base of the solid rock cliffs and the river must be completed; thirdly, a dugway out of the river gorge to the east must be cut from the solid rock wall. All these projects must be finished before another wagon wheel would turn.

Because of the shortage of blasting powder and tools, as well as the limited working space at the top of the Hole, the company was divided into three major work crews. One group worked at the head of the Hole and in the notch itself; a second completed the road from the base of the cliffs to the river; a third was dispatched to cross the Colorado and build a road up the east bank cliffs. All three tasks were undertaken simultaneously.

The exact division of the camp into the various work crews is not known. However, as we have already indicated, the men from Fiftymile camp were given the task of preparing the road on the east side of the river. They walked to the construction site on Monday mornings and remained there during the week. It was a group of these men who met the four scouts as they returned from Montezuma on January 9.

Most accounts are in agreement that Jens Nielson, Benjamin Perkins, and Hyrum Perkins were in charge of the blasting inside the notch itself. The Perkins brothers had migrated from the British Isles, where they had had considerable experience in the coal mines of Wales, and had become proficient in the use of blasting powder. Thus they were the logical men to direct the rock work at the Hole. Other members of the company soon nicknamed them "the blasters and blowers from Wales."

There were two blacksmiths in the San Juan Company, each with a forge and complete equipment. These men were certainly among the most important of the whole outfit, not only because they kept horses and oxen shod but in the essential job of keeping tools sharpened and in repair. One of the smiths was the non-Mormon Wilson Dailey from Harrisburg, Washington County, who had joined the expedition because he considered this an opportunity to get to the mines in Colorado in company with a large emigrant train. Dailey had first established camp back at Fifty-mile Spring but moved over to the Hole as it became obvious that his blacksmithing skill would be needed there. He had brought a small supply of coal with him, as was quite a common custom for blacksmiths who were traveling with overland companies. The other smith was twenty-three-year-old George Lewis from Kanab, who had joined the expedition in company with his father, James Lewis, who was not a black-smith but "went on the trip as helper and guide."[1] Both forges were evidently established at the top of the Hole, where the smiths performed a most vital service. Coking ovens were constructed and operated by the younger men of the expedition. George W. Decker recalled in later life that he had helped in that service.[2] Belt Dailey, young son of Wilson Dailey, remembered (in 1954) having helped run the bellows for his father.

Equipped with picks, shovels, sledge hammers, and chisels, the company set to work with a will. Said Cornelius Decker in later life: "I don't think I ever seen a lot of men go to work with more of a will to do something than that crowd did. We were all young men; the way we did make dirt and rock fly was a caution ... the Cedar boys were a lot of coal miners. The way they did make rock fly was a caution. We had the road made up the other side by the time the Cedar boys got that ledge shot down."[3] Small quantities of blasting powder were received from time to time, although there was always a shortage of that commodity during this early stage of the operation where it was most urgently needed. Hampered by winter storms, the work progressed slowly.

An assault on the major barrier — the forty-five foot drop — was made by lowering men over the edge of the cliff in half-barrels and dangling them there in mid-air while they hand-drilled holes in the face of the cliff and placed small charges of blasting powder. Members of the family of Peter A. Mortensen remember that he was one of those "thrown over the ledge" to help perform this precarious task.[4] This would have been a difficult and hazardous undertaking under the best of weather conditions, but as winter blizzards blew and temperatures dropped to zero, the work was necessarily slowed down. Under existing circumstances, it is remarkable not that this task took six weeks' time, but rather that more time was not required.

On January 22, twenty-five pounds of blasting powder arrived — the largest shipment to reach the camp at Hole-in-the-Rock — giving evidence that Silas S. Smith's fund- and supply-raising campaign was meeting with success. More supplies would arrive from time to time as the company pushed forward. James Monroe Redd, reporting late in life, stated that: "The Mormon Church sent back a ton of giant powder and approximately that much steel in picks and crowbars to Panguitch with orders to get it to the camp as soon as possible and at any cost, which they did."[5] Kumen Jones adds that the legislature made an appropriation of $5,000 and the church a grant of $500 for supplies and provisions.[6] However, there seems to be no record of such a grant in the church archives. The powder obtained on the twenty-second was used up in short order on finishing touches on the Hole. The remnant of one drill hole is still visible right at the top of the Hole.

While men were being "thrown over the ledge" and with pick, chisel, and hand drill gradually widening the fissure at the top and cutting a sort of trench approach to it from the west, others were busy below. At the bottom of the notch, about a third of the total distance to the river, was another sheer drop of approximately fifty feet. This had to be blasted away or otherwise disposed of. Well aware of the shortage of blasting powder and of the difficulty being experienced at the top of the Hole, Benjamin Perkins conceived the idea of avoiding this second sheer drop by tacking a road onto the face of the cliff and thus building a by-pass around that fifty-foot chasm. At this point the notch widens out into a sort of canyon, affording enough room for this type of construction.

For a distance of some fifty feet along the face of this solid rock wall men were instructed to chisel and pick out a shelf wide enough to accommodate the inside wheels of the wagons. Perkins declared that he would now build the face of the cliff up so that the outside wheels would be level with the inside ones. To accomplish this he instructed the blacksmith to widen the blades of drills to two-and-a-half inches; then with these tools men were instructed to drill a line of holes, each ten inches deep and about a foot-and-a-half apart, parallel with the shelf that had been chiseled out, and about five feet below it. Perkins is said to have marked the spot for each hole. At that point the cliff falls off at about a 50° angle, so that while they swung the sledges the workmen had to be held in place with ropes secured by their fellows.

In the meantime men had been sent to scour the river bank and adjacent area as far back as the Kaiparowits Plateau for oak that could be cut into stakes. When the row of holes was completed, approximately twenty-five feet along the face of the cliff, these stakes, each two feet in length, were driven firmly into the holes. On top of the stakes poles were secured to the ledge and brush, rock and gravel added until the face of the cliff had actually been lifted and a wagon road literally tacked on. This is one of the most remarkable portions of the whole road. It is rightly named "Uncle Ben's Dugway" in honor of its engineer. Although the stakes have long since vanished, allowing the poles, brush, and gravel to slip into the canyon below, the drilled holes are still clearly visible and some of the masonry rockwork is still in place.

During the first week in January Charles Hall, accompanied by his two sons, John, age 25, and Reed, age 19, arrived at the Hole with lumber and timbers for a boat or ferry that he had been commissioned to construct. It will be recalled that Hall had already contributed considerably to the success of the expedition as explorer and as builder of the small boat that was at that time being used to ferry workmen back and forth.

While the San Juan expedition had been pushing southward from Forty-mile Spring Hall and his sons had been busy in the Escalante Mountains cutting the necessary materials for the new craft. Some accounts state that Hall had floated part of the heavy timbers down the Escalante River; however, since the normal flow of that stream is so small during the winter low season this seems rather unlikely. He probably did gather some drift logs and possibly some railroad ties that would have floated down the Colorado all the way from Green River, Wyoming, but most of the materials he and his sons brought from Escalante by wagon.

Understanding the problems of boatbuilding and the necessity of having close-fitting joints and seams, Hall had designed the ferry and cut most of the lumber to specification at the Escalante mill, where necessary machinery was available. A brief account of these activities in ferry building has come to us through the pen of Roxanna Dorrity Hall, wife of Reed Hall.[7]

Charles Hall and sons were called by Pres. John Taylor to go to [the] Colorado river and put in a ferry to ferry the pioneers across who were going to Bluff to settle that place in 1879. Charles H. and his sons John and Reed went to [the] river and worked on putting the boats together which they had cut out and fitted in Escalante and all ready to put together. Charles Hall and sons gathered pitch pine wood and made a kiln piling the wood up the kiln and had a hole below; they set the pitch pine a fire and the pitch or gum run down into vessels, and they took it and stopped the cracks between the planks to keep the boats from leaking. The Hall family all went down there; they planted fruit trees and grapes near a spring, raised good gardens...

The fact that the boat was prefabricated made the assembling job at the river much easier and less time-consuming. All this material was carried down through the Hole by hand, since the trail was not yet in condition for wagons or pack animals. The kiln for pitch was constructed right at the river's edge in order that the caulking material would be readily available. All these activities point to the efficient planning of Charles Hall.

In addition to the Hall family, many persons helped in the building of this craft. One account states that half the citizens of Escalante assisted.[8] Numerous members of the San Juan expedition also participated, especially those who had brought carpenter's tools with them. Among those known to have helped are George W. Sevy, Joseph Stanford Smith, William Mackelprang, and Mons Larson;[9] there were doubtless many others. By the time the road was ready for wagons the ferry was also completed, so that there was no delay in ferrying the outfits across the stream — according to some accounts, two wagons at a time.

All these building activities were going on at the same time. Material blasted from the cliffs at the top of the Hole was used to make the necessary fills below, in places more than fifteen feet deep because of the huge boulders that had lodged in the crevice. Most of this artificial fill has been eroded away, leaving the bottom of the notch very rough and rugged, much as it must have been before the pioneers began to work on it. Still to be seen, however, are some of the points of jagged rock cliffs picked off to allow the wagon hubs to scrape by, and some of these points are twenty feet above the present floor of the gorge. There are also names of some of the pioneers chiseled in the face of the crevice wall at least twenty feet above the present floor. Nearby are deep scratches, where wagon hubs scarred the wall in 1880 and 1881. In one place about two-thirds of the way to the bottom of the crevice there is definite evidence that rocks and boulders have slipped and tumbled into the crack since the road was abandoned in 1881. One massive block tumbled into the crevice early in 1956, almost completely blocking the upper part of the notch.

Today there are more than a hundred and fifty chiseled and picked steps visible inside this famous gorge, giving it the appearance of a huge winding staircase. These steps have been the cause of a great deal of discussion and wonderment. Why, wonder most people who view the steps, did pioneer road builders construct a stairway for the wagons to jolt over? The answer is simple: These steps were not built by the Hole-in-the-Rock expedition but picked and chiseled from the solid stone some two decades later, twenty years after the Hole-in-the-Rock route had been abandoned in favor of Hall's Crossing,[10] by citizens of Escalante who were establishing an Indian trading post at the base of the Hole. Steps were constructed to facilitate the packing of goods from the trading post to and from the top of the canyon rim. Some of the steps may have been cut by miners, who also conducted some extensive operations in that vicinity shortly before and after the turn of the century.

Miners were also responsible for two pieces of old road currently observable there. One of these leaves the floor of the Hole-in-the-Rock gorge at a point about two-thirds of the way down to the river and leads out to the top of Jackass Bench, where it is lost in a maze of rocks and brush. Today considerable rock masonry clearly marks this old abandoned road, and many visitors to the spot mistake this for the road built by the San Juan pioneers. But that original road kept rather close to the bottom of the gorge all the way to the banks of the Colorado.

A second stretch of road later built by miners was constructed along the west bank of the Colorado, downstream from the base of the Hole, and could easily be followed for about a half-mile, where it ended abruptly in a tangle of huge boulders and loose debris. This road once extended almost all the way to the junction of the Colorado and San Juan rivers. Segments of it were clearly visible in several places before Lake Powell covered the region. It is possible that the upper portion of this road was cleared by the San Juan expedition as wagons were readied for the ferry and loose livestock bunched for the plunge into the icy waters of the Colorado. But the lower part of it certainly was not related to the Hole-in-the-Rock expedition.

As pointed out by most people who visit the Hole today, wagons could not be driven through there now; however, we must remember that when this was a wagon road it was kept in repair. Most of those huge boulders that block passage today were covered by smaller rocks, gravel and sand that had been thrown into the gorge from above. No horse could climb down through that crevice today with the trail in its present condition, especially since the rock fall of 1956. It is doubtful that a dog could make it either; perhaps a mountain sheep could. It must be realized that nearly a century of disuse has eroded away most of the original pioneer road and rendered the route impassable for animals and vehicles. But for at least a year after its completion in 1880 this was the major highway from southern Utah settlements to San Juan County. Much traffic went over it both ways. Scores of wagons were driven up through that notch as well as down, impossible as this may seem to those who visit the spot now.[11]

By the evening of January 25, 1880, the hard-working crews pronounced their work completed. The road was ready, all the way to the Colorado and up over the steep cliffs to a broad, relatively flat bench on the east side. The ferry was also ready and waiting. Early the following morning they would put the road to test.

Using as few words as possible, Platte D. Lyman, chief chronicler for the expedition, entered the following in his journal: "Jan. 26, 1880. Today we worked all the wagons in this camp down the Hole and ferried 26 of them across the river. The boat is worked by 1 pair of oars and does very well."

During the passing years a great deal of controversy has developed regarding the identity of the person who drove the first wagon down that narrow defile. The men of that day evidently did not consider it a matter of great importance: Lyman has accorded the matter no space in his journal. However, in view of the conflicts that have developed in recent years it is to be regretted that he did not give us the name of that first driver. A great deal of speculation could have been averted.

No fewer than six men are now claimed (or have been claimed by their friends, relatives, and descendants) to have been the driver of the first wagon. Some of these claims can be eliminated in short order. George B. Hobbs, it will be recalled, stated forty years later that his was the first wagon down. But later in his own account he states that his outfit was still camped back at Fifty-mile Spring. George W. Decker, also writing late in life, remembered that Joseph F. Barton drove the first wagon down.[12] But Barton was also camped at Fifty-mile Spring and arrived at the Hole after all the wagons that had been stationed there had made the descent. His own account of his thrilling ride down the Hole will be related later. There is one account that gives George W. Sevy the credit of being that first driver.[13] At least one man claims that Charles Hall actually drove that first vehicle, in addition to all the other services he had performed in behalf of the company.[14] In a statement supposedly written or dictated by James Monroe Redd, the claim is made that "James Pace's wagon was the first wagon down the hole in the rock which was so narrow that it crushed the water barrel on the side of his wagon."[15]

The most commonly accepted version states that Kumen Jones drove Benjamin Perkins' outfit on the first perilous descent. This case rests partly on the testimony of Jones himself, the only member of the expedition to claim the honor. He says:

Long ropes were provided and about twenty men and boys would hold onto each wagon as it went down to make sure there would be no accidents through brakes giving way or horses cutting up after their long lay off. I had a well broken team. This I hitched to Benjamin Perkins' wagon which I drove down through the "Hole."[16]

A great majority of people contacted during the preparation of this book seem to be of the opinion that Jones actually drove the Perkins wagon and that this was the first one to make the attempt.[17]

Later outfits experienced more difficulty than did the first one. Although a crowd of men and boys were on hand to hold back that first wagon, there actually was very little for them to do, for the wheels mired into the loose sand and gravel and pushed a veritable avalanche down the chute in front of the vehicle. The more wagons that passed that way, the more loose material was pushed down toward the bottom and the more difficult the stretch near the top became. After a dozen or more wagons had been taken down, the upper part of the notch was left smooth, slick, and very treacherous.

The method of descent needs some clarification. Wagons were prepared for the venture by rough-locking the hind wheels, not merely cross-locking them. This method of braking, well known to freighters of that era, consisted of wrapping a heavy chain several times around the felloe and tire of the wheel, then fastening the loose end to the wagon box or running gears in such a manner that the wrapped part of the wheel would be at the bottom and hence would help hold back the vehicle by digging into the ground. With two wheels so locked, the wagon would have a very effective brake.

In addition to this, long ropes and chains were attached to the rear axle or some other part of the running gears so that a dozen or more men could hang on behind the wagon to help slow it down as it plunged into the abyss. On occasion a horse or mule was hitched behind to pull back,[18] but this proved to be rather rough treatment for the animal as he was usually thrown to the ground and dragged down the steep bumpy grade. Danielson B. Barney tied "two large cedar trees to his wagon" to hold it back during the drive down.[19] Some accounts mention the planting of a large cedar post at the top of the Hole and throwing a hitch around this, either with a rope or chain, to ease the first part of the trip. These means were all used, and very effectively too, since not a single wagon was lost while making the perilous descent. Women and children usually were happy to walk down to the river rather than risk their lives in the wagons, although a few brave souls evidently preferred to ride.[20] Even walking was very difficult after most of the sand and gravel had been pushed to the lower portion of the notch, leaving the upper third slick and hazardous.

Rumors have spread that wagons were dismantled and lowered over the cliff a piece at a time and that even some of the horses and cattle were lowered over the ledges by use of bellybands and a windlass. There seems to be absolutely no substantial basis for these stories, which evidently had their beginning in the imagination of some later visitors to the Hole-in-the-Rock who found there the remains of an old winch that had been used by miners in 1899[21] to help lower a dredge through the Hole to the river below. The wagons were all driven down that narrow defile with horses or oxen hitched to the front, a driver in the wagon, and as many men hanging on behind as could find footing. On January 26, 1880, all the wagons of the camp at the Hole were driven down to the river and twenty-six of them ferried across the same day. Since there were probably some forty outfits in this camp, about fifteen of them were forced to remain overnight on the west bank at the base of the Hole and were probably ferried across early the following morning.

There are a few accounts of that hazardous descent written by the original participants or based directly on their verbal accounts. Most of these narrations are very sketchy and incomplete. However, some are worthy of reproduction here, for they tell the story as only a participant could possibly tell it. Let us first recount the experiences of Joseph Stanford Smith and his family as told by one of his grandsons, Raymond Smith Jones. Jones had often heard his grandfather tell of the experiences of the Hole-in-the-Rock pioneers and based the following account on those narrations. Smith had been one of the most active leaders in helping build the road through the Hole and on January 26 was kept busy most of the day working inside the notch lending necessary assistance to each wagon as it made the difficult journey to the river.

At last the word came that all the wagons were down, and the crossing on the ferry began. Stanford looked around for his family and wagon, but they were nowhere in sight. He dropped his shovel and climbed to the top of the crevice.

There, huddled in a heap of tattered quilts on packed dirty snow he found his wife, her baby swathed in blankets in her arms.

"Stanford, I thought you'd never come," she exclaimed.

"But where are the other children, and the wagon?" he asked.

"They're over there. They moved the wagon back while they took the others down." She pointed to a rusty stovepipe showing above a huge sandstone boulder.

For a moment Stanford's face flushed with rage. He threw his hat on the ground and stomped it — as was his habit when he was angry.

"With me down there helping get their wagons on the raft, I thought some one would bring my wagon down. Drat 'em!"

"I've got the horses harnessed and things all packed," Belle breathlessly assured him as they ran toward the wagon. Stanford hooked up the team, two at the tongue, and old Nig tied to the rear axle. The fourth horse, a cripple, had died at 50-Mile spring.

The children woke up, tumbled from their bed in the wagon, and wanted to help. Stanford climbed in and unlocked the brakes — and paused long enough to give each of the youngsters a bear hug.

Arabella climbed in and laid the baby on the bed and Stanford started the team toward the crevice through which the wagon must be lowered to the river.

"I'll cross-lock the wheels. Please throw me the chains, Belle."

She did as he asked, and then jumped down to help. Stanford took her arm and they walked to the top of the crevice, where hand in hand they looked down — 10 feet of loose sand, then a rocky pitch as steep as the roof of a house and barely as wide as the wagon — below that a dizzy chute down to the landing place, once fairly level but now ploughed up with wheels and hoofs. Below that, they could not see, but Stanford knew what was down there — boulders, washouts, dugways like narrow shelves. But it was that first drop of 150 feet that frightened him.

"I am afraid we can't make it," he exclaimed.

"But we've got to make it," she answered calmly.

They went back to the wagon where Stanford checked the harness, the axles, the tires, the brakes. He looked at Belle, and felt a surge of admiration for this brave beautiful girl. They had been called to go to San Juan, and they would go. With such a wife, no man could retreat.

"If we only had a few men to hold the wagon back we might make it, Belle."

HOLE-IN-THE-ROCK. This is the Hole-in-the-Rock as it appears from the top looking down through the notch. A small triangle of the Colorado River can be seen, three-fourths of a mile away. Today Lake Powell covers the bench seen on the opposite side of the river.

— *Bureau of Reclamation photo*

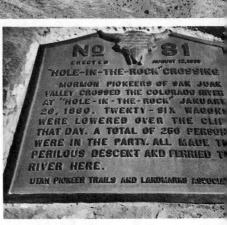

AIR VIEW OF HOLE-IN-THE-ROCK. From the air one gets a better view of the Hole-in-the-Rock vicinity. The dotted line shows the approximate route of the old wagon road: (1) Hole-in-the-Rock, (2) Register Rocks, (3) Cottonwood Hill. (Inset is a plaque which was placed at the river's edge in 1939. However, it was subsequently moved to the top of the "Hole" as Lake Powell waters began to fill the canyon.)

— *Bureau of Reclamation photos*

NO. 81
ERECTED   AUGUST 12,1939
"HOLE-IN-THE-ROCK" CROSSING
MORMON PIONEERS OF SAN JUAN
VALLEY CROSSED THE COLORADO RIVER
AT "HOLE-IN-THE-ROCK" JANUARY
26, 1880. TWENTY-SIX WAGONS
WERE LOWERED OVER THE CLIFF
THAT DAY. A TOTAL OF 250 PERSONS
WERE IN THE PARTY. ALL MADE THE
PERILOUS DESCENT AND FERRIED THE
RIVER HERE.
UTAH PIONEER TRAILS AND LANDMARKS ASSOCIATION

RIVER VIEW OF HOLE-IN-THE-ROCK. This view shows the depth of the canyon and the steepness of the old road as indicated by the dotted line. The canyon rim is approximately 1,800 feet above the river level. The distance from top to bottom via the wagon road is approximately three-fourths of a mile. Impossible as it seems today, this was a two-way wagon road for more than one year. The upper third of the road drops 50 feet for every 100 feet forward. Lake Powell water will never cover that upper third.

— *Bureau of Reclamation photo*

DANCE HALL ROCK. Here San Juan pioneers danced to music supplied by violins. The dance "floor" is just beyond the two figures in the picture.

— D. E. Miller photo

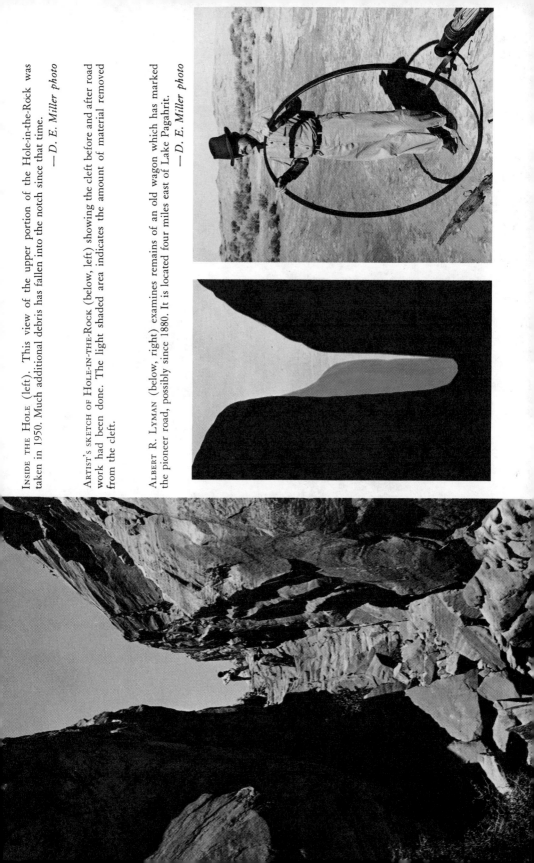

INSIDE THE HOLE (left). This view of the upper portion of the Hole-in-the-Rock was taken in 1950. Much additional debris has fallen into the notch since that time.

— D. E. Miller photo

ARTIST'S SKETCH OF HOLE-IN-THE-ROCK (below, left) showing the cleft before and after road work had been done. The light shaded area indicates the amount of material removed from the cleft.

ALBERT R. LYMAN (below, right) examines remains of an old wagon which has marked the pioneer road, possibly since 1880. It is located four miles east of Lake Pagahrit.

— D. E. Miller photo

UNCLE BEN'S DUGWAY. At the base of the notch at Hole-in-the-Rock, pioneer road build[
avoided a fifty-foot sheer drop by tacking a segment of the road to the side of the cliff. T[
was accomplished by: (1) cutting a shelf (dotted line) for the inside wagon whee[
(2) drilling a row of holes (arrows) some five feet below and parallel to the shelf; (3) dr[
ing oak stakes into the holes, then filling with logs, brush, and gravel to provide a tra[
for the outside wheels. The dugway is named in honor of its engineer, Benjamin Perkin[

— *Bureau of Reclamation ph*[

Silas S. Smith (left), president of the San Juan Mission.
— *Courtesy Edith Dibble*

Platte D. Lyman (right), first assistant and actual field captain during most of the Hole-in-the-Rock trek.
— *Courtesy Lucretia L. Ranney*

Aerial photograph looking north over the Hole-in-the-Rock. Dotted line shows route along base of Kaiparowits Plateau. Lake Powell has now partially filled Glen Canyon. (F) Fifty Mile Point, (H) trail through Hole-in-the-Rock, (J) Jackass Bench, (R) Register Rock.
—*Bureau of Reclamation photo*

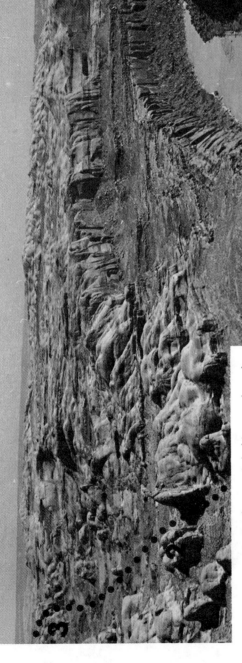

"IMPASSABLE COUNTRY." This view is looking east from the rim of the Colorado River gorge at Hole-in-the-Rock. Dotted line indicates route of wagon road: (1) Dugway road out of the river gorge, (2) Register Rocks, (3) Cottonwood Hill. Below: portion of the dugway (1) out of the river gorge.

— D. E. Miller photos

REGISTER ROCKS. In this view we are looking back through the Register Rocks to the Hole-in-the-Rock (H). Dotted line shows route of old road to a point where it disappears in the Colorado gorge (arrow). Once across the river, the old road followed a course between Register Rocks. Inset: One name carved at Register Rocks, "E. L. L.," stands for E. L. Lyman.

— *Bureau of Reclamation photos*

LITTLE HOLE-IN-THE-ROCK (left). This is actually the upper portion of Cottonwood Hill.

COTTONWOOD HILL (below, left). This is the major dugway in the center of Cottonwood Hill where pioneer engineers built up and over "impassable" country.

THE CHUTE (right). Very little work was required in the Chute, but a road had to be cut from solid rock from the Little Hole-in-the-Rock to get to it. Dotted line indicates route.

THE BACKBONE (below). Across Grey Mesa the old wagon road can still be seen. The narrowest part of the mesa is sometimes called the "backbone." Colorado drainage is on the left; San Juan on the right. Near this spot, John Rio Larson was born February 21, 1880, in the midst of a howling blizzard.

— *D. E. Miller photos*

SLICK ROCKS. The road down from the top of Grey Mesa was blasted out of the rock along a route "pointed out" by a mountain sheep as George Hobbs tried in vain to lasso the animal.

— *Lynn Lyman photo*

OUT OF SOLID ROCK. This is a portion of the pioneer road down from the top of Grey Mesa.

— *C. G. Crampton photo*

LAKE PAGAHRIT. Until 1915 beautiful Lake Pagahrit filled Lake Canyon above a natural sand dam. The Hole-in-the-Rock road ran right across the dam as indicated by the dotted line. On this photograph the dam and lake are sketched in.

— *Bureau of Reclamation photo*

LAKE PAGAHRIT as it appeared before the dam washed out and its waters thundered down Lake Canyon in November, 1915.

— *Courtesy Albert R. Lyman*

CASTLE RUIN (left). Expedition explorers discovered this ancient Indian ruin and a trail leading from it to Clay Hill Pass. Castle Wash is named in its honor.

— *D. E. Miller photo*

SALVATION KNOLL (right). Named by four explorers on Christmas day, 1879. From the top of this knoll the men could see the Blue Mountain and were thus able to locate their position.

— *D. E. Miller photo*

COMB RIDGE. Hole-in-the-Rock pioneers found no way to build a road through this barrier so were forced to follow Comb Wash — immediately in front of the ridge — southward (right) to the San Juan River.

— *Ernst Koehler photo*

SAN JUAN HILL. Finding no route for a wagon road along the San Juan River, the pioneers cut this road from the north river bank to the top of the Comb Ridge. It proved to be one of the most difficult segments of the entire route.

— *D. E. Miller photo*

WILEY REDD examines the partially eroded Hobbs inscription. Mr. Redd directed the search which led to the discovery of the inscription, May 14, 1960, in a gulch between Comb Ridge and Butler Wash. The inscription reads: "G. B. Hobbs Jan. 1."

— *D. E. Miller photo*

BLUFF CEMETERY. The Bluff cemetery overlooks the once prosperous community of Bluff. Many of the stalwart Hole-in-the-Rock pioneers lie buried here. The grave marker shown is that of Platte D. Lyman and his wife Adelia.

— *Bureau of Reclamation photo*

THE NAVAJO TWINS. This natural rock formation is a major landmark at Bluff. At its base stands Sunbonnet Rock, where on May 31, 1958, the Sons of the Utah Pioneers placed a plaque in honor of the San Juan Mission.

— *Bureau of Reclamation photo*

LELAND W. REDD paused briefly before the San Juan Mission plaque prior to offering the dedicatory prayer, May 31, 1958.

— *D. E. Miller photo*

"I'll do the holding back," said Belle, "on old Nig's lines. Isn't that what he's tied back there for?"

"Any man with sense in his head wouldn't let a woman do that," he cried.

"What else is there to do?" she countered.

"But, Belle, the children?"

"They will have to stay up here. We'll come back for them."

"And if we don't come back?"

"We'll come back. We've got to!" answered Belle.

Carefully she set three-year-old Roy on a folded quilt back from the crevice. Between his short legs she put the baby and told him: "Hold little brother 'til papa comes for you."

She told Ada to sit in front of her brothers and say a little prayer. She kissed each one and tucked quilts snugly around them. "Don't move dears. Don't even stand up. As soon as we get the wagon down papa will come back for you!"

Ada turned to Stanford, "Will you come back, papa?" He could only nod a yes and turn away with tears. "Then I'm not afraid. We'll stay here with God 'til you and mama get the wagon down." And Ada began her little prayer: "Father in heaven bless me and Roy and baby until our father comes back."

To take Belle's mind off the children, Stanford told her to test Nig's lines. "Pull back as hard as you can. I bet you couldn't pull the legs off a flea." Arabella wrapped the lines around her strong supple hands. Stanford got aboard. "Here we go. Hold tight to your lines." Arabella smiled at her little brood. "We'll be right back," she called.

Stanford braced his legs against the dashboard and they started down through the Hole-in-the-Rock. The first lurch nearly pulled Belle off her feet. She dug her heels in to hold her balance. Old Nig was thrown to his haunches. Arabella raced after him and the wagon holding to the lines with desperate strength. Nig rolled to his side and gave a shrill neigh of terror. "His dead weight will be as good as a live one," she thought.

Just then her foot caught between two rocks. She kicked it free but lost her balance and went sprawling after old Nig. She was blinded by the sand which streamed after her. She gritted her teeth and hung on to the lines. A jagged rock tore her flesh and hot pain ran up her leg from heel to hip. The wagon struck a huge boulder. The impact jerked her to her feet and flung her against the side of the cliff.

The wagon stopped with the team wedged under the tongue and Stanford leaped to the ground and loosened the tugs to free the team then turned to Arabella. There she stood, her face white against the red sandstone.

He used to tell us she was the most gallant thing he had ever seen as she stood there defiant, blood-smeared, dirt-begrimed, and with her eyes flashing dared him to sympathize.

In a shaky voice he asked, "How did you make it, Belle?"

"Oh I crow-hopped right along!" she answered. He looked away.

He walked to the apparently lifeless form of Nig, felt his flank. It quivered under his hand and Nig tried to raise his bruised and battered head.

Stanford then looked back up the crack. Up there on the sharp rocks a hundred feet above him waved a piece of white cloth, a piece of her garment. Why she had been dragged all that way!

"Looks like you lost your handkerchief, Belle." He tried to force a laugh, instead he choked and grabbed her to him, his eyes going swiftly over her. A trickle of blood ran down her leg making a pool on the rocks. "Belle, you're hurt! And we're alone here."

"Old Nig dragged me all the way down," she admitted.

"Is your leg broken?" he faltered.

She wouldn't have his sympathy; not just yet anyway. "Does that feel like it's broken?" she fairly screamed, and kicked his shin with fury.

He felt like shaking her, but her chin began quivering and he had to grin, knowing by her temper she wasn't too badly hurt. He put his arms around her and both began crying, then laughing with relief.

They had done it! Had taken the last wagon down — alone. Stanford put Belle on the bed in the wagon, found the medicine kit and cleaned the long gash in her leg.

"Darling, will you be all right?"

"Of course I will. Just leave me here and go as fast as you can for the children."

"I'll hurry," he flung over his shoulder and began the steep climb up the incline they had just come down.

He passed old Nig, who was trying to regain his feet. He climbed too fast and became dizzy. He slowed down, and looked around. He had driven a wagon down that fearful crevice, and dragged his wife behind. Her clothes and flesh torn, she had gamely said she'd "crow-hopped right along." God bless her gallant heart! He kicked the rocks at his feet and with tears streaming down his face lifted his hat in salute to Arabella, his wife.

"Papa! Papa!" a faint call came from far up the crevice.

He answered: "Papa's coming, Ada!" His voice echoed and re-echoed among the rocks as he called to the children over and over.

At last he reached the top to find the three little ones sitting where their mother had left them.

"God stayed with us," said Ada. "The baby's gone to sleep an' my arm's 'most broke," said Roy. Little George woke up and smiled a toothless grin.

Stanford Smith lifted the baby tenderly in his arms, took his son's hand in his, and with Ada clinging to his pocket, went down to Arabella.

Stanford's wagon lumbered out of the canyon, the team limping painfully. Old Nig followed behind on trembling legs, his hide torn and bleeding in places.

Just before they reached the river's edge, five men came into view just ahead of them, carrying chains and ropes.

"Look Stanford," she said. "They are coming to help."

He cracked his whip and shouted to his team and bore down on the men evidently without any intention of stopping. They jumped out of the road just in time.

"We came back to help you," one of them began, but Stanford cut him short. "How's the ferry, boys? Any of it left for us?"

"Brother Smith, we didn't—" Again he was cut short. Stanford hadn't gotten over the bitterness he felt when his family and wagon were left stranded above the Hole-in-the-Rock. He glanced at Arabella. She was pale. He remembered her gallant conduct, and was ashamed of his own ill temper.

"Forget it fellows. We managed fine. My wife here is all the help a fellow needs." Arabella's smile forgave his petulance. They went down to the ferry, followed by the abashed men. The wagon was loaded onto the raft. Arabella lay on a pallet at the raft's edge and watched red cliff walls recede, then closed her eyes and slept. When Stanford lifted her to the wagon an hour later she was completely relaxed.[22]

Joseph F. Barton was among those camped back at Fifty-mile Spring. On January 26, as the wagons began the dangerous drive down, he hurried back to camp and soon had his outfit rolling toward the entrance of the notch. However, he arrived late in the afternoon and found that all the wagons of the camp at the Hole had already made the descent. But let Barton tell his own story:[23]

... by means of a long rope and 10 men the wagons were lowered thru the hole and set on their way for the River (¾ of a mile distant) before any of the teams of camp no. 2 put in an appearance. The writer happened to be some distance in advance of the balance of company no. 2 and reached the dreaded road just at Sundown and knowing that if he waited for the ten men and rope he would camp on the rim that night but after taking a Survey of the cavity & putting on ruff lock and urging his team considerable finally got them to face what seemed almost next to death. However the next ½ minute landed team wagon and driver at [the] first station about 300 ft down the hole in the rock right Side up, where upon examination he found that the chain to ruff lock had broken but thru a providencial act the chain had flipped a lap around the felloe in Such a manner as to Serve for a lock.

Nathaniel Z. Decker's account runs as follows:[24]

My father helped Uncle Jim to get his outfit on its way and all the others who needed help and he hooked up his two wagons and six horses and mules and when he got to the hole there was none to help hold back with ropes tho some had promised to be there and would have been had they known he was there but no one showed up so he said there isn't any chance for a wagon to tip over and the animals ought to out run the two locked wagons and putting mother and us five children out he seated himself on the front wagon and started. Down they went in a flash and landed in the soft ground at the end of the slick rock slide . . . but one big mule was dragged and seriously hurt. How mother and the rest of the kiddies got down without harm; I suppose they were too scared to get hurt. I could hardly keep my feet under me it was so steep and slick. Looked like each wagon had slickened the bottom of the road till it was too slick to stand on.

Henry John Holyoak remembered that in order to get horses to face that terrible chasm they had to drive up to the Hole, "then push on the wagons, against the horses to start them thru."[25]

Milton Dailey recorded the following:[26]

The first forty feet down the wagons stood so straight in the air it was no desirable place to ride and the channel was so narrow the barrels had to be removed from the sides of the wagon in order to let the wagon pass through. It had to be rough locked on both hind wheels and then a heavy rope attached behind to which about eight men held back as hard as they could to keep the wagon from making a dash down the forty feet. The women and children took hold of hands and slid down this forty feet as they couldn't walk.

This record of the perilous descent through the Hole-in-the-Rock would not be complete without quoting briefly from a letter by Elizabeth Morris Decker[27] written to her father and mother a few days after that event:

We crossed the river on the 1st of Feb. all safe; was not half as scared as we thought we'd be, it was the easiest part of our journey. Coming down the hole in the rock to get to the river was ten times as bad. If you ever come this way it will scare you to death to look down it. It is about a mile from the top down to the river and it is almost strait down, the cliffs on each side are five hundred ft. high and there is just room enough for a wagon to go down. It nearly scared me to death. The first wagon I saw go down they put the brake on and rough locked the hind wheels and had a big rope fastened to the wagon and about ten men holding back on it and then they went down like they would smash everything. I'll never forget that day. When we was walking down Willie looked back and cried and asked me how we would get back home.

Even with all the precautions taken there were bound to be minor damages to property as wagons scraped through that narrow passage. Some empty water barrels were crushed and chicken coops broke loose, releasing poultry into the canyon. But the fowls were easily caught again as there was no place for them to hide or make good their escape. It is a credit to the skill and courage of the expedition that no major tragedy occurred; not a single wagon is reported to have tipped over or have been seriously damaged. Some animals were rather badly mauled, but all came through alive.

FOOTNOTES

1. Letter from Lettie Y. Swapp, historian of the Lewis family, March 7, 1955.

2. George W. Decker, Reminiscences (Appendix IX).

3. Cornelius I. Decker, Like Sketch (Appendix VII).

4. Letter to Lucretia L. Ranney, December 30, 1954, from Mrs. Eva Martin, daughter of Peter A. Mortensen.

5. James Monroe Redd, statement dictated to James McConkie, 1931 (Appendix XIII).

6. Kumen Jones, Preface to the Writings of Kumen Jones, 11.

7. This account was taken from the original handwritten copy.

8. Samuel Rowley, Autobiography (Appendix VI).

9. Raymond S. Jones, "Last Wagon Through the Hole-in-the-Rock," *Desert Magazine*, June 1954, 23–25, makes the claim for Smith. *L.D.S. Biographical Encyclopedia* (Andrew Jenson, ed.), Volume I, 800, mentions George W. Sevy as boatbuilder. A brief life sketch of Mons Larson furnishes information regarding his contribution; family records supply information for Mackelprang.

10. In 1881 Charles Hall located another, and what was considered to be better and more easily accessible, crossing some twenty miles upstream from the Hole-in-the-Rock at the mouth of Hall Creek, and moved his ferry to that point.

11. See Lyman's journal entry for May 6, 1880, for one account (Appendix IV). Many others could be assembled. Note Henry John Holyoak's statement (Appendix XIV).

12. George W. Decker, *op. cit.*

13. Some members of the Sevy family make this claim for George W. Sevy and state that they have some evidence to support their assertion; however, I have been unable to secure documentary proof.

14. Robert A. Berry made this claim in conversation with me, 1954.

15. From the Memory of Uncle James Monroe Redd, *op. cit.*

16. Kumen Jones, "General Move to the San Juan Mission" (Appendix V). Charles Redd, "Short Cut to San Juan," *Brand Book*, 18, states positively that Kumen Jones was the first to score the Hole with wagon hubs, indicating that his father, and probably other members of the Redd families, understood this to be true. Mary Jane Wilson, daughter of Benjamin Perkins, also confirms this account. (Jesse M. Sherwood, Life Sketch of Mary Jane Wilson, 9.)

17. However, Kumen Jones seems to have confused the issue himself for he also wrote:

> There is a controversy as to who drove the first wagon down through the Hole-in-the-Rock. Now the honor, if any honor belongs to that distinction, goes to Uncle Ben Perkins. Owing to the outstanding part he took in overseeing the job of blowing and blasting the roadway down through the notable "Hole," it was the unanimous decision of all that the honor of driving his outfit down first belonged to Uncle Ben. But his team was not trusty and he came to the writer of this account [Kumen Jones] and asked me to hitch my well–broke team on to his wagon, and he drove down. So there you are.

This quotation is taken from a biographical sketch of the life of Benjamin Perkins: "Benjamin Perkins, 1844–1926," by Albert R. Lyman (on deposit in the B.Y.U. Library). When Lyman was preparing the biography he evidently inquired of Kumen Jones, who must have given him the material here quoted. Nevertheless, it is my opinion that Jones, in writing the above statement, was merely trying to do honor to Benjamin Perkins; and that in spite of the contradictory statements he really did drive the first wagon. Of course evidence to the contrary may yet be discovered.

18. William Naylor Eyre, Brief History of William Naylor Eyre (Appendix XII). See also the account of Joseph Stanford Smith's experiences as quoted below.

19. Laura May Barney Moody (daughter of Danielson B. Barney), letter to Lucretia L. Ranney, 1954.

20. Mrs. William Hutchings reported that her three daughters "Sade, Ella, and Lydia, were the first white girls to be let down through the Hole-in-the-Rock in wagons." Cited in a letter from Mrs. Wm. L. Hutchings, July 1954.

21. Herbert E. Gregory (probably on his 1918 reconnaissance) reported concerning the Hole-in-the-Rock expedition's work at the Hole: "Wagons were taken apart and carried down on the backs of men and horses, or lowered by ropes. Rusty ringbolts embedded in the cliffs and the remains of a roughly made windlass bear witness of the method employed." (Herbert E. Gregory and Raymond C. Moore, The Kaiparowits Region, U.S. Geological Survey Professional Paper 164, 12.)

Concerning the taking of a dredge through the Hole, Jode Porter, an old-time settler of Escalante, remembered late in life that he had shod the horses belonging to an outfit which was taking a mining dredge to the Hole-in-the-Rock. Said Porter: "I not only shod all 16 of the horses that day in October of 1899 but I shod a saddle horse as well." (Statement taken by Kenneth Reed and loaned to D. E. Miller, January, 1956.)

22. Raymond Smith Jones, op. cit., quoted by permission of Desert Magazine. Contrary to the inference of this account, Smith's wagon was not the last one to go through the Hole-in-the-Rock. His was probably the last of those camped at the top of the Hole to make the descent, but half of the company were still camped back at Fifty-mile Springs.

23. Joseph F. Barton, Writings (Appendix X).

24. Letter from N. Z. Decker, April 17, 1954.

25. Henry John Holyoak, History of Henry John Holyoak, op. cit.

26. Milton Dailey told this story to members of his family; his daughter, Madalena Dailey (Gardner), recorded it. The copy reproduced here was sent to me in a letter from Birt Gardner, July 21, 1954.

27. See Appendix VIII for the complete letter.

CHAPTER IX

THROUGH "IMPASSABLE" COUNTRY
TO CLAY HILL PASS

It's the roughest country you or anybody else ever seen; it's nothing in the world but rocks and holes, hills and hollows. The mountains are just one solid rock as smooth as an apple.

—*Elizabeth Morris Decker*

There is no physical evidence today to mark the exact location of the ferry landings on either side of the Colorado at Hole-in-the-Rock, and none of the accounts supplies any details regarding this matter. It is very likely that the ferry operated from a point near the base of the Hole. Since a pair of oars supplied the only power, the ferry drifted downstream several rods at each crossing. Before making a return trip, it would have to be pulled back upstream to a point well above the landing site on the opposite bank. A near tragedy occurred on one of the initial crossings when a gust of wind, quite common in the river gorge, swept the raft far downstream and there was some danger that it might be sucked into the rapids and lost. Such a catastrophe would have been a serious set-back to the already travel-worn pioneers.

Only meager descriptions of the ferry and its operations have been preserved in the writings of members of the Hole-in-the-Rock expedition. However, through details from numerous different accounts we are able to gain a fair picture of the boat in operation. One reference gives the dimensions of the ferry as eighteen feet long and sixteen feet wide; large enough to accommodate two wagons at a time, together with the teams belonging to each. William N. Eyre describes it in these words:

It was a raft large enough to hold two wagons and a man on the back to paddle. When the raft was paddled to the other bank, four men would jump into the water and pull the raft to shore with the aid of ropes which were fastened to each corner of the raft. We would then unload it and the current would take it to the other shore once more. . . . The cattle and horses swam across.[1]

Joseph Stanford Smith remembered:[2]

We had no cable to tie to, but had to use paddles in ferrying across the Colorado. But luck seemed to be with us. The collection of debris from our blasting and from floods prior to our coming had formed sort of a wing dam across the stream, backing the water up at that point so that it was fairly calm for crossing. The ferry barge was pushed up tight against the bank and we drove our teams and wagons onto it. We had made the ferry large enough to hold the entire outfits safely, with room to spare, but to save possible trouble, we always unhitched and unharnessed the horses while crossing, so that if they became frightened, and tumbled into the stream, there would be no accident and they would be able to swim across. . . . The ferry landing constructed on each side of the stream avoided any frightening of the teams as they drove on and off the ferry. They seemed to think it was a regular bridge.

Several accounts of the river crossing mention the fact that a young man was accidentally knocked overboard by unruly oxen. This was evidently young Alfred A. Barney. His daughter Ada B. Plumb, after studying the writings of her father later wrote the following account of this incident:[3]

When they went to cross the Colorado River at Hall's Ferry, or Hole in the Rock, they had five cows and two yoke of oxen. The oxen were yoked up. Alfred was on the corner of the ferry where the cows were. When they were about one third of the way across the river, the oxen began hooking and crowding the cows. They finally crowded the cows and Alfred off into the river, and then the oxen jumped off. Alfred got out all right. The cows and oxen swam back to shore. There were nine men besides Alfred on the ferry to help take the cattle across. They could not turn the ferry around, so they went on across, and towed the boat up stream, then crossed back after Alfred and the cattle.

Recalling what was doubtless the same incident, young N. Z. Decker later stated:[4]

An old gentleman and his son drove a wagon onto the Ferry boat with two yoke of oxen. The lead oxen were nervous and when the outfit got located they decided to take the leaders off but when they got them loose and tried to turn them around they bolted and jumped over the railing pushing the boy over with them. The old man fluttered here and there trying to locate the boy and was about to jump over after him but the oxen came up spurting water way up into the air and about the same time the boy came up and swam to shore several rods below the boat. Asked why he came up so far down from the boat he said he dove to get away from the oxen. The father said, "Thank God. If I had jumped over I'd have drowned. I can't swim a lick. I didn't know the boy could swim."

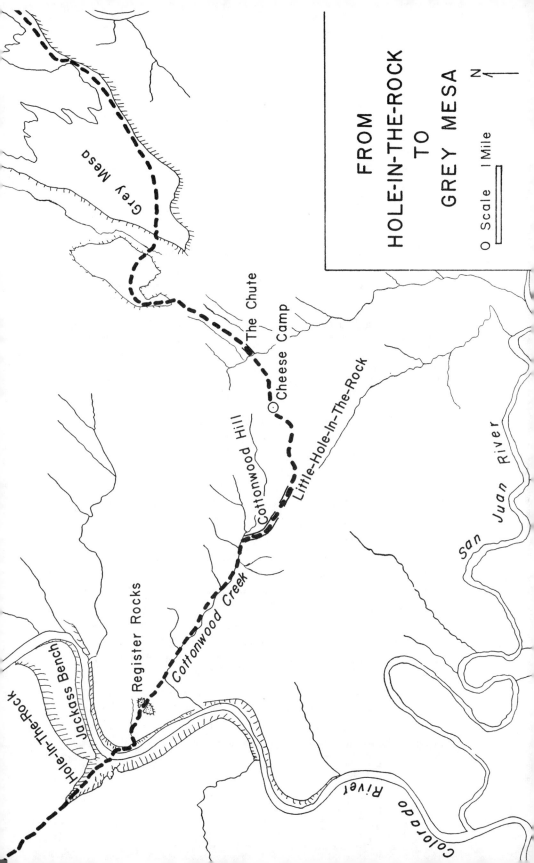

FROM
HOLE-IN-THE-ROCK
TO
GREY MESA

N

Scale   1 Mile

Grey Mesa

The Chute

Cheese Camp

Cottonwood Hill

Little-Hole-In-The-Rock

San Juan River

Register Rocks

Cottonwood Creek

Jackass Bench

Hole-In-The-Rock

Colorado River

This incident is the nearest approach to a major accident involved in the river crossing. Boat crews — Charles Hall and his two sons with the aid of expedition personnel — must have worked very efficiently in order to transport twenty-six wagons across the stream before the end of the first day, January 26, 1880. Hall and his helpers had planned well.

Before all eighty-three wagons had made the crossing the weather turned much colder. By February 1 shore ice had formed along the banks and extended several feet out into the water, considerably narrowing the 350-foot river and at the same time complicating the operation of the ferry boat. It now required much ice-breaking in order to bring the craft close to the bank. Loose cattle and horses forced to ford the stream also encountered this difficulty with ice. Young Henry John Holyoak recalled:[5]

> While crossing the river they had me on the back of the boat to watch the 2 pair of oxen yoked together. One was a mean ox so that's why they had them yoked and had him chained to the wagon wheel. About half way across the ox broke the chain loose and the mean one made a dive at me and I dropped down in the bottom of the boat and they went over the top of me into the water. We had to cut the ice so they could get out on the bank.

Within a day or two after the last wagons had crossed, but while some were still camped on the bar immediately across from the Hole-in-the-Rock, the river froze over completely, and large numbers of otters and beaver came out and played on the ice, providing some interesting recreation for the onlookers.

The large drove of loose cattle and horses were bunched in small herds on the west bank, and forced into the icy waters to ford the stream under their own power. Cowhands were required to make several crossings on horseback. George W. Decker recalled later in life that he had forded the river at least twenty times while completing this task.[6]

The first obstacle on the east side of the Colorado was a sheer wall some two hundred fifty feet high. However, as indicated in the previous chapter, work crews had already cut a dugway from the face of this cliff and thus prepared a road out of the river gorge. This road is a rather steep, narrow, dangerous cut that angles up the face of the cliff and then follows along a shelf not far from the top into the mouth of a small gorge that breaks through the solid rock approximately a quarter of a mile downstream from the ferry landing. The road continues up this small gorge for about a hundred yards, then leaves it by means of another short dugway up the south side, coming out on top of the first benchland above the Colorado. Then by means of a series of diagonals and short dugways, the road reaches the Register Rocks about a mile from the river. I took the liberty of naming the Register Rocks the first time I traversed that part of the old trail because of several names of the original company found chiseled into the face of the solid stone at that point. The old road runs just at the base of the northernmost of these two cliffs, and it was here that some of the expedition members took time to record their names on this huge rock slate. After the road was abandoned in 1881, a massive block of stone fell from the face of this cliff and effectively blocked the passage until it was removed by jeep explorers.

The pull from the Colorado up through this region was relatively easy, and expedition wagons were soon rolling up Cottonwood Canyon. The Cottonwood is a small stream of crystal-clear water that heads in the broken country directly east of the Hole-in-the-Rock. It flows almost due west to a point about a quarter of a mile east of the Register Rocks, then turns toward the south, dropping into the Colorado gorge about a mile below the Hole-in-the-Rock crossing. The pioneers reached this stream right at the bend in a fairly open valley and followed it upstream. In the spring of the year Cottonwood is indeed a beautiful and peaceful little canyon, not deep and rugged as are most canyons in that country. The stream meanders at a gentle slope along the valley floor, dropping here and there into natural rock tanks which form excellent swimming pools. Most people who hike that way (not very many have done so) avail themselves of the opportunity to enjoy a refreshing dip.

The old road is clearly visible as it winds its way along the stream bed, following the line of least resistance. Road makers found it necessary to cross the small creek several times, but this was a matter of little difficulty. At one point, because of impassable rock formations, the pioneers found it necessary to leave the floor of the canyon and build a road high along the north bank. But this was not a major task, by comparison with their previous experiences.

The vanguard of the company moved eastward up Cottonwood Creek some three miles to a grove of cottonwood trees and established camp there on January 30. This site was soon overcrowded, however, and a second camp was located about a half-mile downstream to the west. The severe winter weather moderated somewhat and the company experienced more enjoyable camp life. Regular religious services were held at both camps. For the first time on the trek the expedition found favorable forage for their stock, plenty of wood for campfires, and an abundant supply of pure fresh water. The women took advantage of this situation and conducted the first major wash and cleanup campaign since the expedition had left the settlements.

The trekkers were detained at their camps on the Cottonwood for some ten days while additional road work was being completed, for expedition leaders had already decided that here was the most feasible place to build a road out of the canyon and up over the steep sandstone buttes to the east. The emigrants had now arrived at the point beyond which most of the earlier explorers had decided that no wagon road could be built. Now they must get to work and build a road through the "impassable" country. A distance of approximately five miles separated them from the top of Grey Mesa (sometimes called Wilson Mesa), and a road would have to be built almost every foot of the way, most of it to be hewn from the solid rock.

The first portion of this road is known as Cottonwood Hill, which extends from the floor of Cottonwood Canyon to a small tableland about a mile distant. Cottonwood Hill consists of three major and distinct portions which I have named the Sand Hill, the Dugway, and Little Hole-in-the-Rock. The first hundred yards of the old road consist of a relatively mild dugway which is still clearly visible. Teamsters had little difficulty there. But this terminates in a very steep hill of fine drifting sand in which is was almost impossible to build a roadbed and keep it from slipping down the steep face of the hill. That portion of the road has been completely obliterated by the shifting sands; it is a real struggle to climb up there on foot nowadays.

Above the sand hill is a short, fairly level stretch of road extending along the top of a ridge and leading to a solid sandstone butte from which the major dugway had to be cut. This region had been considered impassable by earlier scouts. But on February first a thousand pounds of blasting powder arrived in camp, evidence that President Smith, still absent from his company, was doing an effective job of procuring supplies. The powder was put to use and a road was soon being blasted from the face of the cliff. Anyone who has climbed a mountain realizes that the ridge or peak immediately in front often appears to be the top of the mountain. So it appears here. The first glance leaves one with the feeling that the road was built right to the top of the highest peak. But when one climbs to the top of that peak, there is still a higher one beyond.

From the top of the sand hill a good view of the road ahead appears as it angles up the north face of that huge mountain of solid sandstone. At first appearance, one is struck with the notion that the pioneers came to this solid barrier and decided to build a road over it just to prove that it could be done; and today it appears to have been an almost impossible task. But the road is there in clear view. A climb up that steep, narrow dugway brings wonders at every step how wagons could ever have been driven along the steep sloping shelf. However, as the climber finally gains the top of the butte and surveys the surrounding country, he sees that the pioneer road engineers planned well; the road could not have been constructed in any other place.

From the top of the dugway the road leads directly to what I have taken the liberty of naming "The Little Hole-in-the-Rock" because of its natural rock formation. Here is a V-shaped notch which leads directly to the top of the small mesa which some of us have called the "Little Mesa" to distinguish it from Grey Mesa, four or five miles farther east. From the top of the Little Hole, the road veers to the left and, keeping on the high ground, eventually winds in a meandering course of a mile or more to a relatively flat camp site known as Cheese Camp.

The stretch of road just described was completed while the pioneers were still camped on the Cottonwood. Wilson Dailey and George Lewis had set up their forges in camp and were kept busy making horseshoes and nails for horses and oxen in preparation for the difficult climb ahead.[7] Wagons and other equipment, damaged in that mad dash down through the Hole-in-the-Rock, were also repaired at this time. Also during this ten-day stop at the foot of Cottonwood Hill several men went back along the road to Escalante in an attempt to round up cattle that had been left behind. However, they returned a few days later to report that the snow was too deep for their jaded horses; most of the cattle not already with the expedition would have to remain behind, to be rounded up when summer came.

It required seven teams of horses or as many yoke of oxen to drag the heavy wagons up those steep slopes of Cottonwood Hill. The first movement began on February 10 and the company soon found itself at Cheese Camp, halted again at the end of the road, faced with more solid rock walls, gulches, and ledges, through which a passage must be cut.

There were some accidents on the Cottonwood Hill. Henry John Holyoak remembered that:

the road was steep and the chain broke and the wagon turned over, the tongue went up in the air and lit upside down in the road so we had to take it to pieces and pack it up on top so we could put it together. We had a hive of bees and had to wait till we could sack the bees before we could start packing the pieces of wagon and the load up the hill. That took a lot of work to get things together.[8]

N. Z. Decker also remembered: "Mother drove up on a sidling hill and tipped the wagon over. Her baby was in the back of the seat but was not hurt, but mother was in a frenzy with fright."[9] Laura May Barney Moody, daughter of Danielson B. Barney, wrote: "One horse was crowding the wagon off the grade and tipped the wagon over and Bird Ella was in the wagon. She was rolled up in a feather bed and it didn't hurt her, but it broke up all the dishes and everything they had on the wagon."[10] Joseph Stanford Smith pointed out that the following precautions were taken to avoid just such accidents: "Two men followed beside each wagon holding the rear wheels onto the grade with ropes, but it was a hazardous trip all the way . . ."[11] Cottonwood Hill continued to be one of the most difficult stretches of the old road as long as it was in use as a highway. Platte D. Lyman, bringing a wagon load of flour from Escalante to Bluff during May, 1880, tipped his wagon over at that point;[12] there were doubtless many other similar accidents.

Cheese Camp was so named because while the wagons were halted there a few men from Panguitch (Amasa M. Lyman being the only one identified in any of the accounts), coming into camp to help with the construction of the road, brought two hundred pounds of pork and forty pounds of cheese, among other supplies, obtained from the Panguitch Tithing Office. Since forty pounds of cheese would not go very far toward feeding two hundred fifty people, the decision was made to auction it off. As yet I have found no satisfactory explanation as to why tithing cheese could or should be auctioned off or paid for at all by members of the company. But this seems to have been the method of distribution. The cheese auction caused enough excitement and interest to give the camp a permanent name.

While road crews were busy working the difficult terrain ahead, another important incident occurred at Cheese Camp. Livestock could be driven forward while wagons were forced to wait for the road. Some members of the company who were driving a large herd of horses, probably intended for trade with the Indians, declared that they were going to drive the animals ahead, leaving the major portion of the camp behind. To some of the men this proposal appeared to be an attempt on the part of the horse owners to get out in front and take advantage of the scanty grass and other vegetation along the way. This would place the teams and oxen at a distinct disadvantage as they lumbered along several days later.

Accounts of this incident indicate that near bloodshed resulted before the controversy was settled. For a time wagon owners rode with rifles slung across their saddles, threatening to stop the movement by force if necessary. However, no violence resulted. The horsemen agreed to drive as rapidly as possible across Grey Mesa and into the country beyond, so that their animals would have little time to pick off the far too meager supply of forage. This, they argued, would be better for the company in the long run as it would leave fewer animals to contend for the vegetation when the wagons began to roll again. Lyman does not mention this incident in his journal, although other writers have expressed some indignation that the horsemen were allowed to get away with this maneuver. Charles Redd, for example, wrote the following: "Many in the company were bitterly sorry when a compromise was made . . . . Some of the party never quite forgot this incident, and never quite forgave the men."[13] Cornelius I. Decker, who was present at the time, recorded what seems to be a logical and sensible statement regarding the settlement of this affair: "So they went ahead, which was the best to be done; so we got rid of that nuisance."[14]

This conflict at Cheese Camp is the first and only major point of friction recorded in all the annals of the Hole-in-the-Rock expedition — that is, until they reached Bluff. Under the stress, strain, and hardships of the trek, as it was prolonged far beyond expectation, it is remarkable that additional difficulties of this nature did not develop. The fact that the emigrants got along so well together under the trying circumstances demonstrates that high-caliber citizens composed the body of the company. Most of them realized that harmony and unity were absolutely necessary for the mission to succeed; they were willing to sacrifice minor personal desires for the good of the entire expedition.

Also at Cheese Camp George Hobbs fitted out a pack train to take food supplies to those already located at Montezuma on the San Juan. It

will be recalled that he and three companions had scouted the region all
the way from Hole-in-the-Rock to Montezuma during the latter part of
December and early part of January and had found the Harriman and
Davis families desperately in need of supplemental food supplies. These
scouts had promised to return to Montezuma with the necessary supplies
inside of sixty days. Realizing that the wagon train would require much
longer than two months to reach the destitute families, Hobbs now prepared a pack train to take supplies to those in need. He left Cheese Camp
February 15 and eventually arrived at Montezuma barely in time to relieve
those who were about out of food. For an account of his expedition, see
his own narrative, Appendix XI.

From Cheese Camp the pioneer road was built up a small dry (un-
named) canyon, over and through solid rock ledges and buttes, and eventually dipped down into the upper reaches of what is often referred to as
Wilson Canyon,[15] to the base of the "Chute." Since most of this road had
to be cut from the solid rock, it is still plainly visible. The pioneers' objective of building where they did was to reach the bottom of a natural U-
shaped notch that extends about a quarter of a mile up from the floor of
Wilson Canyon to some relatively flat slickrock country five hundred feet
above. This place is quite properly called the Chute. Very little road work
was necessary inside it; however a few fills had to be made in the bottom
of the U to make it wide enough for wagons to scrape through. Although
the grade through the Chute seems prohibitive today, the Hole-in-the-
Rock trekkers found it easier than many places they had already traveled.
Here, at least, there was no danger of slipping off the road or tipping over
— there was simply nowhere to tip or slip. If this natural route had not
been discovered, several additional weeks of back-breaking labor would
have been required to cut a road through or over this most difficult rock
formation. In view of what they had already done, no one would assert
that the pioneers could not have accomplished such a task.

From the head of the Chute the old road follows along the top of a
rocky ridge to the base of Grey Mesa, some two miles distant. It is clearly
visible most of the way, but can easily be lost in some places where no road
work was necessary and the wagons left little imprint on the solid smooth
stone. In describing the terrain through which the road had just been
completed, Elizabeth Decker made this observation: "It's the roughest
country you or anybody else ever seen; it's nothing in the world but rocks

and holes, hills and hollows. The mountains are just one solid rock as smooth as an apple."[16]

After coming that far the road engineers found little difficulty in building a road to the top of the Mesa. A series of short dugways placed the company on top of a natural ledge that angles in a northerly direction up toward the summit. About a quarter of a mile of this gentle slope brought the wagons to the top of what might be called a western extension of Grey Mesa, for it is separated from the major portion of the tableland by a rather deep gulch which drains off to the north. Having already traversed some of the roughest and most broken country in America, the pioneers had little difficulty in dipping down into this gulch and out on the other side. An examination of the available records, plus close inspection of the region, leads to the conclusion that members of that original company considered this "extension" as part of the mesa proper.[17]

Once the summit was reached, there was easy wheeling for seven and a half miles. There were no rocks, ledges, or other obstacles here — nothing to bar the way — just a flat, sandy tableland. The major plant growth consisted of a generous amount of shadscale with some grass, supplying better forage for livestock than the company had seen for many a long week. Although this pioneer road was abandoned in 1881, cattle kept the trail open. (By 1960 prospectors had blasted out a passable jeep road to the top of the mesa. Thus it is now possible to travel with relative ease in the wake of those original wagons.) Pioneer wagons were now rolling along the backbone that separates San Juan from Colorado drainage. Here the Great Bend of the San Juan sweeps up to the foot of the mesa and presents an impressive sight as it winds through its straight-walled channel a thousand feet below. Inasmuch as most of the people who have traveled this old road since 1881 have done so during the summer, it is sometimes difficult to realize that a foot of snow covered the ground when the first pioneer wagons rolled that way late in February of 1880.

Among the great heroines of the West were the pioneer mothers who often brought children into the world under most difficult and trying circumstances. We have already noted the birth of two babies since the beginning of the trek and now, on the top of Grey Mesa, in the midst of a howling blizzard, the third child of the expedition was born. This was the son of Mons and Olivia Larson.

At an earlier date Mr. Larson had established a residence at Snowflake, Arizona, and had returned to Santaquin, Utah, in the spring of

1879 to move his wife Olivia and their two children to the new home site. By fall of that year he had completed all necessary arrangements and was either about to start the trek or had already begun the move when he learned of the large San Juan Mission expedition that was to try a new route by way of Escalante. Larson was a close friend of Silas S. Smith so, believing that the new route would be shorter and easier, he decided to travel with the Hole-in-the-Rock expedition as far as Montezuma. Had he chosen to go by the already well-established route via Lee's Ferry he and his family would have been in their new home long before the Hole-in-the-Rock-expedition crossed the Colorado, and the expectant mother would have at least had a roof over her head by the time the baby arrived. But there are many "ifs" in history. As week after week dragged on into month after month, the time arrived for the birth of the child. Ellen J. Larson Smith, daughter of Mons Larson, has compiled the following fascinating account of the circumstances surrounding the birth of her brother:[18]

The canyon on the other side of the [Colorado] river required only fifteen days of work to get to the plateau [Grey Mesa] above. The Larsons and two other parties had been left by the main group during the climb upward. Olivia had been walking a good deal of the day with Moroni and Andrew on each arm, it was so cold that the children's feet had become frost bitten and were purple. The father and mother sat up nearly all night doctoring their children. The wagons were strung all along the roadside, some had reached the top of the plateau above and some were still below the Larsons.

It was February 21, 1880, when the Larsons reached the top of the plateau. A blizzard was raging and it was in this terrible snowstorm, exposed to the desert winds, that Olivia gave birth to a boy. The boy was born while the mother was lying on a spring seat and her husband was trying to pitch a tent so the mother could be made more comfortable. With the help of sister Seraphine Smith Decker and brother Jim Decker, she was placed in the tent and made as comfortable as circumstances would permit. The boy was named John Rio (since he was born near the San Juan river). He grew to be a fine stalwart man and reared a fine family. The day after the baby came a hard wind raised the tent upward, Olivia reached up and took hold of the pole and held it down.

Steven A. Smith tells of the incident of the baby's birth for he arrived upon the scene just before the mother had been put into the tent. He had been left with two wagons and only one team when his father, Silas S. Smith, had gone back to Salt Lake City from Escalante in order to secure an appropriation from the Legislature for road building supplies, dynamite, picks and shovels. These were given him to be sent to the company, but his legislative work had delayed him and the snow became so deep he couldn't get back to join them. Steven

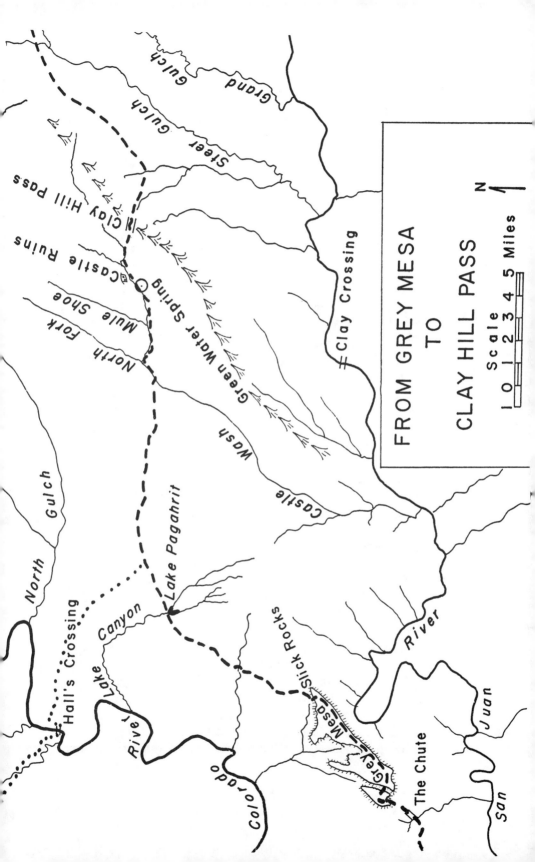

FROM GREY MESA
TO
CLAY HILL PASS

Scale
10 1 2 3 4 5 Miles

N

Grand Gulch

Steer Gulch

Clay Hill Pass

Castle Ruins

Mule Shoe

North Fork

Green Water Spring

Clay Crossing

Castle Wash

North Gulch

Lake Pagahrit

Lake Canyon

Hall's Crossing

River

Slick Rocks

Grey Mesa

The Chute

Colorado

San Juan

River

would keep up with the wagon train and when they would stop he would take his team back for the wagon which was left behind. It was when he was bringing in the second wagon that he saw these people camped off to the side of the road, as he says, "On the backbone between the Colorado and San Juan rivers." "What are you stopping here for?" he asked, surprised that they should be where there was neither protection from the weather, a tree or a spring. To his surprise he was informed "That Sister Larson had a new son . . ."

The third day after the birth of the Larson baby, the Larsons and the Deckers moved on to join the company which had gone ahead. Mrs. Z. B. Decker wanted Mrs. Larson to ride with her because they had a stove in their wagon, but Mons wanted her to ride with him because he would not trust her with another driver. Because of Olivia's unusual vitality, she was able to be up the fourth day, packed her belongings and climbed into the wagon, travelling all day over rocky roads. She said the baby never had colic. If it wasn't snowing she could bathe him, otherwise, this wise young mother of twenty-three, who now had three babies, rubbed him well with flannel instead of bathing him.[19]

After an easy seven and a half mile trip across the top of the Mesa, the expedition found itself at the point where George Hobbs and his companion explorers had been led over the brink by a mountain sheep. Here the mesa terminates abruptly, and there is no natural "chute" down its precipitous slopes. The only way to take wagons to the sandy and boulder-studded valley a thousand feet below was to literally cut a series of dugways from one ledge to the next one below — all out of solid rock. When completed the road was less than a half-mile long, but it took a week to accomplish the task. On the crest of the mesa rim remnants of one pioneer wagon, worn out and deserted at that point, can still be seen. But the other eighty-two outfits began the descent on February 28, all reaching the bottom without serious accident. Cornelius I. Decker, who was driving one wagon and trailing another, left this simple description of the descent: ". . . we had to drive down a sharp hill too, where my lead wagon was on one side of the top of the hill and my trail wagon on the other side. It was raining and slippery, but I got down alright. . ."[20]

Today that portion of the old road lying between the Hole-in-the-Rock and the east base of Grey Mesa (approximately seventeen miles) is by far the roughest stretch of the present jeep trail. It was one of the most difficult parts of the whole undertaking, as viewed by pioneer road builders of 1880. This was the region that explorers of the company had found to be completely impassable, yet the road had been blasted through that rough country in one month. In May, 1954, a group of us, guided by Lynn, Henry, and Edward Lyman, took three jeeps from

Blanding to the base of Grey Mesa, from which point some of us hiked out over the old road as far as Cheese Camp in order to explore and map the route.[21] We had previously hiked from the Hole-in-the-Rock to Cheese Camp, so had now covered all of that most difficult and inaccessible portion of the old road. There is simply no way of describing the country or understanding the nature of the obstacles to be overcome without having made such a reconnaissance. Furthermore, it would be foolhardy indeed for anyone not well acquainted with that wild country to try to drive a jeep into the region. Without the help of experienced guides we would never have reached our destination, but would have become hopelessly lost in the maze of canyons, gulches, and buttes with which that country is so generously blessed.

From the base of Grey Mesa the old road, still visible a good deal of the way, follows a northeasterly direction toward Lake Pagahrit, approximately seven miles distant. Here was a beautiful body of clear, fresh water, indeed an unusual and unexpected sight in that desert country. The lake seems to have been gradually formed in past ages as sand drifted into Lake Canyon, slowly building a massive obstruction or dam behind which the water from natural springs and occasional storms accumulated. The old road ran right across this natural dam. When the pioneers arrived there the lake was a J-shaped body of water approximately fifty feet deep near the dam, nearly a half-mile long, and about a quarter of a mile wide in the widest place. Numerous kinds of birds were found there and vegetation grew in abundance, furnishing a very pleasant setting for a few days of rest and another major washday for the pioneer train. Members of the expedition noted with interest the obvious value of this site for a cattle range and subsequently made good use of it.[22]

But the once beautiful Lake Pagahrit is no more. In 1915 three days of unprecedented sudden and heavy storms filled the natural reservoir to capacity; rapidly rising waters flooded over the dam, soon cutting a channel down through the soft sand; and the waters of Lake Pagahrit thundered down Lake Canyon into the Colorado. J. A. Scorup, veteran cattleman of the region, was an eyewitness of this unfortunate flood. In recalling the event, Mr. Scorup wrote: "To the best of my recollection, the Hermit Lake [Lake Pagahrit] went out Nov. 1st, 1915. My brother and I were there with a bunch of cattle, and it rained so hard, there was an awful flood and the lake went out."[23] Since that time the canyon has cut deeper and deeper as the sand and sediment have washed downstream toward the Colorado. As a result, it is now extremely difficult to find a spot where the canyon can be crossed at all.

While some members of the Hole-in-the-Rock expedition were washing clothes, resting, repairing gear, and actually enjoying camp life on the shores of the lake, work crews were out in front completing the road into Castle Wash and on to Clay Hill Pass. This part of the trek was comparatively easy. The sand in Castle Wash was deep in places, slowing down jaded teams, but the weather was relatively mild and two or three good springs furnished necessary drinking water.

By March 5 the forward wagons were assembling at the top of Clay Hill Pass, the only place where a road could have been built over that mountain barrier. Here was another drop of approximately a thousand feet, and a road had to be built all the way. However, this was a different kind of road work. Sticky blue clay was not pleasant to work with, but it was easier than the solid rock that had confronted the expedition during most of its journey. Even so, another week was required to complete the three miles of road that would take wagons safely to the bottom and onto Whirlwind Bench below. Although a better road, suitable for trucks and touring cars when it is kept in repair, has been built through Clay Hill Pass in recent years, the cuts, fills, and rock work of the old road are still plainly visible, many portions of it too steep for a jeep.

While road crews were engaged in this task, Lyman, Sevy and Bryson went ahead on a five-day reconnaissance to scout the country to the east and mark the route. Finding it necessary to head the various tributaries of Grand Gulch, these men kept fairly close to the Red House Cliffs and marked the road all the way to the base of Elk Ridge, by way of Steer Gulch, Cow Springs, and Dripping Spring Canyon. A side exploration was also conducted to the south, across Whirlwind Bench, all the way to the San Juan. Platte D. Lyman, Joseph Lillywhite, and Edward L. Lyman conducted this reconnaissance and arrived at what is now known as Clay Crossing of the San Juan. Here they found approximately two hundred acres of level land, heavily timbered with cottonwood trees, but the area was not nearly large enough to encourage the planting of a settlement there.

While these explorations were under way, the road down Clay Hill Pass was completed and wagons began the descent on March 13. At the bottom of the Pass another howling blizzard buried the camp, ripped wagon covers, and tipped over tents. The weather turned bitterly cold, resulting in a great deal of discomfort to camp personnel. On March 15 Lyman made this brief entry in his journal: "Last night was the coldest night I ever experienced, it was impossible to be comfortable in bed or anywhere else."

FOOTNOTES

1. William N. Eyre, Brief History of William Naylor Eyre (Appendix XII).

2. Quoted by Lydia Hammond Fielding in her Biography of Joseph Stanford Smith, 4.

3. Letter from Ada B. Plumb, February 23, 1955.

4. Letter from N. Z. Decker.

5. Life History of Henry John Holyoak (Appendix XIV).

6. George W. Decker, Reminiscences (Appendix IX).

7. Madalene Dailey Gardner, Milton Dailey's Life, as cited in a letter from Birt Gardner, July 21, 1954. This citation mentions as blacksmith, the activities of Wilson Dailey only, but it is assumed that George Lewis was employed in the same type of activity.

8. Holyoak, *op. cit.*

9. N. Z. Decker, *op. cit.*

10. Letter of Lucretia L. Ranney, 1955.

11. Cited from Lydia Hammond Fielding, *op. cit.*

12. See Lyman's journal entry for May 20, 1880 (Appendix IV).

13. Charles Redd, "Short Cut to San Juan," 21.

14. Cornelius I. Decker, Life Sketch (Appendix VII).

15. This canyon drains southward into the San Juan; it is shown and identified on some maps. However, local cattlemen insist that this is not Wilson Canyon at all; but that Wilson Canyon drains northward from the north base of Grey/Wilson Mesa and empties into the Colorado. Eventually this region will be properly surveyed, mapped, and drainages officially named.

16. See Mrs. Decker's complete letter (Appendix VIII).

17. See Platte D. Lyman's Journal and accompanying footnotes (Appendix IV).

18. Ellen J. Larson Smith, Life Sketch of Mons Larson.

19. Vague and sketchy reference is made at times to a Jenson baby born on the top of Grey Mesa, but I have been unable to identify a Jenson family among the Hole-in-the-Rock personnel. I consider it likely that the name of "Jenson" has somehow become confused with "Larson," for the ones who speak of the "Jenson baby" fail to mention the birth of John Rio Larson. I should be happy to receive any information regarding other births during the expedition.

20. Cornelius I. Decker, *op. cit.*

21. The jeep road had not yet been opened to the top of and across the mesa at that time.

22. Albert R. Lyman wrote an excellent description of Lake Pagahrit before it was lost. "Lake Pagahrit," *Improvement Era*, October, 1909, 934–938. This lake is also known as Hermit Lake.

23. J. A. Scorup, letter to D. E. Miller, April 18, 1953.

CHAPTER X

TRAIL'S END

The thought of level bottom-land was extremely sweet.

— *Charles Redd*

From the bottom of Clay Hill Pass to the head of Grand Gulch, at the foot of Elk Ridge, less work was required on the road, and the company could travel at speeds limited only by the ability of their nearly worn-out teams to drag the heavy wagons forward. As a result the company soon spread out, with the stronger teams moving rather rapidly and the weaker ones lagging as much as thirty miles behind. The trek had now settled down to a test of sheer endurance. Road conditions varied with the weather; sometimes two feet of snow slowed wagons to a snail's pace while at other times the wheels sank to the hubs in mud. George Hobbs, returning from his mission of mercy to the Montezuma settlement, noted:[1]

I met many different parties that were on their way to catch up with the main camp which was now at the Elk Mountain. The weaker ones were in the rear, some had an ox and a mule hitched together, some had cows and heifers in their teams, one I noticed was a pair of mules with an ox on the spike with a young girl riding the ox, to keep him in the road, all made inquiries of me how far it was to San Juan.

A few wagons had to be left standing by the roadside with their loads intact, to be picked up later in the season.

Somewhere in this area an old Ute Indian rode into camp. Amazed at the spectacle of a wagon caravan in that wild country he at once wanted to know whence they came and whither they were bound. When informed of the route the wagons had taken, he simply threw up his hands in disbelief: No wagon road could possibly be built through that region! Most persons who have traversed that route will agree that he had good reason to doubt the honesty of anyone who would tell him such a story.

As the company approached the base of Elk Ridge, the cedar forest became more and more dense, requiring a crew of choppers to go in front to blaze a trail for the wagons. Natural clearings in this huge forest were called "Flats," such as Grand Flat. These flats were natural camp sites, and various segments of the expedition made use of them. Thus the emigrants from New Harmony established themselves for a few days at what became known as Harmony Flat.

Grand Gulch was headed about the middle of March and the company turned toward the south, as choppers cleared the way through the cedars, into and out of numerous gulches and draws such as Kane Gulch, where satisfactory water was found. Snow Flat, evidently so named because it marked the edge of the snow line, was reached after another week of difficult travel. From that point a steep, winding road had to be constructed down the "Twist" into the lower reaches of Road Canyon and on to Comb Wash where the company arrived late in March.

Expedition members found Comb Ridge an impassable barrier. The Comb is a ridge of solid sandstone extending southward from Elk Ridge beyond the San Juan and into Arizona. When approached from the west it presents a sheer, solid wall approximately a thousand feet high. The top is scalloped in such a manner as to present the appearance of a cockscomb; hence its name. There is no natural break in this solid rock wall except the one cut by the San Juan River at a point some ten miles downstream (west) from Bluff. Although the four expedition explorers (Redd, Hobbs, Sevy, and Morrell) had found an old Indian trail that led through the Comb by way of Navajo Hill, where Highway 47 crosses that barrier today, the Hole-in-the-Rock trekkers found Navajo Hill impassable for wagons and continued southward, down Comb Wash, all the way to the San Juan River.

After a ten-mile pull from the mouth of Road Canyon down the sandy bottom of the Wash, the company finally found itself on the north bank of the stream they had been trying so desperately to reach. From that point they had hoped to be able to build a road along the north bank to the site of Montezuma, nearly thirty miles to the east, but found that the river had cut so close to the perpendicular cliffs that no road could possibly be built that way. An examination of the country, however, showed that if the wagons could somehow be hauled to the top of Comb Ridge they might, with relatively little additional road work, roll northward along that rocky crest until a place could be found to cross Butler Wash lying immediately to the east. No major barrier would then separate them from their desired destination.

But to get to the top of the Comb required the building of another dugway up the face of that solid rock barrier, which the pioneers promptly named "San Juan Hill" — almost two decades before Theodore Roosevelt and the Rough Riders stormed a hill of the same name in Cuba during the Spanish-American War. The road up San Juan Hill is one of the most fantastic of all sections constructed by these indomitable pioneers. It angles up the face of that cliff in a manner which defies description. I first examined this spot in March, 1953, in company with Dr. C. G. Crampton. Albert R. Lyman had described the region and told us where to look for the old road; but even then we could hardly believe it when our eyes caught the faint line angling up the face of that solid rock wall. What we saw from the benchland near the river bank looked as though it might have been an abandoned horse trail — but surely not a wagon road. However, there was nothing else in sight and no other place for a road, so we climbed up the face of that huge rock swell for a closer look. And sure enough, there was the old road up San Juan Hill!

The pioneers required several days to build this San Juan Hill road, during which time members of the expedition camped on the north bank of the river. Here the women enjoyed a brief and well-earned rest at their most comfortable camp site since leaving Lake Pagahrit. Vegetation was sparse, making it necessary to drive livestock across the stream in search of better grazing on the south side. But there was plenty of wood for campfires and an abundant supply of water.

After nearly six months of constant road building and travel under most trying circumstances, San Juan Hill proved almost too much for the worn-out teams, weakened by a long winter of hard work without sufficient feed. Wagons, harnesses, and other gear, also badly worn by the long ordeal, would be taxed to the limit before the summit of Comb Ridge could be reached. Charles Redd has recorded a most graphic description of that last great pull.[2]

Aside from the Hole-in-the-Rock, itself, this was the steepest crossing on the journey. Here again seven span of horses were used, so that when some of the horses were on their knees, fighting to get up to find a foothold, the still-erect horses could plunge upward against the sharp grade. On the worst slopes the men were forced to beat their jaded animals into giving all they had. After several pulls, rests, and pulls, many of the horses took to spasms and near-convulsions, so exhausted were they. By the time most of the outfits were across, the worst stretches could easily be identified by the dried blood and matted hair from the forelegs of the struggling teams. My father [L. H. Redd,

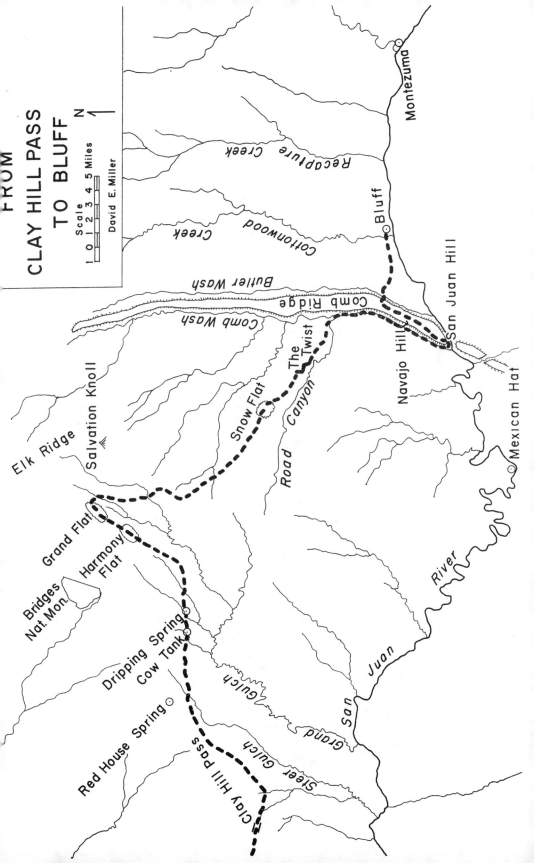

FROM
CLAY HILL PASS
TO BLUFF

Scale
1 0 1 2 3 4 5 Miles

David E. Miller

N

Elk Ridge

Salvation Knoll

Bridges
Nat. Mon.

Grand Flat

Harmony
Flat

Dripping Spring

Cow Tank

Red House Spring

Clay Hill Pass

Steer Gulch

Grand Gulch

San Juan River

Mexican Hat

Snow Flat

Comb Wash

The Twist

Road Canyon

Comb Ridge

Butler Wash

Navajo Hill

San Juan Hill

Bluff

Cottonwood Creek

Recapture Creek

Montezuma

Jr.] was a strong man, and reluctant to display emotion; but whenever in later years the full pathos of San Juan Hill was recalled either by himself or by someone else, the memory of such bitter struggles was too much for him and he wept.

The first three days of April were spent in this grueling task.

Once on the summit, the road continues northward along the top of Comb Ridge for a couple of miles, then drifts off to the eastward, following a little wash which leads to the bench that separates Comb Ridge from Butler Wash. Still continuing northward, the old abandoned road crosses present Highway 47 about a mile west of the bridge across the bottom of Butler Wash. The pioneers built another set of dugways into and out of that deep, difficult gorge two or three miles north of the present bridge.

As they rested in exhaustion from the last intensive strain, for the first time they began to see themselves for what they were: weary, worn out, galled, both teams and men. For so long they had walked and slept and eaten and lived on sloping uneven ground that the thought of level bottom-land was extremely sweet. Yet one woman spoke for the whole group when, recalling this last phase of the journey she said later, "I was so tired and sore that I had no desire to be any place except where I was." Someone pointed out to her that Montezuma wasn't even twenty miles away, and that some of the head wagons were already over Butler Wash and onto dirt road — even then it made no difference. When they began to sing "The Latter-day Work Rolls On," she had to sing to keep from crying.[3]

By April 6 most of the outfits had pulled onto the flat river bottom just east of Cottonwood Wash, and although the intended destination (Montezuma) was only another eighteen miles farther up stream, the company simply lost its push. All at once all energy seems to have left them completely. The travel-worn expedition was just too tired to go on. Here were a few acres of what appeared to be good farmland. Here they would stop — at least most of them. Here they would build their homes. At the suggestion of William Hutchings they called the new location Bluff City. Such important tasks as laying off lots, building houses, and digging a canal to bring water to the parched soil were begun at once. With God's help they would now be able to complete the mission to which they had been called.

FOOTNOTES
1. George B. Hobbs, Narrative (Appendix XI).
2. Charles Redd, "Short Cut to San Juan," 23, 24.
3. *Ibid.*

APPENDIXES

With the exception of the lists of personnel, these documents are accounts of the Exploring Expedition and the Hole-in-the-Rock trek written by participants who were old enough at the time to be completely aware of what was being done and of the problems being met and overcome. They constitute some of the major sources from which the history is drawn — in addition to the numerous sources cited and quoted in the body of the text. Some of these accounts were written at the time of the expedition; others were recorded many years after the events therein portrayed. Until now none of these documents has ever been accurately reproduced in print, although excerpts from, and interpolations of, some of them have been used by other writers.

These documents are copied as accurately as possible, using the original spelling, capitalization, and punctuation unless otherwise indicated.

APPENDIX I

HOLE-IN-THE-ROCK PERSONNEL

One of the most difficult tasks associated with this whole study has been the attempt to compile a complete and accurate roster of those who made the original trek. Charles E. Walton was appointed clerk of the expedition, but if he made a list of the personnel it has been lost — along with his other writings. The church evidently compiled no list. Various writers have assembled lists of those pioneers, yet a careful examination reveals that many of the people so listed went to the San Juan country later than the first expedition. It seems to have been customary for some compilers to include all the early settlers of Bluff and Montezuma as among those who pioneered that road through the Hole-in-the-Rock. And since most of the later interest in that expedition has naturally centered on the founders of Bluff and other San Juan County settlements, members of the original company who did not stay in that vicinity, but moved on to Colorado, New Mexico, Arizona or elsewhere, were sometimes lost track of and hence not included on the various rosters. These omissions were not intentional but merely a result of inadequate records and the frailty of human memory.

Mrs. Lucretia L. Ranney has worked closely and diligently with me in assembling the roster presented here. Together we have written hundreds of letters to various members of the expedition, their families and descendants; sought out and interviewed scores of people, and made many phone calls. By means of letters, newspaper and magazine articles, numerous illustrated lectures, radio broadcasts, a television program, and personal interviews I have encouraged anyone who might have additional information, to communicate with me. The response has been gratifying; most people interested have cooperated wholeheartedly. Needless to say, much of the information thus obtained was contradictory (even from members of the same family) and had to be checked, sifted, and verified. As part of this work Mrs. Ranney spent a great deal of time checking marriage and birth dates and other records.

Although most accounts published heretofore mention the fact that the original company consisted of some two hundred fifty persons, when I began this study the various lists that had been compiled contained a total of fewer than a hundred names — and many of those not authentic.

That number has now been expanded to two hundred thirty who quite definitely made the original trek and several more who possibly were along.

In spite of the patient work and care with which this list has been compiled, there are doubtless still mistakes in it; there may be names on the list that should be omitted; there are almost certainly some omitted which should be added. However, in spite of such errors (which are wholly unintentional but merely the result of inadequate records) this is by far the most nearly complete roster of the Hole-in-the-Rock expedition yet assembled.

A. PERSONNEL OF THE EXPLORING EXPEDITION, 1879

Adams, James J.
Allan, Isaac
Bayles, Hanson
Bladen, Thomas
Bullock, Robert
Butler, John (joined the company at his ranch, just south of Panguitch)
Butt, Parley R.
Dalley, Nielson B.
Dalton, John C.
Davis, James L.
   Mary Elizabeth Fretwell
     Edward F.
     James Henry
     Emily Ellen
     John Orson
Decker, James B.
Decker, Zechariah B., Jr.
Duncan, John C.
Dunton, James Harvey
Dunton, James Cyrus
Gower, John

Harriman, Henry H.
   Elizabeth Hobbs
     John Alma
     Elizabeth Constance
     (Plus two other children, as yet unidentified)
Haskell, Thales (joined the company at Moenkopi)
Hobbs, George B.
Jones, Kumen
McGreggor, Adelbert F.
Nielson, H. Joseph
Perry, George E.
Smith, Albert R.
Smith, Silas S.
Smith, Stephen A.
Tanner, Seth (joined the company at Moenkopi)
Thornton, Hamilton
Urie, George
Wallace, Hamilton

B. PERSONNEL OF THE HOLE-IN-THE-ROCK EXPEDITION

Barnes, Noah
Barney, Danielson Buren (Panguitch)
   Laura Matthews
     Buren Onley
     Alfred Alonzo
     Laura May

     Rachel Sophey
     Edson Elroy
     Eliza Melina
     Betsey Maud
     Bird Ella
Barton, Amasa M. (Paragonah)

Barton, Joseph Franklin
    (Paragonah)
  Harriet Ann Richards
  Harriet Eliza
  Mary Viola
Bayles, Hanson (Parowan)
Bryson, Samuel (Woodruff)
Butt, Parley R. (Parowan)
Butt, Willard (Parowan)
Cox, Samuel (Cedar)
  Sarah Gane
  Sarah
Dailey, Milton (Harrisburg)
  Mary Malinda Wilson
  Marion
  Madalene
Dailey, Wilson (Harrisburg)
  Lorana Tilton
    Bade (daughter)
    Belt (son)
Decker, Cornelius Isaac (Parowan)
  Elizabeth Morris
  William
  Eugene
Decker, James Bean (Parowan)
  Anna Maria Mickelsen
    Anna Lillian
    Genevieve
    Lena Deseret (born at Fifty-mile
      Camp, January 3, 1880.)
Decker, Nathaniel Alvin (Parowan)
  Emma Morris
  Sarah Jane
Decker, Zechariah Bruyn, Jr.
    (Parowan)
  Seraphine Smith
    Nathaniel
    Louis
    Constance
    Inez G.
    Jesse Moroni
Decker, Zechariah Bruyn, Sr.
    (Parowan)
  George William

Dunton, James Harvey (Paragonah)
  Mary Ann Doidge Barker
  Ellen Melissa Barker
  Medora Barker
  John Harvey
Dunton, James Cyrus (Paragonah)
  Eliza Ann Prothers
  James Albert
  Mary Allice
Dunton, Marius Ensign (Parowan)
  Emily Hadden
  Marius
Eyre, William N. (Parowan)
Fielding, Hyrum (Parowan)
  Ellen Agnes Hobbs
    Hyrum William
    Thomas Amos
    Joseph Oliver
    Ellen Delcena
Goddard, William P. (New Harmony)
  Ann Krrilla
    Herbert
    Maud Anna
Goddard, Sidney (New Harmony)
Gower, John Thomas (Cedar)
  Harriet Jane Corry
Gurr, William Heber (Parowan)
  Anna Hanson
  William John
Haight, Caleb (Cedar)
Haight, Isaac Chauncy (Cedar)
Hobbs, George B. (Parowan)
Holyoak, Henry (Paragonah)
  Sarah Ann Robinson
    Alice Jane
    Henry John
    Mary Luella
    Eliza Ellen
    Albert Daniel
Hunter, David (Cedar)
  Sarah Jane Urie
Hutchings, William Willard (Beaver)
  Sarah Agnes LeBaron
    Sarah Eliza
    Matilda Ellace
    Lydia Maria

Jones, Kumen (Cedar)
  Mary Nielson
Larson, Mons (Santaquin)
  Olivia Ekelund
    Moroni Mons
    Lars Andrew
    John Rio (born on Grey Mesa,
      February 21, 1880)
Lewis, George (Kanab)
Lewis, James (Kanab)
Lillywhite, Joseph (Beaver)
  Mary Ellen Wilden
    Mary Elenor
    Joseph
    Charles W.
    Lawrence
    John
Lyman, Amasa M., Jr. (Panguitch)
Lyman, Edward L. (Oak City)
Lyman, Ida E. (Oak City)
Lyman, Joseph A. (Oak City)
  Nellie Roper
Lyman, May (Oak City)
Lyman, Platte DeAlton (Oak City)
Lyman, Walter C. (Oak City)
Mackelprang, Samuel William (Cedar)
  Adelia N. Perry
    Samuel William
    Estella
    Margaret
    Lydia
    Minerva
Michelsen, Erasmus (Parowan)
Morrell, George (Junction)
Mortensen, Peter Andrew (Parowan)
  Hannah Maria Smith
Nelson, Peter Albert (Cedar)
Nielson, Jens (Cedar)
  Kirsten
    Hans Joseph
    Margaret
    Jens Peter
    Francis
    Lucinda
    Caroline

Pace, James (Panguitch)
  Hannah Sevy
    Frank
    Preston D.
    Roy
Pace, John H. (New Harmony)
  Pauline A. Bryner
    Elizabeth Mary
Pace, Wilford (New Harmony)
Perkins, Benjamin (Cedar)
  Mary Ann Williams
    Mary Jane
    Caroline Cardelia Thurston
    Katherine
    Naomi
Perkins, Hyrum (Cedar)
  Rachel Corry
    George Wm.
Redd, Lemuel H., Sr. (New Harmony)
  James Monroe
Redd, Lemuel H., Jr. (New Harmony)
  Eliza Ann Westover
    Lula
Riley, Henry James (Beaver)
  Sarah Ipson
    James Morton
Robb, Adam Franklin (Paragonah)
  Sarah P. Holyoak
    Alburtus
    William Heber
Robb, George (Paragonah)
  Caroline Jones
    Mary Ann
    Ellen
Robb, John (Paragonah)
  Sarah Ann Edwards
    Ellen Jane
    Sarah Ann
Robb, William (Paragonah)
  Ellen Stones
    William
Robinson, John Rowaldson
  (Paragonah)

Rowley, Samuel (Parowan)
 Ann Taylor
  Annie
  Samuel James
  Hannah
  Sarah Jane
  Alice
  Elizabeth
  Ida
  Jewell
  John Taylor
Sevy, George Washington
   (Panguitch)
 Margaret Imlay
  George F.
Sevy, Reuben Warren (15 year old
 son of George W. Sevy by his
 first wife, Phoebe Butler)
Smith, Silas Sanford (Paragonah)
Smith, Jesse J. (Parowan)
Smith, John A. (Paragonah)
 Emily J. Bennett
  Emily J.
Smith, Silas (Paragonah)
 Betsey Williamson
  Clarinda Ann
  Silas
Smith, Stephen A. (Paragonah)

Smith, Joseph Stanford (Cedar)
 Arabella Coombs
  Ada Olivia
  Joseph Elroy
  George Abraham
Smith, Samuel (Paragonah)
Stevens, David Alma (Holden)
Stevens, Roswell (Holden)
Stevens, Walter Joshua (Holden)
 Elizabeth Kinney
Taylor, Edmond (New Harmony)
Taylor, Warren (Kanarraville)
Urie, George (Cedar)
 Alice Jane Perry
Walker, Joseph (Cedar)
Walton, Charles Eugene (Bear Valley)
 Jane Hatch
  Charles E., Jr.
  Magnolia
  Leona
Webster, Francis (Cedar)
Westover, George (New Harmony)
Westwood, George (Beaver)
Williams, Sarah (Cedar)
Williams, Thomas (Cedar)
Wilson, Henry (St. George)
Woolsey, Joseph Smith (Panguitch)

In addition to the roster listed above, there are many other persons who possibly made the trek but whose record we were unable to verify. Each of these possibilities has been named by at least one writer interested in the Hole-in-the-Rock expedition. Some of these persons are known to have been present during part of the trek only. Because of this it is rather a problem to determine just who should be included and who excluded. An excellent example of the nature of the problem is that of Silas S. Smith, appointed president of the San Juan Mission. He first caught up with the expedition at Forty-mile Spring on November 24 and returned to the settlements for supplies December 15, before any work had been started at the Hole itself. Thus, Smith was actually with the expedition only about three weeks, for he did not again overtake the company until long after the San Juan had been reached. Just which (and how many) of his sons returned to the settlements with him is likewise unknown. But we list all of the members of the Silas S. Smith family who participated at all — as accurately as we can determine this fact — as part of the Hole-in-the-Rock expedition. So, in order to be consistent, we should include all those who contributed materially in the roadbuilding, even though they did not make the complete trek to the San Juan with the original expedition.

C. Persons sometimes listed as among the Hole-in-the-Rock Company but without definite proof

Christensen, Lars and family
Hudson, El.
Hudson, William H.
Ipson, George
Jensen, Lars Peter and family
Kelsey, Orrin and wife
   Emerette Angell

Mortensen, Charles
Openshaw, Jobe and wife Martha
   Jane Watts
Robb, Alexander
Robb, Samuel
Robb, Thomas
Wilden, James

Some men came out from Panguitch to work on the road; not all have been identified. We know of Amasa M. Lyman, Jr., and Joseph Smith Woolsey as two of these and their names are included in the roster of personnel. Some men returned before the Hole was blasted out. Three of them are: Frank Rysert, James Dorrity, and Arza Judd — as mentioned in Platte D. Lyman's journal.

Many Escalante citizens helped as guides, and in the actual work of road and ferry building. But as far as I can determine, they were never considered as part of the expedition and are not included on the list.

No doubt, with the publication of these lists, descendants of other members of the expedition will present additional names.

APPENDIX II

NIELSON B. DALLEY'S ACCOUNTS OF THE EXPLORING EXPEDITION

Nielson B. Dalley has left us two accounts of the exploring expedition of 1879. The first of these is called the "Diary"; the second is titled "San Juan Exploring Company." The Diary as presented here is a copy of a typewritten manuscript loaned to me by Mrs. Myrtle Janson of Cedar

City, Utah. Although this Diary would seem, at first glance, to have been written on the spot, at the time of the incidents portrayed, there are evidences that at least some of the entries were made sometime later. Note, for example, the last entry which covered a rather extensive period of time yet is listed under the date of May 19.

The second account is a document copied from the original hand written record which was loaned to me by Mary Lyman Reeves who still has it.

A. Nielson B. Dalley's Diary

Names of Exploring Party

Captain Silas S. Smith	John Duncan
Albert Smith	Robert Bullock
Steven Smith	Thomas Bladen
Harvey Dunton	George Perry
Harrison Harriman	John Gower
George Hobbs	George Urie
James J. Adams	Kumen Jones
John Dalton	Joseph Nielson
Delbert McGregor	John Butler
Zacharriah B. Decker	Hamilton Wallace
James Decker	Nielson B. Dalley
Hansen Bayles	
Parley Butts	six wagons[1]
Isaac Allen	Only two women
James Davis and family	Mrs. Davis and Mrs. Harriman

First night spent at Parowan
Second night at Bear Valley.
30 head of cattle
10 head of loose horses[2]

Went four miles above Panguitch to John Butler's ranch. Waited for John to go with us.

April 21.[3] Left Butler's ranch — very fine day. Camped at Sevier — organized.[4] Silas S. Smith, Captain; Robert Bullock, Ass. Captain; James Decker, Singing Master. Supper, prayer meeting, bed.

April 22. All well — (Which was carried out through all the trip.) Hooked up, gathered cattle, and moved to Sink Valley.[5]

April 23. All well. Stormy all day. Got to Johnson's about eight o'clock.[6] Robert Bullock, James Decker, and myself left wagons and started across the Buckskin Mountains with the cattle on the trail to House Rock, arriving there about five o'clock next day.

April 25. Company got in about seven o'clock.

April 26. Got up this morning, gathered in horses — one missing, hunted all day — not found. Moved on 15 miles, camped at Jacob's Pools.

April 27. John Dalton and Nels Dalley chosen to hunt again for lost horse; tracked it 15 or 20 miles. It was evidently being ridden by someone. Did not find horse; company moved to Soap Rock, 15 miles. George Urie and John Gower broke an axle out of their wagon. Company laid over and made an axle out of an old cottonwood tree.[7]

April 30. Started for Lee's Ferry; arrived about sunset.

May 1. Started to work ferrying our teams and wagons across the Colorado taking all day. Silas S. Smith having a small bunch of horses did not want to pay $1.00 a head for their being ferried over, so drove them into the river to swim them across. The river was one-fourth mile across and the horses struck below the landing and had to swim back nearly losing one over the rapids.

May 2. Leaving south side of the river about 1 p.m. to cross Lee's Backbone, a very steep mountain. Cross the mountains very successfully without any trouble and camped at Bitter Springs, seven miles on.

May 3. Went to gather horses and found one of James Davis's mules down with its hind foot through its halter and had dug both eyes out so we had to kill it. Moved on after breakfast with exception of one wagon that stayed with the cattle which had a 60-mile desert to cross. When the company got to Kane Creek, they loaded two wagons with water and came back to meet us; met us about daybreak second morning, and we drove the cattle to Kane Creek.[8]

May 6. Stopped all night and next day went to Moencopi. There we found a colony of Mormon people among them my sister Eliza B. Fornsworth. We stopped there two days and rested our horses; and most of the men went to quarrying rock for John R. Young who was at that time building a woolen mill. We received Indian corn for our work.

May 7. Moencopi was a Moquee village of a small tribe of these Indians, the Main Village being about 40 miles east. We left Moencopi traveling east for about 20 miles, before leaving Moencopi we arranged with Brother Thales Haskell[9] to pilot us through to San Juan River. Our first night from Moencopi was at the head of a wash at or near where young George A. Smith was killed while doing Missionary work among the Indians some years before.[10]

May 9. At this camp there were about 20 Indians (Navajoes) among them.

May 10. Mr. Peoeon[11] a large Navajo Indian who claimed he killed Brother Smith.

May 12. We broke camp as usual after having made friends with the Indians the night before and smoking the Pipe of Peace.

May 13. Traveled all day over rolling benches; quite sandy all the way. Camped at what was called Peocorn Ranch.[12] Some little ponds of water for the horses, but none fit for camp use. Some of the boys took the pick out of the wagon and drove it in the sandstone ledge and a small stream of water came out — plenty for camp use.[13]

May 14. Broke camp about nine o'clock; traveled all day and camped in the Mountainous country, the first wagons, I think, ever to have gone through the country. Brother Robert Bullock met us in the afternoon, he being one of the three men sent ahead to locate the route we should take. The other two men were Kumen Jones and Thales Haskell; they went on to the San Juan River. During the day Parley Butt and Hansen Bayles traded horses with the Navajoes camped near some small lakes.

May 15. In the evening as we had made camp, we had just turned the horses out to feed and the horses mixed up. For some reason those two horses had not met and they did not know which was boss, so they backed up together and started fighting. My horse broke the other horse's hind leg — a nice big fine horse of Silas Smith's our Captain. But it caused no delay as Brother Smith had a bunch of eight or ten loose horses.[14]

May 16. Next morning gathered the horses after breakfast, went on our journey traveling through the Navajo Reservation. Nothing unusual, until night when a bunch of Navajoes about 60 came to our camp and demanded that the boys trade back. As I have noted Hansen Bayles and Parley Butt had traded with them. The Indians being very persistent, Hansen had just taken the horse out of his halter. The Indian came, grabbed the halter, and he and Hansen had a regular scuffle to see who was stronger, the Indian taking the Championship. Our numbers being so much smaller, we persuaded Hansen to call the trade off. So everything was all right and no more trouble. But to show there is a sense of honor in the Indians, he followed us up a day and a half and traded back again. After thinking the matter over, he thought it was not honorable to do that way, so he came and made the trade good though it was to his own disadvantage.[15]

May 17. Camped at what we called the Cane Bed, a small spring. Did not start very early; had to go and make a road across two deep washes — about 25 feet deep. After we had crossed the wash, we traveled down a canyon for a number of miles and we came against solid rock hill. We had to take picks and axes and make notches in the rock so the horses could get footing and then we put eight horses on each outfit it was so steep. We then traveled some five or six miles without a bit of dirt — solid rock, but it was rather smooth, some up and down. Camped five or six miles from the rim.[16]

May 18. Camped five or six miles from the San Juan River at a small spring. After breakfast George Urie and myself took our fishlines and walked on ahead of the teams and wagons and had a mess of fish for dinner. We pitched our camp on the south side of the river for two days. The same evening we arrived Robert Bullock went up the river about a mile to where Peter Schurtz was camped, being an old acquaintance of his and borrowed a canoe which Peter had made to cross the river back and forth, the river being quite high. We wanted to locate a place where we could ford the river to locate a permanent camp for summer. Brother Bullock had some rough experience coming down, not paying much attention to where he was going, the current took him under some fallen trees and skinned his face.[17]

May 19. On the morning of the 19th of May we forded the river and made a permanent camp for the summer. We immediately went to work to put a dam across the river to take out the water. We worked on the dam about two weeks and about the 30th of June Brother Smith chose James Decker, Parley Butt, Hamilton Wallace, and Nielson B. Dalley to go back to Moencopi and get the cattle we had left when we went to the river — a distance of about 150 miles. We arrived about the third of July. During the time they were there the cattle broke into the fields and there was a 17 dollar bill on them. I having a two year old steer, I turned him to the man for the damage. We found all the cattle. But during our stay two of our horses either strayed away or were stolen by the Navajoes which delayed our return two or three days hunting for them. Two boys started with the cattle and two stayed to find the horses. Boys went 40 miles and made camp. There a big bunch of Navajoes came along two riding our horses. Wanted $5 before they would give them up.

[*The typewritten copy of Dalley's Diary ends rather abruptly; I have been unable to locate the additional entries that must have been in the original copy. However, Dalley's second account, after relating that the four men had returned to Moenkopi, goes on to tell of some incidents regarding their activities as they piloted the Davis family and the cattle herd back to the San Juan.*]

B. San Juan Exploring Company

Silas S. Smith Capt of the Co.
Albert & Stephen Barton Paragoonah his sons
Harvey Dunton
James J Adams Parowan
Zacarah Decker
John Dalton   mostley young men
Dell McGregor   unmarried
George Hobbs
Harrison Harriman married Geo. Hobbs sister both went
Isaac Allen
Hans. Bayles
Parley Butts
Robert Bullock Cedar
John Duncan
Tom Bladen
Geo. E Perry
Geo. Urie
John Gower

Kumen Jones
Joseph Neilson
James Davis & family 3 or 4 children.
Nielson B Dalley, Summit
John Butler Panguitch
Hamilton Wallace, Toquerville

Left here 16th April 1879. We out thru Bearvalley & thru Panguitch to Johnson, the Buckskin mts by way of House Rock. Crossed the river at Lees Ferry, named for John D Lee. A few yrs

We stayed at the Mogue villiage at Moyancoppy, Ariz. John W. Young was building a woolen mill there. The Navajo cut the wool with a butcher knife. We were out of grain so we quarried for him for 2 days for grain. We then went East up the wash. (We took a few head of cattle each of us.)

When we got to Ortons or Lafevers the Company organized & I was appointed to drive the cattle. At night we'd sing hymns around the camp fire & have prayer. I helped take care of the cattle during the whole trip. The first night or two we had to corral our cattle so they wouldn't run back. We hobbled our horses then we'd turn them out & hunt them in the morning. We never guarded them & we were very successful until we got to Moyincoppy.

The younger calves were hard to drive so tender footed so Silas Smith ordered us to leave all the cattle at Moyincoppy. There was quite a colony living there & they took care of them.

We camped with in 2 hundreds yards of where young Geo A Smith was shot. Thales Hascal helped to show us the road. The old Indian was in camp that night. We went 20 miles to Peoquans ranch the one who shot Geo A. we went on two days (2 men to a wagon). Hans Bayles & Parl traded horses with the Navajoes they overtook us after 2 days they thot they were beat. Hans didn't want to. the Indians was determined to. So we persuaded Hans to trade back. Then after 2 days the Indians over took us & I guess he had desided it wasnt honest so he wanted to trade again & they did. (we were right in the Navajo country)

We didnt have any more trouble we arrived on the San Juan on the 17 day of May. Kumen Jones says it was 1st of June.

We stayed there until sometime in July Silas sent James Decker Ham Wallace, Parley Butts & Neils Dalley. went back for the cattle.

John Dalton Silas S & son Geo Urie & Robert Bullock I think and maybe Dell Mc went with 2 wagons 4 horses on a wagon went into Colorado, I think Durango for provisions.

We only took a pack Horse, on horses it took us 4 days to get to Moincoppy. The cattle had done some damage $17. We didnt have any money. But I had a 2 yr old steer I had taken along for beef so I turned it to pay the damage bill.

We gathered all our cattle ready to go the night before we were to leave we lost one of my horses & one of Parley Butts. We had turned them out. We hunted them 3 or 4 days but couldnt find them. Parley B & [James B Decker] went on with the cattle. while we stayed to hunt. On the 4th day we got word that Parley Butt [and] James Decker had found our horses.

The Navajos were parading & were riding our horses. They had to pay them $5.00 to get them. We never knew whether they took them from Moincopy or found them on the road back. Ham & I left immediately & overtook them 40 miles in a swampy country the cattle wattered in a muddy pond. We only had to dig 2 or 3 ft to get water to drink. Old peogon appeared again he was peaved at us staying on his lands.

There were 2 boys from S. L. C. stayed with us one night. The old Indian was peaved & began pushing the smallest of the S L around but he was too much for him & he pushed him into one of the water holes at this the S Lers mother dog jumped out of the wagon & grabbed the Indian. the S Ler took his raw hide whip to the dog but the Indian grabbed the ax & was going after the dog. the owner stopped him but the Indian started on him the other S L grabbed a shovel to interfer. But we finally pacified the Indian. We wrote to the Indian Agent & explained the trouble & we went on.

We lost one animal die from drinking alkali water. We traveled some at night as the days were so hot. We made the trip in about 6 days.

We all staked a home stead and built us a log cabin. We made our camp about 20 miles above Bluff. Neils D, James J Adams & the Decker boy built their about 1 mile above Bluff.

We stayed in San Juan 4 months.

We put a dam across the San J. River to get the water on to the land.

The utes came there 2 or 3 times while we were there But they were friendly to us.

Geo Hobbs[18]

Harriman

Davis but these remained there.

The whole Com left we traveled to Monticello & then on thru Emery Co.

John Gower & Geo Urie went back by the Ferry to get their broken wagon It took us close to a month to return.

Those who stayed looked after them & we traded them to the company to left. We came back in the fall & the next fall the Company of colonizers left on a different rout. But they didn't profit by our experience they took a new route over the mts.

1879

1861   Febr Dalley

18

In Pioneer days there were no grocery stores, no yeast cakes, no bakers bread. The Pioneer mothers met every need, they were not afraid of work.

FOOTNOTES

1. This is the only account that I have found which lists "six wagons." Other accounts refer to about a dozen outfits.

2. This listing of the number of livestock is considerably below the estimate given in other accounts. See chapter II, this work.

3. Most accounts agree that the expedition had left Parowan on April 14, 1879.

4. In his other account Dalley says that the camp was organized at Orton's, a few miles north of Panguitch; he also adds his own name as having been placed in charge of the livestock.

5. The route took them to the headwaters of the west fork of Sevier River, over the divide at Long Valley Junction, and into the valley where Alton is now located. See map, page 21.

6. The expedition evidently did not pass through Kanab.

7. Although repairs described here were made, the wagon was evidently abandoned, for Dalley, in his second account, states that Urie and Gower later returned from the San Juan via Lee's Ferry to pick up the broken outfit and returned to the settlements over the same route taken on the outward trip.

8. Kane Creek must have been the place usually referred to as Willow Spring.

9. Dalley's second account also mentions Thales Haskell and his service as guide. No other accounts, as far as I have been able to determine, mention Haskell in this connection.

10. George A. Smith, Jr., son of Apostle George A. Smith, had been killed by the Indians on November 2, 1860.

11. See page 31, n. 21 above for the various spellings of his name.

12. An account located in the L.D.S. Church archives as part of the San Juan Stake History states that the company did not leave Moenkopi until May 13. The camp described here was probably in the Red Lake region.

13. This is the only record containing an account of this incident.

14. The San Juan Stake History account places this event on May 25 instead of the date given by Dalley.

15. This is the only known record of this incident.

16. This must be a description of Chinle Wash and the road out the other side of it.

17. The San Juan Stake History account states that the exploring company reached the San Juan River on May 31.

18. Hobbs did not remain on the San Juan, but returned to the settlements with the main company of explorers. The third man who did remain, in addition to James Davis and H. H. Harriman, was Harvey Dunton.

APPENDIX III

EXCERPTS FROM THE HISTORY OF THE LIFE OF JAMES DAVIS

Sometime before his death in 1920, James L. Davis, was induced by members of his family to compile a brief sketch of his life. The early part of his account deals with his birth and early life in England and his subsequent migration to Utah. He married Mary Elizabeth Fretwell April 23, 1864, and soon moved to Cedar City. We begin our quotations from his life sketch at that point.

The excerpts here quoted are from a typewritten copy which was presented to the Cedar City Camp of the Daughters of Utah Pioneers October 21, 1936.

Excerpts from the History of the Life of James Davis

After our marriage we went by ox team to Cedar City to make our home. We first lived in a dug out in William Shurtz' lot, the first street west of the main road. Two children were born to us, Mary and Edward. We then bought the lot where aunt Sarah Ann Fretwell home stands, and built a log house on it, in which we lived for a number of years. About this time Bro. Dan Jones stopped in Cedar City on his way to preach to the Navajoe Indians. Being called on to preach to the people in Cedar City, he told them that he could go no farther unless he could get a pack animal. The spirit told me to get the animal for Bro. Jones. I was overcome with joy and could scarsely stay until the meeting was over. Next day I brought a nice young mule and gave it to Bro Jones. He turned to Bishop C. J. Arthur and said, "Those are the kind of men the Lord will not part with." I had a feeling within me that the Lord had forgiven me for not paying due attention years before when the spirit prompted me to pay my surplus money to the Bishop as a thank offering.

From this time we were blessed financially. We built a very fine brick house for those days. I was very proud of my home surroundings, and we were very happy, except for the poor health of my wife. She was seldom ever well. So it came as a great surprise, when on Dec. 29, 1878 we were called on a mission to Arizona to help build a settlement there. Erastus Snow, Pres. of the pioneering committee, asked that all who was called be ready by the first part of April. I told him I would be ready by the first part of April.

My wife and I felt very bad at leaving a comfortable home and our friends. Never the less we had been called by the servants of the Lord and we were determined to magnify the call. We disposed of our store, land and a good deal of other property at a great sacrifice. On the 13th day of April 1879, we left Cedar City in company with several young men. Brother H. H. Herriman and family joined us at Parowan. The company consisted of 26 men two women and eight children, the rest not being ready until fall.

Bishop C. J. Arthur Blessed my wife and told her if she would go and do her part her health would be restored, and that she would never be called on to part with another child, for out of our eight children we had buried four. He also told her that the Lord would protect us and our lives would be spared. We traveled many long dreary weeks; we crossed over the same region the Spanish had crossed in 1540. The Indians said we were the first whites to pass that way since that time. Every morning my wife would arrange the children in the bottom of the wagon, then climb to a high spring seat, and drive a team all day. There were only Indian trails to mark the way, so driving was a difficult task. We crossed the Colorado at Lees Ferry, and stopped at a small village called Moencopi settled by some Moquech Oriba, Hopi and Navajos Indians, and a few white people. Among them was Pres. Willford Woodruff and John W. Young, son of Pres. Brigham Young, who was building a woolen Mill to take care of the vast amount of wool the Indians produced.

They advised us with familys to stay there on account of the dangers ahead of us. And let the young men go and find a suitable country to locate. We did so and in two months five of the boys returned and reported finding a place. We started again on our journey. We traveled peacefully until we nooned the third day, then we were in some very bad Indian country. One by the name of Peascon, came to our camp and caused a great deal of trouble. (He was the one that caused the killing of Apostle George A. Smith Sr., the first L. D. S. to be killed by the Indians, and we were close to the place he was killed).[1] This Indian would kick the dirt on our food, and struck our knife blades on the rocks. He would draw his knife across his throat to show my wife and children what he would do to them when he got help. Our boys acted like the time had come for them to kill or be killed. I begged of them not to fire the first shot. The Indians left for help and did not return by night-fall. We expected them to return before sunrise as those Indians were sun worshipers and believed that the sun can see and tell the great spirit all they do, but if the sun didn't see the spirit doesn't know. So when daylight came and the sun came up and they had not returned we felt very much relieved, and had decided to cook our breakfast. I saw at a distance an old Indian coming towards us. He came and told us to hitch up our horses as quickly as possible and travel fast. We did so but was a little doubtful as to the Indians plans. We feared he might be leading us into a trap. The roads were thru deep sand so the horses had to stop often. This seemed to anoy the Indian. He would stand upon the spring seat and look far and wide, then he would urge us to hurry faster. After a time he told us we could stop as long as we liked then travel as slow as we wished. He asked me if I did not know him. He told me my name and where I had come from, and said he had been to my place many times, and we had always given him something to eat, and was good to him. He knew I was there with my family he had watched us on our journey and we did not know it.

He said the Indians were planning to kill and rob us as soon as they could find enough volunteers and he had come to save us by hurrying us out of their territory. In two weeks time we arrived at the San Juan river at a point called Montizuma Ford. I very much liked the look of the country, but my wife felt that we were isolated from all civilization and was very down hearted.

The boys helped us build two small log rooms, one for Bro. Harriman and family and one for us, they then left us. An old man by the name of Harvey Dunton was with us, so our company consisted of three men, two women and eight children. We were nearly a hundred miles thru almost impassable country to the nearest settlement, which consisted of eight familys; on the 2nd of August two weeks after we arrived my wife gave birth to a baby girl. The first white child to be born on the San Juan. One beautiful afternoon just as I was trying to build a fire place which would complete the walls of our room, a friendly Navajo came to tell us that the White River Utes were on the war path and had killed one family up the river,[2] and would be there to kill us about nightfall. He wanted us to go with him and we would be safe. But we remembered that we had been promised that if we did our part no harm would come to us, we fortified the best we could in one room. We made holes in the wall to shoot thru. About midnight the dogs barked and run up the river bank, but after a while they came back, but was very restless for some time. When daylight came we found they [the Indians] had crossed the river a short distance up and were making for the strongholds of the renegade Indians. We felt once more that the Lord was mindful of us.

My wifes health steadily improved. We passed the winter in peace but was very lonesome. In the Spring we had the pleasure of seeing our old friend Bro. Thales Haskell, he being an Indian Missionary and interpreter. Pres. Snow hearing that we had been killed by the Indians had sent Bro. Haskell to see if it was true, and if it was, to give our bones as deasent a burial as possible, and if not to stay until the next company came. When he saw at a distance the smoke coming from our chimney he offered up a prayer of thanksgiving.

We were living on wheat ground in a coffee mill. We had looked all winter for the company that left Cedar City in the Fall to bring us food, but they had never arrived. We were very anxious for their safety. They were our old friends and neighbors. Our wheat gave out and Bro. Harvey Dunton said he would leave and on cleaning out his wagon found a little wheat in a sack which he gave to us saying, he had a good gun and would live on wild game. Just after he had left another Indian missionary by the name of Lewellyn Harris called and told us that the company would be there in about ten days. My wife told him we did not have bread to last two days. He was hungry and ragged and said he wanted to stay three days. My wife told him he was welcome but that she was at a loss to know what to give him to eat. He told her to be of good cheer she had seen her worst time. He stayed his time and after he had gone I asked my wife where she was getting the wheat to make the bread, she said from the sack Bro. Dunton had left. I hefted the sack and there seemed to be as much as when he had left it. And again we knew there was an unseen hand controling our wellfare. It was not until April the 6th 1880, that the second company arrived. Six months after they had left Cedar City.

FOOTNOTES

1. He means George A. Smith, Jr., son of the apostle. For further information regarding this incident see page 33, n. 47, this work.

2. This is a reference to the Meeker Massacre. For further reference to this incident see page 211, this work.

APPENDIX IV

JOURNAL OF PLATTE DeALTON LYMAN

Platte D. Lyman's journal is the only day-by-day account of the Hole-in-the-Rock expedition, written at the time and at the site of the incidents described. Other members of the company may have kept similar records, but if so, they have either been destroyed or lost. Lyman's is the only one known to me. This fact alone makes the journal a vital and indispensable part of the Hole-in-the-Rock story. Without it we would be completely uninformed concerning many important aspects of this memorable trek. Of course, the journal does not record every important event — the author of it could not be everywhere present or see everything that happened.

Silas S. Smith had been called by the church to head the San Juan Mission with Platte D. Lyman as his first assistant. However, Smith was absent from the company during most of the trek, leaving Lyman in the top position of responsibility. As leader of the expedition the author of this journal was in a position to know what the major problems were and what progress was being made. In his account he tells what he saw and felt.

This journal should not be considered merely a record of Platte D. Lyman. It is rather an account of the whole expedition as seen through the eyes of that expedition's appointed leader. The account of the progress of the company as it hewed its way toward the San Juan is not the account of Platte D. Lyman's progress, but the progress of the whole camp. Descendants of that expedition should not feel that undue emphasis is being given to Lyman because his journal is so often quoted, and reproduced here in full. It is indeed regrettable that other similar accounts are not available. But since his is the only one, we should be grateful that such a record was kept and is available for publication.

There are several typewritten copies of this journal: one on file at the Utah Historical Society, one at Brigham Young University Library, one at the L.D.S. Church Historian's Library; and there are many privately owned copies. Some of these seem to be copies of copies and contain many inconsistencies and obvious mistakes. I do not mean to say that all are inaccurate; but all I have examined certainly contain serious errors.

That part of the journal reproduced on the following pages has been carefully copied from the original pen and ink, handwritten copy, now on deposit at the L.D.S. Church Historian's Library. The record is a straightforward account of events as they occurred, recorded on the spot and at the time of the events portrayed. Once written, the record remained in its original form; there were no later corrections or alterations. Only that part of the journal dealing with the Hole-in-the-Rock expedition is here presented — and that comprises only a small fraction of the complete Platte D. Lyman journals.

In preparing this valuable document for publication, I have tried to retain the original form as nearly as practicable — original paragraphing, sentences, etc. I have taken the liberty of adding a few periods and commas where they were obviously omitted in the haste of the writing and (in a very few cases) to help clarify the text. I have made no attempt to completely punctuate the document. No other changes have been made; the original wording, spelling and capitalization are retained, just as Platte D. Lyman wrote them. Footnotes are added where needed to further identify persons, incidents, or places referred to in the journal.

We begin the journal with the entry of October 20, 1879, and end with that of June 2, 1880.

Journal of Platte D. Lyman

Monday, Oct. 20th, 1879. Spent most of the day in loading my wagons, and in the evening sold my house and lot to Geo. Lovell for a span of mules and harness and $100.00 in money.[1]

Tuesday, Oct. 21st, 1879. Started in the afternoon for San Juan drove 12 miles to Badgers Field[2] and camped, stood guard over our stock all night. There is not a particle of feed, and but little water. Our company consists of myself my brothers Joseph, Edward & Walter, my sisters Ida and May, Josephs wife Nellie, Frank Rysert who is working for me, Ole Jensen his mother wife and 3 children, and F. R. Lyman and John Lovell who will help us out a few days with our stock.

We have 6 wagons 39 horses and mules and 180 head of cattle.

Wednesday, Oct. 22d, 1879. Drove 17 miles to Scipio saw mill,[3] no feed. Stood guard over our stock. It has been a hard day on our teams on account of hard hills and heavy sand. The boys lost 10 head of cattle on 8 miles creek.[4]

Thursday, Oct. 23d, 1879. Drove 10 miles and camped on the east side of Round Valley Lake.[5] Coralled our cattle. Feed poor and scarce.

Friday, Oct. 24th, 1879. Drove 20 miles and camped near Ike Colby's close by the Gravelly Ford on the Seveir [*sic*], had good feed for our horses but none for our cattle.[6]

Saturday, Oct. 25th, 1879. Fred and John started back. We lost one of our saddle horses last night. Drove 10 miles and camped at Prattvill,[7] had good feed and our stock stayed without being guarded. This looks like a good country, plenty of water hay & grain.

Sunday, Oct. 26th, 1879. This morning Ole Jensen left us to stop at Richfield as he did not think he was prepared for the trip and his Mother was quite sick.[8]

Drove 10 miles and camped near Monroe found pretty good feed in the stubble.

Monday, Oct. 27th, 1879. Drove 16 miles to Marysvale[9] and turned into a pasture for 1 ct per head. The road today has been mostly heavy up hill, no feed or water the whole distance.

Tuesday, Oct. 28th, 1879. This morning had to pay 1 dollar more for pasturage than we agreed to last night, because unconscionable Mrs Langly[10] thought we were a little late in starting. Drove 6 miles and camped at Bears[11] on the river. Stood guard over our cattle all night.

Wednesday, Oct. 29th, 1879. Lost 1 cow and calf, drove 12 miles to Junction and camped at Riddles grist mill, left 1 calf on the road.

Thursday, Oct. 30th, 1879. Drove 6 miles up the East Fork which we crossed 5 times got stuck in the mud and was delayed 2 hours, the road is very rocky and in places very sideling.

Friday, Oct. 31st, 1879. Drove 8 miles and camped near John Kings place on Kiota Creek[12] good road most of the way, we crossed the river 4 times and got stuck in it one, lost 1 cow and a colt today.

Saturday, Nov. 1st, 1879. Drove 2 miles and layed over on Poison Creek.[13] Shod some of our horses, no feed.

Sunday, Nov. 2d, 1879. Traded my mules for another span and sold 2 give out calves for 100 cwt of beef, and left one sore footed cow, drove 12 miles over rough road and heavy rolling hills, camped 2 miles below Riddles Ranch[14] on the East Fork, no feed.

Monday, Nov. 3d, 1879. Left a give out cow, drove 10 miles and camped in Sweetwater Kanyon,[15] a little feed.

Tuesday, Nov. 4th, 1879. Lost 3 head of cattle and spent some time hunting for them which made us late in starting, drove 3 miles to the summit which is the rim of the Basin, and as far as we can see east and south the country looks very rough and broken, drove 5 miles down the mountain the first part of the road being a muddy steep dugway, the balance of it a good smooth even grade, found a good camp some time after dark with feed and water in abundance. There is a fine growth of white pine all over the hills here.

Thursday, Nov. 6th, 1879. Layed over yesterday and wrote letters, and today rode 13 miles down the Kanyon to Escalante with Joseph Liston[16] and staid over night at the house of his brother Parry, went to the Post Office but got no letters.

Saturday, Nov. 8th, 1879. Returned to camp yesterday, the day was very cold. Snow has fallen all day today.

Monday, Nov. 10th, 1879. Snow fell all day yesterday and is still falling, wrote more letters and sent them to the P.O.

Thursday, Nov. 13th, 1879. The past 2 days have been clear and cold, we have looked after our cattle as well as we could and have hunted deer some, Walter killed one, 3 inches of snow fell last night, but today is fine and warm. We moved ½ a mile down the Kanyon and camped in an old house.[17]

Friday, Nov. 14th, 1879. While in the hills gathering our stock this morning Walter shot 3 deer, but we could only get one of them. Moved 4½ miles down the Kanyon, we have had to leave 25 head of our cattle which we could not find and 1 horse that gave out.[18]

Saturday, Nov. 15th, 1879. Drove 6 miles and camped in Escalante field, have had considerable muddy road today, got stuck once and spent most of the afternoon in getting out.

Sunday, Nov. 16th, 1879. Eddy traded a yoke of oxen for a saddle horse. Bro Silas S Smith and a few wagons from Red Creek[19] came down the Kanyon this evening and camped opposite us. The day has been bitter cold.

Thursday, Nov. 20th, 1879. Have layed over the past 3 days, bought some corn for 2 cts per lb and potatoes for 1. Started on in company with two sons of Walter Stevens and his uncle of Holden.[20] Drove 7 miles beyond Escalante onto the desert and made a dry camp, found some snow and good feed, have had good roads today.

Friday, Nov. 21st, 1879. Drove 3 miles to the 10 mile spring[21] but could get no water for our horses. Here we sent our stock off the road to the east about 7 miles to the Harris Ranch,[22] because of scarcity of water on the road. Eddy and Alma Stevens will stay with them for the present. We then drove 10 miles over a soft sandy road crossing several deep gulches where we had to double teams, and camped at dark at the 20 mile spring,[23] where there is plenty of good feed but very little water.

Saturday, Nov. 22d, 1879. Drove 15 miles and camped after dark at the Kiota Holes[24] where we had to dig for water and got plenty of it. The road is much the same as yesterday and there is plenty of good feed.

Monday, Nov. 24th, 1879. We layed over yesterday and started late this morning and drove 6 miles over very heavy road and was till after dark getting to the Cottonwood Gulch[25] where we found water in a hole ½ a mile above the road, and plenty of good feed.

Tuesday, Nov. 25th, 1879. Joshua Stevens and I walked 4 miles to the main camp at the 40 mile spring,[26] spent most of the day there and walked back in the evening, found Eddy had come in from the herd.

Bishop Schow & bro Reuben Collett[27] of Escalante camped with us on their way down to assist in locating a road across the Rio Colorado.

Wednesday, Nov. 26th, 1879. Bros Schow, Collet Eddy and myself climbed a high point of the mountain close by and endeavored with the aid of field glasses to make out something of the country ahead of us but could not.[28] Returned to camp and found that Joseph had undertaken to move some of our wagons and had them scattered all the way from one camp to the other.

Thursday, Nov. 27th, 1879. Snow fell all last night and is 2 inches deep this morning, hitched up early and got our wagons all into camp at the 40 mile spring, attended meeting in the evening[29] and was called on to speak as were also bros Schow and Collet, bro Smith also spoke, a good spirit seems to prevail and the most of the people feel like pushing ahead if possible, although the prospect is rather discouraging as there is no road beyond here and the country is totally unexplored with the exception of a few miles ahead of us which is the roughest white men ever undertook to pass over.[30]

Friday, Nov. 28th, 1879. By direction of bro Smith I started with 12 others to look out a way for a road across the Colorado and beyond, we have a boat on one wagon and our luggage on another.[31] We drove 10 miles over the roughest country I ever saw a wagon go over and camped at the 50 miles spring. The company is as follows: A. P. Schow, Reuben Collet, Wm Hutchings, Kumen Jones, Saml Rowley, Cornelious Decker, Geo. Hobbs, John Robinson, Jos Barton, Joseph Neilsen, Saml. Bryson, James Riley and myself.

Saturday, Nov. 29th, 1879. Drove 6 miles over rough sandstone hills and sand to the "Hole in the rock"[32] a cleft in the solid rock wall of the Grand Kanyon of the Colorado, which runs about a mile below us, the walls of the Kanyon rise 2000 feet from the water and are in many places perpendicular. We took our wagons 2 miles farther up the river to where the banks are not so abrupt but are still solid sandstone, and took the front wheels from under the boat and lowered it down about 1 mile onto a sandy bench[33] from where we dragged it 1 mile to the river and slid it 200 feet over a rock into the river about 1 mile above the mouth of "Hole in the rock." After supper and a little rest we loaded our luggage into the boat and about midnight rowed it down [to] the mouth of the "Hole" where we tied up and camped. The river is about 350 feet wide, the current sluggish and the water milky but of good taste, the willows on the bank are still leaved in green.

Sunday, Nov. 30th, 1879. One of the boys caught a fine fish called white Salmon[34] large enough for our breakfast & dinner.

We loaded our luggage into the boat and 7 of us got in and started down to find the mouth of the San Juan, but after going 1½ miles we ran aground in a rapid and were compelled to turn back to our starting point, from where 11 of us with our provisions and blankets on our backs started up over the bluffs to the east which were at first very rough and precipitous but soon we found a smooth open Kanyon[35] with water wood and grass in it which we followed up for 3 miles and then began to ascend the bluffs which are at first sandy and afterwards steep solid sandstone hills[36] which continue as far as the summit 6 miles from the river,[37] went 1 mile farther and camped in the rocks where we found plenty of water in the rocks.[38]

Monday, Dec. 1st, 1879. Started out to the east and after going a mile or two we found the country so rough and broken and so badly cut in two by deep gorges all in solid rock that we gave up all idea of a road being made there,[39] we then went back nearly to our camp and struck a Kanyon on a line with the one we followed yesterday which we followed down 4 miles right to the San Juan river,[40] which is about 250 ft wide, with a rapid current, its color is slightly milky but the water tastes very good. The banks are nearly as high as those of the Colorado but not so steep nor solid. The little Kanyon we have followed down is a curiosity in its way. For 2 miles more or less, its width is from 15 to 30 [feet] while the walls of bare rock rise perpendicularly 200 or 300 feet and the bottom is much of the way smooth and level as a floor and is covered with a little stream of water seeping from the crevices in the rock which spreads over the surface so evenly that one can walk for rods at a time without wetting the uppers of their boots although in running water all the time. The grass and willows which grow in small bunches here are very rank and still very green. There are deep holes in places in the bed of the creek where we caught several mud turtles about as large as a mans hand.[41] The country here is almost entirely solid sand rock, high hills and mountains cut all to pieces by deep gulches which are in many places altogether impassable. It is certainly the worst country I ever saw,[42] some of our party are of the opinion that a road could be made if plenty of money was furnished but most of us are satisfied that there is no us[e] of this company undertaking to get through to San Juan this way. We returned to our last nights camp after dark.[43]

Tuesday, Dec. 2d, 1879. Walked back to the Colorado, crossed over and hauled our cart back to the top of the bank which was half a days hard work, and then camped.

Wednesday, Dec. 3d, 1879. Drove back to camp[44] much of the way in the rain which wet me to the skin. In the evening an informal meeting was held in bro Smiths tent when those who had been out reported the result of their explorations, after which on motion of bro Jens Neilsen sen it was resolved unanimously to sustain bro Smith in whatever course he thought best for us to pursue. Bro Smith then said he thought we ought to go ahead and all present expressed themselves willing to spend 3 or 4 months if necessary working on the road in order to get through, as it is almost impossible to go back the way we came because of the condition of the road and the scarcity of grass.

Thursday, December 4th, 1879. Bro Smith called a meeting of the whole camp to take an expression of their feelings in order that bros Sckow & Collet may know what to report to those behind,[45] when it was unanimously resolved to go to work on the road.

Wednesday, Dec. 10th, 1879. Drove to the 50 mile springs and camped, have been four days beside this getting our wagons to this place. In the evening

Alma Stevens & Edward L came in from the herd and brought a fat cow for beef and a little later 2 men from Red Creek[46] came into camp and brought us papers and letters from which we learned that all was well in the settlements.

Thursday, Dec. 11th, 1879. Killed our beef in the morning and loaned most of it to the camp,[47] and afterward rode down to the "Hole in the Rock" with bro Smith where we found about 15 wagons[48] of the company camped, returned to camp in the evening.

Sunday, Dec. 14th, 1879 "Hole in the Rock." Have spent the past 2 days in moving our wagons to this place, and today put our horses down over a trail which we have made to a bench next to the river where there is a little feed and water.[49] There is neither wood water or grass near the camp. Bro Smith came from the 50 mile where his folks are camped and held meeting in the afternoon at which the following travelling organization was effected.

Capt of company Silas S. Smith
Asst Capt " Platte. D. Lyman
Capt 1st Ten Jens Neilsen.   Capt 2d Ten   Geo W Sevy
   " 3rd " Benj. Perkins   " 4th "   Henry Holyoak
   " 5th " Z. B. Decker Jr.   Chaplain Jens Neilsen

Clerk C. E. Walton. Saml Bryson was afterwards appointed Capt of the 6th Ten. Bro Smith returned to his camp, and tomorrow will start to Parowan expecting to be absent 3 weeks from camp, and if possible secure an appropriation from the Legislature to assist in putting the road through.[50] Bp Geo. W. Sevy of Panguitch came in today with several wagons from that place and Harmony.[51] Held meeting in the evening and had a good time.

Tuesday, Dec. 16th, 1879. With a square and level, I determined the grade of the road down the "Hole" to be for the first $\frac{1}{3}$ of the distance to be 8 ft to the rod, and for the second $\frac{1}{3}$ — $5\frac{1}{2}$ to the rod and the last part much better than either of the others.

Wednesday, Dec. 17th, 1879. Realizing the necessity of having the country more thoroughly explored ahead of us, I have talked the matter over with bro Sevy and he has consented to undertake a trip through to the San Juan if it is possible to get through, and today he made a start with Lemuel Redd, Geo Hobbs and Geo Morrell and 4 animals,[52] expecting to be gone about 15 days. There are about 47 men at work on the road and we are making good progress.

Sunday, Dec. 21st, 1879. The wind has blown strong and cold and last night some rain fell, which makes water more plentiful. Today I took the girls down to the river and gave them a ride in the boat.[53] The weather being better we held a meeting in the evening and had a good time. We are making good progress on the road.

Thursday, Dec. 25th, 1879, Christmas. The weather has been so cold and windy with some snow that we have been unable to do much work so far this week. There is dancing in camp this evening.[54]

Friday, Dec. 26th, 1879. The feed has give out on the bench[55] so that we were compelled to move our horses up today and in doing so, got some of them badly cut on the rocks.

Tuesday, Dec. 30th, 1879. Weather cold and foggy have had 6 inches of snow during the last few days. We are just getting at work again.

Saturday, Jan. 3d, 1880. Today we finished the road from the river up to where the solid rock commences, being about ⅔ds of the whole distance.[56] The weather is warm and pleasant during the day but rather frosty at night.

Sunday, Jan. 4th, 1880. Warm and cloudy held meeting in the afternoon and evening and had a good time. During the past week bro Charles Hall of Escalante has brought down the material for a flatboat which he is building and will use as a ferry.

Tuesday, Jan. 6th, 1880. Sent our horses back 10 miles on the road in charge of 2 men, as they are falling away fast while staying here.

Saturday, Jan. 10th, 1880. Bro Sevy and party returned last night all well but badly tired out. We held meeting in the forenoon and heard their report. They have had a hard trip and great credit is due them for the pluck and determination they have shown under the very adverse circumstances which surrounded them. They were lost 4 or 5 days in deep snow and blinding snow storms, were out of provisions and talked seriously of eating a mule but finally reached the camp on San Juan having been 12 days on the road and having travelled 175 miles. They found the settlers in a very destitute condition as regards provision. They stopped 1 day and then started back, and were 11 days on the road and travelled 136 miles but thought a road might be made some shorter. Reported that it was possible to put a road through the worst of it being this end where we are now at work.

Monday, Jan. 12th, 1880. Found one of my mules down in a ditch and so weak it could not stand so I killed it.[57] We are making slow progress on the road for want of powder.

Friday, Jan. 16th, 1880. Received a letter from bro S. S. Smith informing me that he had secured some powder and would forward it as soon as possible.

Thursday, Jan. 22d, 1880. Today we received 25 lbs of giant powder by Arza Judd from whom we leared [sic] that bro Smith is sick at Red Creek. Frank Rysert started for Kanosh on the 20th inst with James Dorrity.[58] We have put in our time to the best advantage on this job and will now be able to move in a few days.

Sunday, Jan. 25th, 1880. Walked back to the herd on Friday, stayed there yesterday and returned to camp today with our teams. Received a few lines from Delia dated Jan 12th saying she had given birth to a fine boy 2 days before,[59] and was getting along very well. Also a letter from Susannah Robison.[60]

Monday, Jan. 26th, 1880. Today we worked all the wagons in this camp down the "Hole" and ferried 26 of them across the river. The boat is worked by 1 pair of oars and does very well.[61]

Wednesday, Jan. 28th, 1880. Snow fell most of yesterday and today but cleared up towards evening.

Friday, Jan. 30th, 1880. Bros Walton and Bryson moved one of my wagons 4 miles up on the creek[62] where we will have to camp for a week or so. We moved the rest of them 1 mile onto the creek and camped. The weather is as cold as we have seen it on the trip.

Saturday, Jan. 31st, 1880. Moved up to the cottonwoods where the rest of the company are camped. Wagons from the 50 mile spring where half of the company have been during the winter began to come into camp today.[63]

By brother Amasa M and 3 other men came in to camp, having been sent from Panguitch to work on the road, they reported that 1000 lbs of blasting powder had been left at the 50 mile by a man sent from Panguitch to bring it to this company.[64]

Sunday, Feb. 1st, 1880. Held no meeting during the day as it was rather too cold but held one in the evening and had a good time.

The weather has been quite cold but is getting warmer and we are making good progress on the road, as we have got the powder in camp and are using it as it is needed.

Sunday, Feb. 8th, 1880. Have had a good force of men out during the past week and have made encouraging progress, as the weather is now very pleasant. Today we held 2 meetings 1 at each camp they being ½ a mile apart.

Monday, Feb. 9th, 1880. Went 2 miles beyond the summit[65] with the Panguitch boys who are going to work, and then returned to camp, the road is going over the same rough country we passed over on our exploring trip and considered impassable for a wagon road.

Several of the boys started back to Potato Valley[66] today for the cattle we have had to leave there. I sent letters to my family and also to bro Erastus Snow.[67]

Friday, Feb. 13th, 1880. Have been busy during the past 3 days moving our wagons up the Cottonwood Hill where it took from 4 to 7 span of horses or the same number of oxen to move 1 wagon. The weather has been very cold and stormy a part of the time. We are now camped 2 miles from the summit at what we call the cheese camp.[68] Two men from Panguitch came into camp a few days ago,[69] they will stop and work on the road. They brought us 200 lbs of pork and 40 lbs of cheese from the Tithing Office to be divided among 70 men. The cheese was sold at auction hence the name of this camp.

Sunday, Feb. 15th, 1880. Four men[70] have started to San Juan on their own hook with pack animals. We held meeting in the evening had a good time.

Tuesday, Feb. 17th, 1880. While camped here we have been building road over and through solid rock, which we have now completed.[71] Snow fell until noon today when it cleared up and the company began to move.

Joseph and I moved 2 of our wagons 2 miles[72] when he camped, and I returned to the old camp.

Wednesday, Feb. 18th, 1880. Joseph brought the teams back and we moved the other wagons up and took his on one mile farther and camped in a gulch running through the bench over which our road now runs.[73] We find plenty of grass here, the first for a long time, and the country is smoother and more open and looks much better. The Henry Mountains lay directly north of us in full view and perhaps 25 miles distant our course is between north and northeast.

Friday, Feb. 20th, 1880. Worked the road yesterday, and today drove 7 miles over a smooth bench close to the banks of the San Juan which runs 1 mile below us in a gorge so deep and with banks so precipitous as to be completely inaccessible,[74] camped at the top of the smooth rock over which we will build a road. Here the bench terminates abruptly, and a rough broken valley full of sand and low reefs of Sandstone lays below us, and to reach it we will have to build a road ½ a mile down through the steep hills and little pockets in the rock which extends from the top to the very bottom.[75]

Saturday, Feb. 21st, 1880. Spent part of the day looking over the rocks for a place to put the road. The constable of Escalante and 2 other men came into camp looking for stolen stock went ahead to see some stock that had been taken on a few days ago.

Sunday, Feb. 22d, 1880. The boys returned from Potato Valley today,[76] found the snow so deep and their horses so weak they could do nothing, brought us letters from the settlements.

Thursday, Feb. 26th, 1880. Amasa and the boys from Panguitch started for home yesterday.[77] The constable and party returned today having found 2 stolen horses in the herd of Jim Dunton & Amasa Barton.[78]

Saturday, Feb. 28th, 1880. Yesterday we finished the road, and today we moved 1 mile and camped.[79] The past week has been very cold and windy.

Sunday, Feb. 29th, 1880. Drove 7 miles over a rough rocky and sandy road to the lake, a beautiful clear sheet of spring water ½ a mile long and nearly as wide, and apparently very deep.[80] Cottonwood, willow, canes, flags, bulrushes and several kinds of grass grow luxuriantly, and it would make an excellent stock ranch. On a point of rock jutting into the lake is the remains of an old stone fortification, built probably several hundred years ago.

Monday, March 1st, 1880. Layed over, wrote letters and shod some of my horses. Lewellyn Harris[81] a missionary to Mexico came into camp from the west and brought us letters & papers.

Tuesday, March 2d, 1880. Drove 7 miles over sand and rock not so rough as coming to the lake, found plenty of grass, and snow water.

Wednesday, March 3d, 1880. Drove 5 miles over road much is it was yesterday, and camped in the Castle Wash.[82] where we found good grass and water our course is now more nearly east. The country looks much better.

Thursday, March 4th, 1880. High wind with some snow last night. Drove 4 miles up the wash. The road has been very sandy, but even and tolerably good. Joseph layed over to let his team rest.

Friday, March 5th, 1880. Moved 5 miles and camped at the head of the wash on the Clay Hill where there is a very abrupt drop of 1000 feet down which we have got to work the road, and three miles farther into the vally [*sic*] beyond.[83]

Wednesday, March 10th, 1880. Returned this evening from a 5 days trip with bros Sevy and Bryson[84] looking for a road across what we call the Cedar Ridge extending 30 miles each way and nearly everywhere covered with a dense growth of cedar and pinion pine. We found gulches with perpendicular banks 1000 feet high running from the extreme north 30 miles into the San Juan on the south, but by going around the head of these we can make a passable road by following an old indian trail.[85] There is plenty of grass and some water most of the way. Found that the brethren had nearly completed the road down the hill.

Friday, March 12th, 1880. Killed a very poor beef yesterday, and today my bro Edward and Joseph Lilleywhite and I rode 12 miles to the southwest where we struck the San Juan where the banks are low and there is a good ford[86] found a small bottom of perhaps 200 acres of good land lying 6 ft above the water and covered with the heaviest growth of cottonwood I ever saw. The river runs with a swift current most of the way.

Saturday, March 13th, 1880. We made ourselves as comfortable as we could last night in a cave with a big fire as we had no bedding, and this morning rode back to camp, some snow fell last night and this is one of the coldest mornings I ever saw. Most of the camp have moved down the hill.

Sunday, March 14th, 1880. Moved down the hill and out 7 miles into the valley and camped,[87] found good water on the rocks.

Monday, March 15th, 1880. Last night was the coldest night I ever experienced it was impossible to be comfortable in bed or anywhere else. Drove 8 miles over fair road and camped, found plenty of feed and plenty of water on the rocks.[88]

Tuesday, March 16th, 1880. Drove 4 miles and camped good feed and water.[89]

Thursday, March 18th, 1880. Drove 3 miles yesterday, and 6 today and made camp in a sage brush opening in the cedars which are now very thick all around us.[90] There is a force of men ahead chopping all the time. There is a good deal of snow and mud making the wheeling very heavy. We left one of [the] wagons and a load in it this morning as our teams are getting very weak.[91]

Friday, March 19th, 1880. Drove 4 miles mostly through sage flats, and camped at the head of the cedar ridge and close to the foot of a high mountain on the north covered with deep snow and pine timber (called by some Elk Mountain). Our course from the Clay hill has been northeast, but now we turn more to the east.

Thursday, March 25th, 1880. During the past 5 days we have worked on the road and moved our wagons along 13 miles over the worst muddy and snowy road we have had, the mud and snow being from 6 inches to 2 ft deep. We are still in the thick cedars and have lost a part of our horses through there being no feed nearby for them.

Friday, March 26th, 1880. Found part of our horses and moved 2 of our wagons 4 miles to Snow Flat[92] where there is some feed, the road much better and the cedars not so thick.

Saturday, March 27th, 1880. Moved our other wagon up to camp, the boys have hunted all day and found nothing, the main body of the camp has gone on.

Monday, March 29th, 1880. By hand of Dan Harris[93] we received letters from our folks, one from Marion[94] to me contained a ten dollar bill for which I am very thankful. I found part of our horses but there are still 4 gone.

Wednesday, March 31st, 1880. Eddy found the last of our horses yesterday, and today we drove 8 miles and camped just before we got into the Comb Wash. The road is dry but rough and rocky and very sandy.[95] The water is very bad and feed pretty good.

Met Kumen Jones and Warren Taylor from the main camp with 6 animals to help us in.[96]

Thursday, April 1st, 1880. Drove 10 miles down the wash through very bad sand to the San Juan river where the company is camped and at work on the road. We cannot follow up the river, so we have to do some work to get up over the bench.[97]

Sunday, April 4th, 1880. Pulled up over the rock 3 miles yesterday, and today went 4 miles to the Butler Gulch most of the way on the rock.[98] Good feed and water.

Monday, April 5th, 1880. Drove 7 miles over heavy sandy road and camped in bottom of the San Juan 2 miles long where we propose to locate for the present.[99] This is 15 miles below where bro Smiths camp was last summer. This land is rich covered with cottonwood and about 6 feet above the river which runs with a pretty good current, but looks as if it would be hard to handle,[100] the climate appears to be mild. There are 3 families by the name of Harris who have been here all winter.[101]

There are about 70 men in our camp, about 85 wagons and we have expended Forty eight hundred dollars on the road in labor counting our time one dollar and a half per day, several men will go above here 15 miles and settle with their families, and a few (principally non-mormons)[102] will go in to the mining districts of Colorado 100 miles east of here.

Tuesday, April 6th, 1880. Looked over the land and selected a site for a town and in the evening held meeting when a committee of 3 weas [*sic*] chosen to manage the work on the ditch which we will have to make, and another of 5 to lay off a field and a town, I being among the latter number.

Wednesday, April 7th, 1880. We began laying off the lots and land and most of the brethren began work on the ditch.

Saturday, April 10th, 1880. As we have finished laying off the land and lots and find the former much less than we expected, it was motioned and carried in meeting this evening, that we draw lots to see who has the land here, and those who draw blanks can go farther up the river and make another location, 22 blanks and 40 numbers were put in the hat and after the drawing was over bro Sevy and I had blanks with a number of others, and each of my brothers drew a number.

Sunday, April 11th, 1880. Held a meeting in the afternoon and evening. James Pace who drew a number proposed to throw the whole thing out and all share alike, this however was not carried. There is some disappointment manifested by those who have drawn blanks, and also a very illiberal feeling by those who are elected to stay here.[103]

Monday, April 12th, 1880. Did not feel well and layed around camp most of the day and attended a very stormy unsatisfactory meeting in the evening, and tried to harmonize the discordant element that is aroused by some of those who drew blanks taking up land for themselves which it was understood was to be used by that part of the company that remained here. After a good deal of debate a motion for the holders of blanks to go farther up the river if a suitable place can be found was carried.

Tuesday, April 13th, 1880. Because of a proposal made by some of the brethren I called the camp together to see if some arrangement cannot be made so that all may continue to work here, as it is out of the question for us to move any farther at present. Spent most of the forenoon in adjusting our difficulties during which a good and conciliatory spirit was generally manifest. It was decided unanimously to throw out the former drawing altogether and all share alike with the understanding the brethren who hold large claims taken up last season, throw them into the hands of the field committee for disposal in the interests of the camp[104] 59 persons then drew 1 lot each and a general feeling of satisfaction seemed to prevail, work which has been almost entirely suspended on the ditch, was resumed this afternoon. Our town lots are 12 rods square being made thus small owing to the limited space suitable for building on. The field lots vary from 8 to 20 acres to the man according to location and quality. The course of the stream here is almost west and the land lays on both sides although we will only utilize that on the north side at present.

The valley is from ½ to 1 mile wide between the sandstone bluffs which rise 300 feet perpendicular, beyond these there are benches partly smooth and otherwise generally covered with grass and 40 miles to the north of us lay the blue mountains the nearest point at which we can reach saw timber. We have learned that an appropriation of five thousand dollars has been made to Silas S Smith to be expended on this road the people are looking anxiously for his coming expecting a little money for their labor during the winter.[105] Last night in our camp a son was born to the wife of Alvin Decker, this is the first birth in this location.[106]

Thursday, April 15th, 1880. Joseph started yesterday for the wagon we left behind.[107] I was quite poorly yesterday but feel better today and am at work on the ditch. Visited father Roswell Stevens in the evening who is very sick and liable to die at any time. At his request I made an inventory of his property and the disposition he wishes made of it which he signed and which was duly witnessed.[108]

Thursday, April 22d, 1880. Most of the camp have moved down onto their lots. We have moved onto our claim and put up a "wikiup" and dug a well getting good water at 16 ft.

I have bought a log house 10 acres of land, a cook stove, table, 3 gals of coal oil, and some work on the ditch, and one town lot, from Geo Harris for 1 horse & 2 cows & calves.[109] We have had a great deal of high wind and a little snow and rain during the last few days.

Sunday, April 25th, 1880. Have had more wind and rain and snow and the weather is still cold and boisterous. Today we held meeting and by unanimous consent named our town Bluff City.[110]

Monday, April 26th, 1880. San Juan county having been organized by the last legislature with Silas. S. Smith as Judge and P. D. Lyman, Jens Neilsen and Zechariah B Decker as selectmen, and C. E. Walton having been appointed County Clerk by Judge Smith the four latter met by appointment of the Judge and held the first term of court for this county and adjourned for 6 weeks after having appointed L. H. Redd Assessor and Collector.

Several members of the camp have started back, some of them for supplies and some intending to remain in the old settlements. I wanted to have started for Escalante but have not been able to find my horses. From a tree near here I learn that the altitude of this place is 4600, distance south of Salt Lake City 328 miles and east of Same 126 miles, according to Government Surveyor Ferdinand Deckert.[111]

Thursday, April 29th, 1880. Have not found all our horses, but made a start today for Escalante with my brothers Edward, Walter and Joseph, the latter going back for the wagon we left. Drove 17 miles and camped at the Navajoe Spring.[112]

Saturday, May 1st, 1880. Helped Joseph to fix up the wagon and he started for camp, and the rest of us went on to Harmony Flat 51 miles from Bluff City and camped.[113] The road is dry and good and the grass is quite green.

Thursday, May 6th, 1880. Camped at the Cottonwood[114] last night and drove down to the Colorado this morning and was ferried over, found several wagons here that started 3 days before I did. The river is 7 feet higher than when we crossed in January.[115] Rested our team and then pulled our wagon to the top of the "Hole" which was a ½ days hard work for 5 horses after packing up all our loose things.[116]

Saturday, May 8th, 1880. Met bro S. S. Smith and a small company bound for San Juan.[117] Received letters from my folks, also learned there was some flour and boots and shoes on the road for our camp. Was told by bro Smith that he did not think the appropriation would pay more than 40 per cent of the expenses of the road.

The grass is very poor on this side of the river, but water is in abundance, the weather is windy and dry and rather cool.

Monday, May 10th, 1880. Met 3 wagons near the 20 mile spring loaded with flour for our camp, learned that some had been left in Escalante.

Wednesday, May 12th, 1880. Left my wagon at the 10 mile spring and rode into Escalante on horse back. . . . I returned to camp in the evening.

Thursday, May 13th, 1880. Drove in to town and loaded in 1000 lbs of flour and Walter and I started for San Juan after parting with Edward who goes on to Oak Creek.

Tuesday, May 18th, 1880. Camped at the 50 mile last night, and drove to the ferry today and crossed my wagon over. The river is very high and still on the rise, which makes it hard to cross, as we have to tow up stream some distance in order to reach the landing on the opposite side.

Wednesday, May 19th, 1880. Crossed our horses and cows over, and moved up to the foot of the cottonwood hill and camped. We have left 2 cows and calves as they are too weak to travel through.

Thursday, May 20th, 1880. Started on this morning, and on the big hill my wagon got loose from the team (which was hitched to the end of the tongue) and ran back and off the dugway and tipped over, breaking the reach, box, bows, flour sacks and some other things and scattered my load all over the side of the hill.[118] Spent the balance of the day in mending up and getting things in shape to move on.

Monday, May 24th, 1880. Layed over yesterday and today at the Lake, and Walter and I walked 8 miles down to the Colorado and 3 miles up the stream to where there is a good place for a road into the river on both sides. Here a stream comes in from the north, which I could trace for several miles by the green cottonwoods on its banks.[119]

Saturday, May 29th, 1880. Met bro Sevy and 4 others between the Grand Gulch and the Canebrake,[120] going to the ferry for flour.

Wednesday, June 2d, 1880. Drove from the Butler Gulch home and found all as well as usual, the water is in the ditch and some seed has been sown which has come up and is looking well, but taken all together, I do not think the prospect very encouraging.

---

1. Platte D. Lyman's mother also kept a journal, excerpts of which add interesting information and will be cited from time to time in these footnotes. I have examined a typewritten copy of this journal in the Brigham Young University Library: the citations are from that copy. On October 20, Mrs. Lyman made this entry: "Platte has sold his house and lot to George Lovell, but I have the privilege of living there and having the fruit off from two rows of trees and a part of the lucerne until Platte comes back, which we expect will be sometime during the summer of 1880." The following day, after recording the fact that the Lyman company had gotten under way, the mother made this entry, which truly reveals the missionary spirit of the San Juan colonization: "May the Lord watch over them and keep them in health and peace

untill they can perform the work that they have been sent by the Apostles to do."
(Autobiography and Diary of Eliza Marie Partridge Smith Lyman, 1820–1885.)

2. Badger's Field was a field owned by George W. Badger of Holden, according to a letter from his son, Frank Badger (November 16, 1954). The letter goes on to say: "The place near the Oak City-Holden road about halfway between these towns has quite long since been abandoned, and now farther up the creek is called Duggins and is owned by Benjamin J. Stephenson, Elbert Stephenson, and a Mr. Stansworth."

3. The old Scipio sawmill was located about three and a half miles south of the town of Scipio, according to an unsigned letter from the Scipio postmaster in answer to an inquiry of October 27, 1954.

4. Eight Mile Creek — eight miles north from Holden — is shown on all earlier maps of Utah. The old road followed by the Lyman party parallels Eight Mile Creek, leading toward the east, up into the mountains, and strikes the U.S. Highway 91 just southwest of the Scipio summit. Losing cattle would become a regular occurrence on this trek.

5. All early maps show Round Valley and Round Valley Lake located about ten miles south of Scipio. Utah State Highway 63 passes that way today. Some present-day maps list the lake as Scipio Lake.

6. "The route followed by Platte D. Lyman is now highway 63 from Scipio to Salina, which joins highway 89 and goes to a place called Vermillion. East of this place is the place mentioned as this Gravelly Ford — namely Rocky Ford.

"At the time mentioned this was the only crossing of the Sevier River that could be made, Ike Colby's place is still standing. This land at the time of entry was owned by Hyrum Colby and Joseph Colby with Ike Colby being a cousin of the other two." Letter from Thomas J. Morley, postmaster; Salina, Utah; November 16, 1954.

7. The site of Prattville is slightly north and a few miles east of Richfield, between that city and Glenwood. It is shown on most early maps of Utah.

8. This reduced the party by five. The old wagon road ran south from the "Gravelly Ford" keeping on the east side of Sevier River all the way; east of Richfield and south through Monroe.

9. From Monroe the old road struck up over the hills to Marysvale, rather than following up the Sevier River through Marysvale Canyon as U.S. Highway 89 does today.

10. Mrs. Langly remains unidentified.

11. Bears on Sevier River; located near the site of the present Piute Reservoir.

12. This would be near the present site of Antimony.

13. Poison Creek is shown on older maps.

14. Riddles Ranch was located in the vicinity of present-day Widtsoe. Other members of the Hole-in-the-Rock expedition, coming from Parowan via Panguitch and Red Canyon mention this ranch as being on the route. The Lyman party camped two miles below (north of) this place on the east fork of the Sevier River.

15. Sweetwater Canyon heads near the summit of Escalante Mountain and runs west through Widtsoe. Utah State Highway 23 follows that canyon today. Sweetwater Spring is located at the base of the mountain, just before the climb to the summit begins. The Lyman party probably camped at or near the spring.

16. Joseph Liston was not a member of the Lyman party, but rather a resident of Escalante.

17. This camp was probably on what is now called "Old Hall's Creek" according to Escalante residents.

18. An extremely heavy loss of cattle. This camp was at or near the old Mort Liston ranch.

19. Red Creek was an early name for Paragonah. Silas S. Smith had been chosen by the church leaders to head the whole expedition. A major portion of the company had already passed through Escalante and established camp at Forty-mile Spring before the two appointed leaders caught up.

20. The two sons of Walter Stevens were: Walter Joshua and David Alma Stevens. The uncle was Roswell Stevens. Walter Stevens listed here (father of the two boys) was not on the trek.

21. The route took the party southeast from Escalante to Harris Wash where Ten-mile Spring is located — ten miles from Escalante. Springs in that region were almost literally in name only.

22. This ranch was located near the junction of Harris Wash and the Escalante River.

23. The Twenty-mile Spring is located on the north fork of Collett Wash. Water is still scarce there.

24. This was in Coyote Gulch. There is no apparent water there today.

25. Cottonwood Gulch is one of the forks of Willow Creek or Gulch.

26. This journal entry shows that both Smith and Lyman, appointed leaders of the expedition, arrived at Forty-mile Spring after the major portion of their company.

27. Schow and Collett had already conducted one exploration of the Colorado at Hole-in-the-Rock and beyond. See Chapter III. Now they had brought a better boat to conduct another reconnaissance. Charles Hall who had built the boat evidently accompanied Schow and Collett at this time.

28. These men had climbed to one of the numerous points on the face of the Straight Cliffs of Fifty-mile Mountain — Kaiparowits Plateau.

29. At that time it was customary in the L.D.S. Church to hold regular Thursday evening meetings. Religious services were held regularly during the entire Hole-in-the-Rock trek.

30. A person must traverse that region to appreciate this statement. But Lyman would soon see rougher country. It seems astonishing that the wise leaders of this expedition should have allowed themselves to be misguided into such wild desolate country with their families and most of their possessions, armed with such meager information concerning the possibility of making a road through to their destination. This was really pioneering! To see this country is to realize that Lyman was not exaggerating.

31. One wagon used on this reconnaissance was that of Cornelius Decker.

32. Just when the Hole-in-the-Rock received its name is not known, but this is the earliest contemporary reference I have seen that actually names it.

33. I infer from this that the boat was left on the rear running gears and the reach probably used as a tongue. At any rate, it was maneuvered down onto Jackass Bench, and thence slid to the river. Compare with entry for December 2.

34. The fisherman was Cornelius Decker who states in his account that two fish — a twelve pounder and a six pounder — were caught. The fish were no doubt channel catfish. This species of fish is plentiful in the Colorado today and little difficulty is experienced in obtaining as many as are needed for food.

35. This is Cottonwood Creek or Canyon.

36. This site was soon to become known as Cottonwood Hill as the pioneers carved a road from the floor of Cottonwood Canyon early in February.

37. The word "summit" does not always mean the same thing in this journal. Here, Lyman obviously means the top of Cottonwood Hill — surely not the top of Grey Mesa. A comparison of actual distances listed in later journal entries and from accurate maps will show the distance from the river to the top of Grey Mesa to be nearly twelve miles. Anyone who has hiked over that part of the old road will agree that it is at least that far.

38. This camp was probably at the top of Cottonwood Hill. Natural rock tanks are often the only source of water in this desert country.

39. These explorers obviously did not reach the top of Grey Mesa; they possibly went as far as the "Chute." The country over which they were passing was rough enough to discourage anyone; a person must see this region to appreciate how rugged it really is. It is accessible today only by hiking, by horseback, or by the use of four-wheel-drive vehicles. Lyman's journal gives an idea of its ruggedness when he says that they gave up all hope of building a road through it. Consider: these men did not believe it impossible to build a road through the Hole-in-the-Rock; but the region east of the Colorado was too rugged! Anyone who has seen the Hole-in-the-Rock can appreciate the implications of this statement. But these same men would soon be building a road over this exact country — where they were sure none could be built.

40. I have made no attempt to locate, identify, or explore this canyon. There are several relatively small streams draining southward into the San Juan which joins the Colorado just a few miles below this point.

41. This information should prove of interest to biologists.

42. This is still one of the wildest, roughest, least known regions in the United States. Anyone in search of farm land would surely be justified in branding it the "worst country I ever saw."

43. This would be the camp at the top of Cottonwood Hill, already referred to.

44. Back to Forty-mile Spring.

45. All accounts of the Hole-in-the-Rock expedition mention these two meetings, but there seems to be considerable confusion regarding what was accomplished in each. Most accounts state that the final unanimous vote to go ahead was obtained on Sunday, whereas Lyman's journal quite definitely sets it on Thursday. All accounts are in agreement that as soon as the decision was reached, a new spirit spread through the camp. The real strength of a united camp could now be demonstrated; and the task ahead would require all the power the company could muster.

It was important that Bp. Schow and Reuben Collett be apprised of the decision before returning to Escalante. Had the report been to turn back, many members of the mission not yet arrived at the main camp, could be turned back at Escalante — or even farther back along the road.

46. These two men from Paragonah (Red Creek) are unidentified.

47. When someone else killed a beef, the Lyman party would probably be partially repaid.

48. The "leaders" were not always out in front of the company breaking trail, so to speak. Although Lyman had been over this stretch of road earlier, this was Smith's first look at the "Hole."

49. This is Jackass Bench (or Jackass Mesa) and is sometimes described as containing 100 acres of good grazing land — not too far from the facts. It is a feature well worth noting and one that might easily be overlooked by the casual visitor to the region. The trail down to the mesa was not through the Hole-in-the-Rock but two miles upstream — the same route used by earlier explorers. No horse could be taken through the Hole-in-the-Rock until it had been blasted out.

50. The territorial legislature did eventually appropriate $5,000 for the construction of this road although the pioneers did not learn of such appropriation until after they had arrived in Bluff. (See Lyman's journal entry for April 13, 1880.) The "three weeks" Silas S. Smith expected to be absent grew into almost five months. He did not again catch up with the company until May 22, more than a month after they had arrived at Bluff. Smith's departure left Lyman in charge.

51. Although Lyman seems to indicate that Sevy, Redd and company had just joined the expedition, Silas S. Smith reported their arrival at Forty-mile Spring on November 29.

52. It seems very clear from this entry that Lyman picked George W. Sevy to head this exploring expedition. For George B. Hobbs' account of the exploration, see chapter VII of this volume.

53. This would be Ida, May, and possibly Nellie Lyman. It is significant that these people should be interested in a Sunday boat ride on the Colorado. Recreation was very essential to the welfare of the company. The boat used was the one brought from Escalante by Bp. Schow and Reuben Collett.

54. What a Christmas! It was too cold and stormy to do much work, but not too cold and stormy for a Christmas dance.

Back in Oak City, Mrs. Lyman was enjoying a bleak Christmas. Her journal contains the following: "Christmas. Not a merry one for me. Cannot think of any thing but the cold, and my friends who are camped on the banks of the Colorado river, without houses or tents and exposed to the inclemency of the weather. May the Lord preserve them from suffering is my prayer continually."

55. Jackass Bench.

56. Lyman failed to note the birth of a baby girl — Lena Deseret Decker — born to Mr. and Mrs. James B. Decker on this day. But this event had occurred back at Fifty-mile Spring; it is likely that Lyman didn't even hear of the birth for several days. He also failed to record the birth of John Rio Larson on top of Grey Mesa, February 21, 1880.

57. This statement speaks volumes concerning the condition of the livestock. The company was really hard pressed to find enough feed to sustain the large herd.

58. As far as I can determine, this is the only reference to Arza Judd and James Dorrity in connection with the Hole-in-the-Rock expedition.

59. Lyman's wife was Adelia, but he always refers to her as Delia. This baby was Albert R. Lyman, born January 10, 1880.

60. Adelia Lyman was staying with her sister-in-law, Susannah Robison, at that time.

61. There was no cable across the river so the ferry drifted downstream at every crossing and had to be hauled back again by use of teams of horses before each crossing. When the river was high and the current swift, this became somewhat of a problem. See Lyman's journal entry for May 6, 1880, on this subject.

62. This would be about four miles from the Colorado River on Cottonwood Creek. There is a large grove of cottonwoods at this spot today. It was from this point that the road was soon to be cut out from the creek bottom up Cottonwood Hill, and eventually over and through solid rock to the top of Grey Mesa. A second camp was established about a half-mile downstream, to the west.

63. Members of the Fifty-mile camp lost no time in catching up with the rest of the party. As soon as the Hole was ready for use, they began to move, at least one wagon (belonging to Joseph F. Barton) arriving at the canyon rim and making the

perilous descent on January 26, the same day the first wagons were driven down. See Barton's own account of this experience, Appendix X, this work.

64. These "3 other men" or the man who brought the powder have not been identified. This much needed powder would have been invaluable at the Hole.

65. "Summit" could possibly mean the top of Grey Mesa. However, it seems more likely that Lyman meant the top of Cottonwood Hill. He had escorted these men out to work on the road and the section then under construction was Cottonwood Hill and the two mile stretch between the top of that place and the Chute.

66. See journal entry for February 22, for the outcome of this journey.

67. The journal kept by Lyman's mother back in Oak City records the reception of several letters from Platte and other members of her family. I have been unable to locate any of these letters.

68. Identifying and locating Cheese Camp has been somewhat of a problem. A careful examination of the journal and the terrain, however, places it about three-quarters of a mile west of the Chute and some two miles east of the top of Cottonwood Hill. Two miles from the summit probably means two miles short of the top of Grey Mesa.

69. These men remain unidentified. However, they may be the men referred to in the entry of January 31.

70. This was the day George B. Hobbs started with a small pack train to deliver food to the settlers at Montezuma. Hobbs indicates that two of the Robb boys, John (Jack) and Adam, caught up with him before he had gone far; they were driving a herd of horses. Lyman's journal entry for February 26 indicates that James Dunton and Amasa Barton had also gone ahead — possibly at this time. For Hobbs' account of this — his second winter trip to Montezuma, see Appendix XI, this work.

71. This is the region of about a mile on either side of the Chute.

72. This would take them about a mile beyond the Chute and bring them to the base of what might be called a westward extension of Grey Mesa. See map, page 121.

73. West of Grey Mesa and separated from it by a rather deep gulch is another, much smaller mesa, flat on top, sandy, and covered by a rather thick growth of shadscale and some grass, giving it much the same appearance as Grey Mesa. It seems that Lyman considered this smaller mesa as part of Grey Mesa, which is quite logical. Joseph Lyman's wagon evidently camped in the gulch separating the two mesas or the two parts of the same mesa. It's the only spot that fits the description.

74. This at the point where the Great Bend of the San Juan swings right up to the base of Grey Mesa. It is a remarkable sight. The road follows along the south rim of the mesa and terminates abruptly at the northeast end.

75. This point is usually called the "Slick Rocks." It is the spot where a mountain sheep led George B. Hobbs over the only possible route to the valley below. See Hobbs' account, Chapter VII, this work.

76. Because of these deep snows, the Hole-in-the-Rock expedition would have been unable to return to their old homes via Escalante. They were literally going in the only direction possible — forward.

77. There is no indication of the number of men who left the company that day; probably the three men who had come with Amasa Lyman on January 31 and the two who had brought pork and cheese to the Cheese Camp. They had remained until the road down the Slick Rocks was almost completed and hence, had made a real contribution to the success of the expedition.

78. This does not say that Dunton and Barton had stolen the horses in question. It is very likely that the animals had strayed into the herds of the expedition as the

latter passed through the Escalante region. The fact that no arrests were made would tend to indicate that no man was actually accused of stealing.

79. In other words, they drove down the famous Slick Rocks and camped not far from the base of Grey Mesa.

80. This is Lake Pagahrit or Hermit Lake, located at the forks of Lake Canyon.

81. The Hole-in-the-Rock road was intended to be a highway into southeastern Utah, New Mexico, and beyond. Harris was evidently the first traveler to try the new road. See his letter describing this trip in *Deseret News,* April 5, 1880. Harris did not remain with the company, but pushed on toward his mission field, arriving in Montezuma well ahead of the expedition. (James L. Davis, History of the Life of James Davis, Appendix III, this work.)

82. Castle Wash was named for Indian ruins found in a cave there; not because of the natural rock formations, according to Albert R. Lyman.

83. The pioneers had reached Clay Hill Pass.

84. Sevy had been through the region as one of the four scouts a few weeks before, but neither Lyman nor Samuel Bryson had any knowledge of it. This five-day reconnaissance probably took the trio well up toward Elk Ridge.

85. The same Indian trail located and followed by the four scouts about six weeks earlier.

86. This was no doubt at a point called Clay Ford.

87. It is actually three miles from the top of Clay Hill Pass to the bottom. Seven additional miles would have taken the party into Steer Gulch.

88. This camp was probably at Cow Tank

89. Probably in Dripping Spring Canyon.

90. This camp was near the west end of Grand Flat.

91. This wagon was recovered May 1, 1880. See journal entry for that date.

92. Snow Flat, another clearing in the Cedars.

93. Dan Harris had accompanied the four scouts (Sevy, Redd, Hobbs, and Morrell) on their return from the San Juan early in January, 1880. He had then taken pack animals with supplies back to the site of Bluff later that same month. (See Hobbs' account, Appendix XI, this work.) Just what his activities had been since that time is unknown. He had probably gone into Colorado and brought back the reports mentioned here since it was quicker to send letters to San Juan via Colorado than over the old road by way of Hole-in-the-Rock.

94. Francis Marion Lyman.

95. They had traveled from Snow Flat down the "Twist" and camped near the mouth of Road Canyon.

96. The major part of the company was already at the mouth of Comb Wash on the San Juan where that stream cuts through Comb Ridge.

97. This is one of the greatest understatements of the entire journal. Building a road up the famous "San Juan Hill" was one of the major undertakings of the whole expedition.

98. Three miles would have taken them up San Juan Hill and to a point a short distance south of where present Highway 47 cuts through Comb Ridge; that would have been a full day's work. The next day's journey of four miles took them to the crossing of Butler Wash, somewhat north of the present highway crossing.

99. This was Bluff. Almost every account states that the company arrived in Bluff on April 6, yet Lyman definitely arrived there on the fifth.

100. The San Juan certainly did prove "hard to handle." A major task of the new settlement was that of canal or ditch building. It is interesting to note how much of the future pages of Lyman's journal is devoted to this subject.

101. The Harris families had moved in from Colorado during the fall of 1879, having heard that a settlement was to be established there. Hobbs and fellow scouts had eaten "Christmas" dinner with them. (See Hobbs' account, Chapter VII, this work.)

102. The only non-Mormons that I have been able to identify were Noah Barnes and the family of Wilson Dailey.

103. This is the first reference in Lyman's account that indicates any ill will in the company.

104. Members of the exploring expedition of 1879 had staked out claims in suitable locations all the way from McElmo Creek to the site of Bluff.

105. This was the first authentic news of the $5,000 appropriation. It is interesting to note that Smith had not yet caught up with his company.

106. This first baby born in Bluff was named Alvin Morris Decker, born April 12, 1880.

107. Joseph was evidently delayed until April 29 when he actually left with Platte D. and others.

108. Roswell Stevens was an old man, a veteran of the Mormon Battalion. He subsequently died May 4, 1880, being the first of the company to die since the expedition left the settlements in October, 1879, with the possible exception of the baby born at Escalante. (See Chapter IV for a discussion of this incident.) He willed all his property to the church. Burial was in a casket fashioned from an old wagon box.

109. George Harris was not of the Hole-in-the-Rock company, but was already at Bluff when the expedition arrived.

110. The honor of suggesting the name goes to William Hutchings, according to George B. Hobbs.

111. The survey had just been completed and the information carved in the bark of the tree trunk.

112. Navajo Spring is located at the foot of Navajo Hill in Comb Wash where present Highway 47 cuts through Comb Ridge.

113. Harmony Flat had been so named because some of the pioneers from New Harmony had camped there temporarily on the original trek. It is located just west of Grand Flat. The present highway from Blanding to the Natural Bridges National Monument passes through both Grand and Harmony flats.

114. Very likely right at the foot of Cottonwood Hill.

115. Although seven feet higher, the river would not be much wider, because of the nature of the channel at this point. High, rushing water would make the crossing very difficult.

116. Lyman and his party had traveled from Bluff to the Colorado and pulled up through Hole-in-the-Rock since April 29, a total of eight days. It had taken the company four months to cover the same distance on the outward trek.

This entry supplies definite proof that wagons were driven up through the Hole-in-the-Rock. From this reference it can be assumed that several wagons went that way on May 6, 1880. There are numerous other references to the fact that wagons were driven up through the Hole, statements of some writers to the contrary notwithstanding.

117. Lyman's party probably camped at or near the top of the Hole the night of May 6. The next day they would probably travel to Fifty-mile Spring. On May 8

they met Smith and party headed for the San Juan, no doubt somewhere on the road between Forty-mile and Fifty-mile. Smith had not been with the company since December 15, 1879. All the work of building the road from Hole-in-the-Rock to Bluff had been done during his five months' absence.

118. This accident probably occurred on the narrow dugways of the center section of Cottonwood Hill where the road was carved from the face of sandstone buttes.

119. This reconnaissance had taken the men down Lake Canyon to the Colorado River. They had then worked their way up the southeast bank to a point opposite Hall's Creek which they could see coming in from the north. As far as I can determine, this was the original survey of what was to become Hall's Crossing, established in 1881. To be sure, other men had preceded them to the spot, but not with the intention of locating a crossing for wagons.

120. This would be at Cane Spring where the old road crossed Cane Gulch, south of Elk Ridge.

APPENDIX V

KUMEN JONES: GENERAL MOVE TO THE SAN JUAN MISSION

Kumen Jones was one of the leaders of the San Juan Mission. However, he did not undertake to write an account of this famous expedition until approximately a half-century after the Hole-in-the-Rock trek. Then, for some reason or other, he eventually wrote three accounts instead of one. The account reproduced here is chapter four of The San Juan Mission to the Indians contained in The Writings of Kumen Jones. The other two accounts are contained in Preface to the Writings of Kumen Jones and The Journal of Kumen Jones.

The material quoted here is preceded in Jones' writings by a chapter dealing with the exploring expedition of which he was a member.

General Move to the San Juan Mission

When the first exploring party which was sent out had found what was considered a feasible location for a settlement on the apparently rich bottoms of the San Juan River, their leader, Silas S. Smith, took steps to have a shorter way explored for moving the pioneers into this new location. He wrote the Church Authorities to have some scouts from Escalante sent out to look over a way from that point to the San Juan River. He gave them general directions as to distance and location on the map.

Charles Hall and A. P. Schow were sent out from Escalante and they came down as far as the west rim of the Colorado River Canyon. After looking down through the "hole-in-the-rock" through which they could see water and a canyon leading out from the river up to a flat looking country, this party returned and reported clear sailing for a wagon road to San Juan. This latter report was founded more on a desire to encourage travel through the village of Escalante than to find a feasible place for a permanent road. All who have seen the first old trail from Escalante to the settlement at Bluff on the San Juan River, all who will ever see it, will say that the above scouts must have failed in their task.[1]

Immediately after the explorations of Charles Hall and Bishop Schow, preparations were begun for the second pilgrimage to the San Juan Mission, as it was then called. The Saints were advised to provide themselves with provisions, clothing, seeds, and implements to last at least one year.

By the latter part of October 1879, the greater part of the Pilgrims that were to make up the company booked for the San Juan Mission were on wheels headed for the Colorado River at a point east of the Escalante Desert. There were only a few in this company who made the first trip. [That is, the exploring expedition.]

By early November the greater part of the company had gathered at "Forty Mile Spring," which was down on the Escalante Desert forty miles from the town of Escalante. The company was made of Saints from practically all the counties from Weber south to Washington. After the arrival of President Smith at the rendezvous, matters took on a serious aspect. Scouting parties had been out as far as the Colorado River and met the vanguard of the moving company, informing us that an impassable barrier had been discovered at the river. A council was called and other scouts were sent ahead and about two weeks were spent investigating up and down the river with the result that nothing more favorable was found than the Hole-in-the-Rock. This was an opening in the solid wall through which we could see the river about 2000 feet below.

By this time it was getting well along in November and an extra heavy fall of snow on the Escalante Mountains back of the company had blocked the road and effectually prevented us from returning home. Even at this early date failure seemed to stare us in the face. After another council, several young men of which I was one, were sent out on an exploring trip for the purpose of bringing back an official report as to the possibilities of getting the company through the Hole-in-the Rock.

We had not gone far when we met a party of prospectors returning with burro packs. The prospectors told us it would be useless to attempt to make a road where the proposed route had been pointed out, saying, "If every rag or other property owned by the people of the Territory were sold for cash, it would not pay for the making of a burro trail across the river." However, we went on and crossed the river. The boat improvised for that purpose was about ten feet long and the same width as a wagon box. One shovel and one spade were used for oars, and two of us hauled water out while two plied the oars. The water being low in the river, we crossed without any serious difficulty. Several of the boys were detailed to look over the country at and near the river and four men, George Hobbs, William Hutchings, George Lewis, and myself were fitted out with a blanket each and lunch for a few days scouting farther out in the country.[2]

After about a weeks tramping, we all returned and gave in our reports. There were about as many different kinds of reports as there were men. For example we four who were out fartherest toward San Juan reported as follows: first. It would be out of the question for the company to attempt to get through on this route; second, with some assistance from the Legislature which was about to convene and the united effort of all the camp, the company could get the wagons and stock through but no permanent road could be made; third, a good road might be made over the proposed route in a few weeks without much trouble; one scout did not report.

Several meetings were called by the men at the head and it was finally the almost unanimous decision to go to work and make a way to get through. One thing that influenced for this decision was the fact that on account of deep snows on the mountains over which the company had just passed, it would have been impossible to return home for several months. Another contributing element was the fact that many in the company had been called by their church leaders as on a mission and that served as an urge to go through. It was this same principle that urged on Father Escalante 103 years earlier when he and his party went through all kinds of hardships in this same neighborhood in the winter of 1776.[3] He was bent on finding a better and shorter trail connecting the missions of Santa Fe and California.

When the company decided to go to work for this church and make a way to get through, we made a decision that has affected the San Juan Mission for all time. The country would have been settled, but it would have been under a different lineup, for that same bunch could not have been got together again. The miracle of this decision came just as soon as the leaders of the company gave orders to sail on, sail on. It went through the company like an electric shock and all was good cheer and hustle. Captain Smith started back with a large team and light buggy. With him went some of his sons with horses to assist in breaking a trail through the snow.[4] The next the company heard from him he had been successful in obtaining, through Church Authorities, necessary tools, powder provisions, experienced miners, and five-thousand dollar appropriation from the territorial legislature then in session, he had obtained all of which made it possible for the company to blast and work out our way through.

While visiting the Legislature Captain Smith had San Juan County organized and officers appointed. These were as follows: James Lewis of Kanab, Judge; Charles E. Walton Sr., Clerk; Platte D. Lyman, Jens Nielson, James B. Decker, Selectmen; Benjamin Perkins, Accessor and Collector, and Kumen Jones, Superintendent of schools.

Several extra men were soon sent out by Capt. Smith to assist in the roadwork.[5] These were mostly men who had had experience in mining where powder is used. Good progress was made and a hearty good feeling prevailed throughout the whole camp.

In the camp consisting of ninety or more men, about thirty women and sixty children, moving in eighty-three or more wagons through an extremely rough country, one would naturally look for some trouble and a few accidents, but this was not the case. All was hustle and harmony.

About December 17 it was decided to send men out to look over the proposed route to ascertain whether it was possible to get through to the San Juan at the point where the former explorers had made "locations" during the summer before, and for this purpose George W. Sevy, L. H. Redd Sr., George Hobbs, and George Morrell were chosen, or volunteered.[6]

Before this party of scouts started out, a general meeting was held at Forty Mile Spring where the situation was discussed.[7] The Saints were encouraged by the principles laid down in the ancient as well as modern scripture that "a religion that does not require sacrifice, if or when necessary, of all things does not have the power within it to save in the Celestial Kingdom."

The four scouts took with them only four animals, a small quantity of provisions and bedding, expecting to replenish their lunch bags when they arrived at the camp of those who had remained on the San Juan the fall before. In this they were somewhat disappointed, as provisions had run very low with this camp. In fact the outlook was so slim in the provision line that the explorers did not feel justified in remaining long enough to recuperate after their long hazardous journey and they at once prepared for the return trip, only remaining at the river camp one day. The trip out had taken twelve days but the return trip took eleven days.

The exploring trip of those four men will always be remembered by all those who were acquainted with it, and more especially by those who took part in it, as one of the hardest and most trying in the way of perserverance and persistant endurance of any undertaking connected with the San Juan Mission. It was one, also, in which the participants must have had the assistance of our Heavenly Father. It has been a source of wonder to all those who since those early days, have become acquainted with the country through which these explorers had traveled. How they ever found their way through deep snow and blinding snow storms in such a broken timbered country, all cut to pieces with deep gorges, for such a long distance, without compass, trail, and most of the time no sun, moon, or stars to help them in keeping their course is a mystery. The only answer is that a kind providence came to their assistance in answer to their humble fervent prayers. They endured difficulties and grilling experiences almost unbelievable with snowstorm, boxed canyons, thick cedar and pine forests, and food shortage. Their experience almost made the journey of the good Catholic Escalante, look like a picnic party.

Just before reaching the camp of the few men left of the party who went out in the spring, the four scouts met two miners who were making a start to hunt for the lost Pashelkine mine, reported by Navajos and others as being very rich in silver. The mine had been worked by Navajos but had been lost, as the few Indians who worked it were killed off by the soldiers when they were being rounded up several years before to be taken to Santa Fe. These prospectors tried to persuade the Mormon scouts to go out with them, promising that they would lay over for them and would let them in on the big mine, which they said was a "sure" thing. Had the Latter-day Saints scouts fallen for this wild proposition, it might easily have resulted in failure for the San Juan Mission, at least at that early date. The two miners, Merick and Mitchel, were killed by the renegade Pahutes and Navajos as they were returning with their pack animals loaded with ore supposed to be from the lost mine. The Mormon men would most likely have met the same fate and the company could not have got the news of what became of them for a month or two. A great portion of the camp were discouraged because of the rough country and other difficulties and such an event would have been enough to finish the whole undertaking.

When the four explorers returned, they reported that it would be possible to make a road through to the San Juan, as by far the roughest and most difficult country was at or near the Hole-in-the-Rock or within a few miles of the Colorado River where the work was being pushed as fast as possible with tools that were in the camp.

A long and interesting story could be written about the travels and workings of this large, well organized, good natured, jolly camp, but for the purpose of this story, just a few points will be noted. The great majority went to work in earnest and a good healthy Christian atmosphere prevailed in the camp. The Sabbath was observed at all times and under all conditions. Every evening hymns were sung and prayers said. Occasionally dances were held, especially while we were at the Hole-in-the-Rock where nature had made the smooth flat rock floor on purpose.

January 26, 1880, after about six weeks work and waiting for powder, a start was made to move the wagons down the "Hole."

Long ropes were provided and about twenty men and boys would hold onto each wagon as it went down to make sure there would be no accidents through brakes giving way or horses cutting up after their long lay off. I had a well broken team. This I hitched on to Benjamin Perkins' wagon which I drove down through the "Hole."

All went smooth and safe. By the 28th most of the wagons were across the river and work had commenced again on the Cottonwood Canyon, another very rough proposition. There was a very important work to be attended to in addition to road making. This was the matter of finding forage for the work horses. A great many animals were needed to move the eighty odd wagons of the camp, and the open country was limited and many hands were occupied with finding feed.

After working and traveling nearly two and one-half months, the future site of Bluff was reached on the sixth day of April, 1880. Surely the Hand of Providence had been over the traveling pilgrims. No serious accident had befallen any of them. There had been only two "tip-overs." Three babies had been born on the way,[8] with the assistance of an old time nurse or two and the blessings of the Good Father Above. Most everyone had been kind and helpful and good natured. In every rough place men had rallied around steadying the wagons down with long ropes or pushing and rolling wagons up the bad hills. Provisions were anything but plentiful, but good health prevailed and the roughest wagon road in North America had been gone over without any serious smash-ups or breakdowns. About 325 miles had been traveled, 210 of which had been through an unsettled country over which a wagon had never gone before. The main portion of the camp had been five and a half months on the journey and all of us as well as the faithful work teams, were ready for a rest. However many were more or less disappointed in the country and if their teams had been able, many more would have accompanied the few who moved on.

Besides H. H. Harriman and family, George Hobbs,[9] and James L. Davis and family who had remained on the river since the Silas S. Smith exploring party came in the summer of 1879, the company found their old friend and neighbor, Thales Haskell, who had been sent in by the Church Authorities to act as Indian interpreter. This was a pleasant surprise to all.

When I look back upon the large company traveling and blasting and working through a country of that nature, six months in the midst of one of the severest winters, it looks to me that there was something more than human power or wisdom associated with it. When this bedraggled company of tired pilgrims straggled into the present site of Bluff, many of the teams which consisted of horses of all sizes and descriptions, oxen, mules and burros, were unable to proceed further for at least some time. Some remained at Bluff on that account, but most of those who settled at that point did so from religious and conscientious motives, and under the protection and blessings of a kind Providence were prospered and preserved to accomplish, at least in a large measure, the mission assigned to them, that of cultivating and maintaining friendly relations with all Indians whose homes were near the section where the State of Colorado and the Territories of Utah, New Mexico, and Arizona corner together.

Footnotes

1. This statement by Kumen Jones seems to be the major source of the general understanding of most of those who have written about the Hole-in-the-Rock expedition concerning explorations of the route by Escalante citizens prior to the general migration of settlers. Yet this statement does not harmonize with other sources concerning the method by which the short-cut route via Escalante was chosen. See Chapter III this work for further discussion.

2. There were two explorations from the Forty-mile camp; Kumen Jones was a member of each. However, in this account he runs the two expeditions together, failing completely to distinguish between them. See Chapter V above.

3. Escalante did not pass very near to the "neighborhood" described here. "The Crossing of the Fathers" where the Spaniards crossed the Colorado is located some forty-five miles downstream from the Hole-in-the-Rock. And that was as near as the Escalante party came to the route of the Hole-in-the-Rock expedition. An excellent account of the Escalante expedition is "Pageant in the Wilderness" by Herbert E. Bolton, *Utah Historical Quarterly*, volume 18.

4. Just how many of Silas S. Smith's sons were on the trip is difficult to determine. It is, therefore, virtually impossible to know which of them accompanied him on his return to the settlements. He actually left the company on December 15. In "Preface to the Writings of Kumen Jones," the author states that the Utah Territorial Legislature appropriated $5,000 while the L.D.S. Church made a grant of $500 for supplies and provisions.

5. In the main, these men remain unidentified.

6. See George B. Hobbs' account of this remarkable exploration, Chapter VII, this work.

7. The expedition was actually camped at Fifty-mile Spring and at the top of the Hole — not at Forty-mile.

8. In Preface to the Writings of Kumen Jones, 16, he says that "Several babies had been born." James Monroe Redd speaks of three births. See this work page 48 for discussion of the first birth en route.

9. This is a mistake. Hobbs had rejoined the expedition long since, and was not at Bluff when the main company arrived.

APPENDIX VI

SAMUEL ROWLEY'S AUTOBIOGRAPHY

Since only a few members of the Hole-in-the-Rock expedition ever took time to write a report of that memorable trek, every account written by any of them takes on added importance. Samuel Rowley was one of the leading members of the expedition who, later in life, found time to write an autobiography which included a brief report on the Hole-in-the-Rock trek. Just when the record was written is not known, but in 1928 Albert R. Lyman had opportunity to study and copy it — or parts of it. Finding important information regarding the migration to San Juan County therein, Lyman sent excerpts from Rowley's autobiography to the L.D.S. Church Historian who promptly inserted them into the San Juan Stake History. It is from that source that the account reproduced here is taken. What became of the original is not known.

While copying these pages from the Rowley original, Mr. Lyman found occasion to make numerous comments regarding certain statements in the text. These are included in some of the footnotes below. As a preface to the actual autobiography, Lyman adds this bit of information about its author: "Samuel Rowley was born in Worstershire, England, in 1842, of Latter-day Saint parents. He crossed the plains with Captain Willey's handcart company, made his home for a while in Nephi, and later in Panguitch and Parowan, from which place in 1879, I begin with his account."

Samuel Rowley's Autobiography

At the quarterly conference of the Parowan Stake I was called to go to the San Juan to settle that country, and not being able to go in the spring, we went the next fall. Leaving Parowan on the 23rd of October, 1879, going by way of Little Creek Canyon and over the divide into Bear Valley, down Bear Creek to the Sevier River by way of Panguitch, Red Canyon and the East Fork of the Sevier, off up Sweet Water Creek and over the mountains into Escalante Canyon. We found there a part of our company from Beaver, among them was our present townsman, George Westwood. Our company from Parowan also waited for the part of the company from Cedar City.

The people of Escalante, on hearing of our coming, held a convention and raised the price of everything we would be likely to need, almost double what it was before.[1] Before we left our homes we were told that the country had been explored, and that the road was feasible. But now we found that someone had been mistaken.

Moving out ten miles into the Escalante Desert, we camped near a spring we found down in a wash, the water of which was so hard that peas and beans would not cook in it. In looking around a day or two later, some of the women found some water in pockets that was used for such purposes.

Unable to move our wagons till the road was builded, we fitted out some pack outfits and laid out the road to the west bank of the Colorado River.[2]

The river, from where we stood, appeared to be from five to seven feet wide.

The only place between Navajo Mountain on the south, and the mouth of Grand Gulch on the north, where we could make a road to the river, was to go down a chasm which led down towards the river, and terminated abruptly in a cliff of solid sandstone, where we let a man down by means of a rope, and by measuring the rope we found it to be forty-seven feet.[3] Understanding the real situation, we now returned to the camp at Ten-mile Spring.

On the Escalante Desert a meeting was called to discuss the situation. We were without tools and other material for making the road. At the meeting it was decided that Silas S. Smith should go to the legislature and get an appropriation for the material for the road. Silas S. Smith having had charge of the company, Platte D. Lyman was chosen to take charge during Smith's absence.

During the interval we made the remainder of the road across the desert, and moved on to the Fifty-mile Spring, it being the nearest water to the Hole-in-the-Rock, which was now the big obstacle in our way.

While waiting the action of the legislature, we, with half of the Escalante people, built the ferry-boat.[4]

The road being made down the Hole-in-the-Rock and up the other side, the company crossed the river the first week in February (1880), going up Cottonwood Canyon to its head. We had to make another halt while we blasted a dugway up the sloping side of a solid sandstone bluff.[5]

Getting upon the surface of the earth again, we traveled on about one day's journey when we had to halt again for some days. While this work was going on, part of our number went back to gather stock that had been left on the Escalante Desert.

The road is now made down the Slick Rock, and we move on to the Lake. This is a very romantic scene. The Lake is from five to eight rods wide, and about forty rods in length, the south end of which is called the head of the lake terminates at the base of two solid sandstone bluffs, about a rod and a half a-part, back of which is a beautiful strip of meadow in beautiful contrast with the mounds of sandstone which contribute largely to the makeup of this part of the country.[6]

In moving on our road we wound around between these knolls of stone. We soon came to a slight divide of this same formation which was very severe on animal's feet. We now traveled up Castle Wash some nine miles when we came to Oak Springs, which is up on the side of the hill.[7]

Here we make another halt while we make the road down Clay Hill, which occupied some weeks.[8] This being accomplished, we moved on. Our company being composed largely of young married men, when we came to the top of the hill, they would detach their lead horses, and their young wife would drive them down the hill while the husband brought down the wagon with one team. My wife had driven a pair of horses all the way while I drove three yoke of oxen. But here I had to drive her team down the hill. A snowstorm has now come on, and in going back up the hill after my ox team, I saw several women in the shelter of some rocks holding their husband's lead horses. In bringing my team down, I turned two yoke of cattle loose, and brought my two wagons down with one yoke of oxen.

Now we are at the foot of the hill without wood, and but very little water. It is dark and still snowing, — my two yoke of oxen gone, I didn't know where. My wife made a small allowance of sling and put me to bed without supper.

The next day our scattered company was gathered up, and we moved on a distance that occupied two days, and we were confronted by a box-canyon, walled in with irregular ledges with an occasional huge rock broken off.[9]

Here we wheeled to the left and traveled up the side of the gulch till we formed a crossing and went down the other side to within a stone's throw of where we camped the night before.

It's the month of March now, with a foot of snow, and frost coming out of the ground. No chance to dodge a mudhole on account of standing cedars and pines.[10]

We wend our way down off the Cedar Ridge. We next find ourselves in the Comb Wash getting mired in the quick sand, ourselves and our animals suffering with thirst, some of the latter becoming unable to pull their loads farther. Eventually we reach the San Juan River at the mouth of the wash.

Here we let our animals rest while we make a very difficult piece of road; a very steep dugway a quarter of a mile in length.[11] It took us up onto a kind of table land, rather rock, along which we followed along with some difficulty to the Butler Wash.

The remaining six or seven miles was made without much difficulty. The company arrived here adjacent to the present site of Bluff on the 6th day of April, 1880.

On investigation the following day, it was found necessary to blast a trail up from the head of a small box-canyon which led up from the northeast corner of the prospective town.[12]

This being accomplished, we set about to ascertain where our canal would come. The canal being surveyed, we went to work in earnest to get the water out. When the canal was finished and we went to turn the water in, the river had gone down and left the head of the canal above the surface of the water. We tried to raise the water by means of a dam, but failing this we extended the canal up to where a perpendicular cliff formed the north bank of the river. Here we tried again to tap the river, but with the same failing result. . .

Late in the summer (1881) the Navajoes stole the best horse I had, without which I had no team, for it required four horses to make a team in that country. My provisions were running short by this time, and I had to return to Iron County to work for supplies. So I had to pay the Indians twenty-five dollars ransom for my horse.

On this journey we suffered much for water; my dog perished, and a mare belonging to George Ipson fell in the harness being overcome with the heat and thirst.

(When we arrived at the river) after taking care of our animals, the next thing to consider was how to get across, the boat being on the other side. We decided to take the side-boards from one of the wagons, place them side by side, lash a ten-gallon keg crosswise upon them, and [Z.] B. Decker, a member of the Mormon Battalion, volunteered to sit astride of those boards, using a spade for an oar, and row himself across to the ferry-boat, in which he was successful. Taking the boat from its moorings he worked it up the west bank to where the stream butted against the cliff. All being ready, he started for the east side rowing for dear life. It was by the smallest margin that we were able to catch the rope when thrown to us by the gallant old soldier. The river butted against the cliff on the east side immediately below where we stood. And thus we were able to cross the stream.[13]

Traveling up Grand Gulch,[14] at noon of the second day we stopped at a pool of highly-colored water in the wash, which proved to be so minerally we could not use it. Lars Christensen and myself each mounted a horse and started in quest of water. We soon found a pool of rain-water, which had run down from the cliff some time before, it being literally full of pollywogs, However, it answered our purpose after undergoing a separating process.

That night we reached Grand Tank by taking the left-hand fork of Grand Gulch and traveling between two mountain walls wide enough apart for a wagon to pass, tho for a distance of about two miles it was somewhat wider in places. This tank would remind one of the mouth of a tunnel, or of an old-fashioned brick oven built in the wall and extending into the rock mountain farther than we could see. Here we laid over one-half day. We did not see the sun till eleven o'clock in the morning on account of the towering cliffs.[15]

Moving on we crossed the divide and down Silver Falls Canyon. In the mouth of this canyon is a cave in which, on our return to San Juan, we drove eight wagons in and camped.

On reaching Escalante Creek we found it necessary to rest our animals, and our provisions were almost exhausted. Lars Christensen and myself started horse-back for Escalante for supplies. We had not gone more than a quarter of a mile when we met the ferryman, going to the Colorado River. By him the Escalante people had sent ample provisions to last us through...

Footnotes

1. Whether this is a fact or not, members of the Hole-in-the-Rock expedition seemed to think that prices had been jacked up just to take advantage of the situation.

2. A very interesting bit of information contained in no other account. This road survey work was accomplished from the Ten-mile Spring, according to Rowley.

3. Another bit of information not found in other accounts.

4. Many unidentified people, no doubt, assisted with this work. Charles Hall of Escalante directed the construction.

5. Cottonwood Hill.

6. Lake Pagahrit. Albert R. Lyman adds this comment: "Being very familiar with all the road from Slick Rock to Bluff, and particularly familiar with The Lake, I must remark that Brother Rowley, far from exaggerating, has the lake and the meadow above it entirely too small."

7. "The oaks died from around this spring, and it became known as Clay Hill Spring." — Lyman.

8. It actually required about one week.

9. "The desert at the foot of Clay Hill is a wide dry stretch of black shadscale, from which the company would naturally want to go eastward, both because their destination lay in that direction, and because they could see a tree-covered region in that direction. But yawning gulches made it imperative that they turn to the northeast and the north, and from every attempt to go east they would have to hunt their way back along the ragged rim of some impassable box-canyon." — Lyman.

10. "Here, as in his account of the making of the road into the Hole-in-the-Rock, he passes without comment a long hard struggle, for it was a long painful story of trial and error, misshap and delay between their entry into the cedars north-east of Clay Hill to their getting down into the Comb Wash on the east side." — Lyman.

11. San Juan Hill.

12. "This small canyon, Cow Canyon, at first a dangerous trail, and then a more dangerous wagon-road, has for a number of years been a highway [Utah State Highway 47] over which cars travel in perfect safety." — Lyman.

13. "It is to be inferred here that this crossing was not made at the Hole-in-the-Rock; Halls Crossing farther up the river was discovered sometime soon after the settlement at Bluff, and the lower crossing was not used again, becoming impassable for need of repairs." — Lyman. The Hole-in-the-Rock road was actually abandoned early in 1881.

14. This "Grand Gulch" is not to be confused with the Grand Gulch east of Clay Hill Pass. The gulch referred to here must surely have been present Hall Creek.

15. This must have been the Muley Twist Canyon.

APPENDIX VII

EXCERPTS FROM: SKETCH OF MY LIFE BY C. I. DECKER

Cornelius Isaac Decker was a son of Zechariah Bruyn Decker, Sr. The early part of this sketch deals with a brief account of the elder Decker and his activities related to the Mormon Battalion and the discovery of gold at Sutter's mill in 1848. After his return to Utah, Zechariah settled at Parowan where Cornelius was born February 11, 1855. The sketch contains a brief account of its author's youth and subsequent marriage to Elizabeth Morris of Parowan, 1875. Seeking land of his own, young Cornelius Decker soon went into Arizona and established title to land at Snowflake where he built a house and prepared to make his home. While on his return to Parowan in the spring of 1879 (presumably to move his family and belongings to the new site), he met Silas S. Smith's company of explorers headed for the San Juan. Cornelius' brothers James and Zechariah, were members of that company and the young man possibly first had his thoughts directed toward the Four Corners region at that time. At any rate, he continued to Parowan where he arrived May 1, 1879.

During that summer there was a great deal of talk about the proposed colony in the San Juan Valley and Cornelius seems to have caught the "San Juan Fever." Shortly after the first contingents of the Hole-in-the-Rock expedition had left Parowan, Decker and his family were on their way also — headed for the San Juan. We begin his account at that point.

The record presented below has been carefully copied from the original handwritten copy loaned to me by Edgar T. Decker, son of Cornelius Isaac Decker. The original is a pencil manuscript written in long hand on two-hole loose leaf paper, tied together with a shoe lace. The account was written during 1936 and 1937 when its author was over eighty-one years of age. In preparing this record for publication, I have found it advisable to add some punctuation and correct some (but not all) spelling mistakes in order to insure clarity of the narrative. The exact wording of the original has been retained.

Excerpts from: Sketch of My Life by C. I. Decker

I had got the idea of moving to a new country. Everybody was bragging the San Juan up saying what a good country it was for farming and raising stock, so I concluded to sell my rights at Snowflake and go to the San Juan country. So I sold my rights at Snowflake to John Hulet. I got 4 good cows for it, then began to get ready to go to San Juan country. I sold my place in Parowan to Mrs. Pickering for a wagon, three horses, seven cows. I broke two young mares of father's, hitched them in with my four and trailed my one wagon;[1] started for the San Juan country in November 12th, 1879. We drove up into Little Creek Canyon 4 or 5 miles and camped. Then we drove over to the Severe River the second night, 3rd day we drove South East of Panguitch 5 miles; 4th day we drove over the Escalante Divide down into the canyon. 5th we drove down to Escalante and loaded in some seed wheat and a few beans then went on down the desert to a spring 10 miles below Escalante; then to the 40 Mile Spring. That Night Silas S. Smith and his company caught up with us.[2]

We held a meeting that night to see what we would do about the work that was ahead of us. We decided to send S. S. Smith back to the legislature as it was in session at that time, to plead for us and to send us some powder & drills and hammers to shoot our way through the rocks that were ahead of us.[3]

Charles Hall had brought a little boat down there with him so the next day myself, Samuel Roly, and two or three Cedar boys took the boat with my lead team and trail wagon on down to the river 15 miles away to see what the prospect really was like.[4] We hunted around a while before we tried to get down to the river. We decided that the only feasible place to get down to the river was to shoot a road down through a solid rock ledge 40 ft. straight down.[5]

We had to take the little boat half a mile above there to get it down to the river. By using a forty foot rope I had, we slid it and rolled it on some cedar chunks we found, down to the river. Then we got into the boat and went across the river and walked up the other side a ways to see the prospect of making a road up the other side. It looked favorable[6] so we camped there that night. I set a couple of fish hooks that night and caught two large fish, one about 12 lbs. and one about 7 lbs.[7] We ate the large one for breakfast; the other I took back to camp with me. We reported what we had found so we all decided we had better go on as it would be almost impossible to go back over the Escalante divide with our wives and babies and all of our loose stock, as the snow had fallen about 3 ft. deep then and still snowing.

So we drove on down to the river — at least the Cedar boys did. Us Parowan & Paragonah boys stopped at a spring we called 50 Mile Spring about 4 or 5 miles from the river. We was afraid there would not be water enough for all of us there on the bluff at the top of the river. They had to depend on the water that was in the holes in the rocks for everything, and the rains and snows that should come. As luck would have it, they had plenty of water so the Cedar boys, Kanarrah & Beaver boys camped right on top of the Hole-in-the-Rock and us Parowan & Paragonah boys camped back at 50 Mile Spring.[8] We would go down to the river Monday morning and stay till Saturday evening then we would go to our camp and stay. Monday morning again we went down and camped on the other side of the river and worked from the river up the other side. I don't think I ever seen a lot of men go to work with more of a will to do something than that crowd did. We were all young men; the way we did make dirt and rock fly was a caution, S. S. Smith had us plenty of powder there in a week and the Cedar boys were a lot of coal miners. The way they did make rock fly was a caution. We had the road made up the other side by the time the Cedar boys got that ledge shot down.[9] It took about 6 or 7 weeks to get it so we could all cross the river onto the other side.

Bro. Platt Lyman and his company done their part toward it too. I always had a great respect for Bro. Lyman. He was a man that everybody liked. We moved our camp across the river about Jan 7th or 8, 1880.[10] (I forgot Bro. Platt D. Lyman had been with us all the time; he always done his part.)

At the meeting we got three men to go ahead, pick out the road for us to follow. So picked George Sevy from Panguitch and George Hobbs of Parowan. There was one more but I can't think of his name.[11] There was an old dim Indian trail that crossed the river just about a half mile below the ferry there,[12] that they (the boys that went to look out the route) crossed the river on their horses. We carried their packs across on the little boat. This Indian trail was a guide to them all the way through. They tried to cut off three or four times but had to come back to the old trail every time they would get headed off by a deep gorge. They finally just stuck to the trail. It lead them in a northeasterly direction till they got up near the foot of the Elk Mountains; then they crossed the Grand Gulch. Then it led them back in a southeast direction down to the San Juan River. When they got there Hobbs could see where he was wanting to get to. They were within a days travel of where they wanted to go to. Hobbs found his folks all well but they were nearly out of everything; they were no doubt mighty glad to see their brother come with something to eat.[13] They turned and came back to us just as we were getting the road done across the river.[14] We were all mighty glad to see them come back again. They told us we were over the worst of it. That was sure good news to us.

The day after we got our wagons & teams across the river I went back across the river after some cows of mine. I went afoot. I found them and brought them to the river, but I had to carry a calf about a mile & half on my back. I got mighty tired before I got to the river. I got to the ferry just dark but the ferry-man had gone up to our camp on the other side of the river and both boats were on the other side of the river. I seen I was in for it that night. I began rummaging for some matches to make a fire but could not find any, so I just tramped up & down the bank of the river all night long to keep warm. The ferryman came down about 10 o'clock the next day. I was getting mighty hungry and tired too — I hadn't had anything to eat for 24 hours. The ferryman brought the ferry boat over to where I was and we drove the cows on and ferried them over ourselves. It was noon before I got them up to our camp. I was ready for something to eat; I ate my dinner and rested the rest of the day.

The next day we had to climb a sand hill.[15] It took us about a week to make the road up that sand mountain — it was almost pure sand. We got the road made up the sand hill into some of the roughest country teams and wagons were ever driven over. The rocks were like great hay stacks. We made a road through between the hay stacks, but we had to keep on the old Indian trail.

Right there, while we were in that rough country, there were a few boys that had a lot of loose horses along. They got in a hurry to get their horses out of the way of the teams so they decided to go on to where they could get a little wider range for them. But a few of the teamsters thought it would be eating the grass away from their teams. It caused quite a disturbance in the camp, but it soon blowed over. They said if it was any danger of them eating the grass away from the teams they would hurry on and not endanger the teams. So they went on ahead, which was the best to be done; so we got rid of that nuisance.[16]

We traveled through those big rocks for about 10 miles. It was rough going but we got through allright without much trouble. Two of us had six horses and two wagons; it was pretty close driving but we got through without much trouble. After about 10 miles of that we got onto a little smoother going;[17] then we got to what we called the slick rock. It kept us there about a week.

There was an old gentleman had got off his road. He started for Snowflake Arizona and he got hemmed in. On account that big snowstorm he could not get back. His wife gave birth to a child while we were working road down the slick rock. They called him Rio Larson.[18] I have seen the boy out here in Colorado since I came to Sanford though he lives in Arizona now.

Soon as we got the road finished down the slick rock we drove about 10 miles and came to a very pretty little lake.[19] It was about a mile long and a half mile wide. But before we got to that lake we had to drive down a sharp hill to where my lead wagon was on one side of the top of the hill and my trail wagon on the other side. It was raining and slippery, but I got down allright and drove to the lake that night.[20] We camped at the lake for three or four days so the women folks could do their washing as we had been on dry camping for about 10 days. Before leaving the slick rock some of us took a ramble down to the San Juan River to look at it. Although it was in March the vines were beginning to bloom down in those deep gorges that faced the sun. A perfect carpet on the bottom of the gorges, they were pretty to look at.[21]

Well, when we had rested a couple of days at the lake we hitched up and drove up what we called Castle Wash about 15 miles. We got to a steep hill; we had to work the road down it. We called it Clay Hill it had so much hard blue clay on it. It took us 4 or 5 days to work the road down it. We got down all right into quite a pretty little valley — it looked like it was about 10 or 15 miles long by about 3 or 4 miles wide. We went diagonally across it, following the Indian trail, and we got into one of the prettiest cedar forrests I had ever seen. We kept on the trail till we got to very near the Elk Mountain, then we crossed what we called the Grand Gulch at the foot of the Elk Mountain. Then we followed the trail down to the San Juan. Chopping cedars out of the road was the most of the work we had to do. We were 10 or 12 days going through that cedar forrest; there was some of the prettiest cedars there I had ever seen.

The night we got down into Comb Wash, just before we got to the San Juan River, our meat and everything else had give out on us. My dear wife and my two little boys had to eat dry bread for their supper. There is where I thought my heart would break; to see them go to bed with nothing but dry bread to eat. My dear wife never did have much of an appetite, with the best of stuff to eat. That hurts me yet when ever I think of it. Yet none of them said a word; even those two little boys ate their dry bread and never said a word about it. I tell you that cut me to the quick. I never slept much that night; I was trying to think what could I do to get them something to eat. The next morning was no better, but that day about noon we landed on the San Juan River about 10 miles from our destination; my brother Alvin killed a calf and gave us quite a big piece of it.

We camped there three days and worked the road up to Butler Wash;[22] then we hitched up our teams and drove to our destination — Bluff City we called it — on the 6th day of April, 1880.[23]

FOOTNOTES

1. This means that Decker had six horses hitched to one wagon and was trailing the other, a practice quite common among freighters of that day.

2. This does not mean that the Decker outfit arrived at Forty-mile Spring in one day from Ten-mile. We should not expect this account, written more than a half century after the events had taken place — when its author was over eighty years old — to be entirely accurate concerning dates. The Decker outfit evidently reached Forty-mile Spring November 24.

3. Smith was not sent back to the settlements immediately upon his arrival at Forty-mile Spring, but on December 15, after he and advance units of the company had reached the Hole-in-the-Rock.

4. Platte D. Lyman says that Reuben Collett and Andrew P. Schow had brought the boat from Escalante, but other accounts agree with Decker, that Hall had brought the boat. It seems logical to assume, therefore, that all three men, Hall, Collett, and Schow arrived together at Forty-mile Spring and that they brought the boat with them. There seems to be general agreement that Hall had built the boat.

That one of the two wagons, long known to have been used on this reconnaissance, was that of Cornelius Decker is here revealed for the first time.

5. Almost every account stresses this forty-foot cliff at the top of the Hole-in-the-Rock. It was the major obstacle to be overcome as road-building activities eventually got under way.

6. Most accounts emphasize the idea that most of the men of this exploring group agreed that no road could be built that way. Compare Chapter V, this work.

7. Until now the identity of the fisherman has remained a mystery to all except members of Cornelius Decker's family. Decker lost the two hooks in the San Juan River shortly after the company reached Bluff. See: Letter from Elizabeth Decker dated May 10, 1880, at Bluff, Utah, Appendix VIII, this work.

8. No other account, as far as I have been able to determine, indicates just how the expedition was divided — who camped at Fifty-mile Spring and who at the Hole. Of course, there were many from towns not mentioned here; just where all of those families camped is not known.

9. I have long been of the opinion that the road through the Hole and that on the east side of the river were being worked at the same time. This record confirms that belief. The division of labor described here is very interesting. It is such information that adds value to this Decker account. Most accounts mention the *shortage* of blasting powder at the Hole. Smith's major shipment did not arrive until the company had crossed the Colorado.

10. This is a mistake in the memory of Mr. Decker. Elizabeth Decker, in a letter written shortly after the event, states that they crossed February 1 — which would be about right.

11. There were four instead of three scouts. The other two were George Morrell and Lemuel H. Redd, Sr.

12. This is the only mention (in any of the records that I have seen) of an Indian trail crossing the Colorado near the Hole-in-the-Rock. Most accounts state that the Indian trail was first located by the four scouts as they explored in Castle Wash. Yet Decker mentions the trail several times in describing the route, long before Castle Wash had been reached by the wagons. Compare with Hobbs' account, Chapter VII, this work.

13. These people got no relief from the four scouts who had run out of food four days before they reached the site of Bluff December 28, 1879.

14. Hobbs and his three companions arrived at the river camp in time for dinner on January 9, 1880.

15. Cottonwood Hill.

16. Some accounts have made a great deal of this conflict in the camp. Decker's description of the incident is probably about right.

17. Grey Mesa.

18. This was the third child born en route — John Rio Larson, son of Mr. and Mrs. Mons Larson; the date: February 21, 1880. For further reference to this incident see Chapter IX, this work.

19. Lake Pagahrit.

20. This is a description of driving down the Slick Rocks at the east end of Grey Mesa.

21. This is the only account that indicates that some adventurers climbed down those steep slopes from Grey Mesa to the San Juan.

22. That is, they built the road up San Juan Hill, one of the most difficult places on the whole trek, and then to Butler Wash.

23. The account goes on to trace the life of its author during the early days at Bluff and later in Colorado. Although very interesting, there is no place for the remainder of the record in this work.

APPENDIX VIII

LETTERS FROM ELIZABETH MORRIS DECKER

Elizabeth (Lizzie) Morris Decker was the wife of Cornelius I. Decker. During the course of the Hole-in-the-Rock trek, and shortly after the expedition arrived in Bluff, she found occasion to write letters to her parents, Mr. and Mrs. William Morris who still resided in Parowan. These letters were made available by Edgar T. Decker, son of Cornelius and Elizabeth.

A. Letter written at Grey Mesa, February 22, 1880

Harrys Slideoff[1]
Feb. 22, 1880

Dear Father and Mother, we received yours of the 23 of Jan. and Feb. 2nd and was more than glad to hear from you. I got yours of the 23 about a week ago but did not have a chance to answer it. Some men start from here tomorrow for Escalante and we thought mabe it would be the last chance we would get to write. We crossed the river on the 1st of Feb. all safe; was not half as scared as we thought we'd be, it was the easiest part of our journey. Coming down the hole in the rock to get to the river was ten times as bad. If you ever come this way it will scare you to death to look down it. It is about a mile from the top down to the river and it is almost strait down, the cliffs on each side are five hundred ft. high and there is just room enough for a wagon to go down. It nearly scared me to death. The first wagon I saw go down they put the brake on and rough locked the hind wheels and had a big rope fastened to the wagon and about ten men holding back on it and then they went down like they would smash everything. I'll never forget that day. When we was walking down Willie looked back and cried and asked me how we would get back home. Willie wants me to tell George that him and his pa had a more than a good ride on the river, him and Genie got their valentines just two days too soon and was nearly tickled to death. They have got them yet and show them to everybody in camp. Cornelius has gone back after stock and will be gone for 10 days while the rest of the men work. We have got to another big rock, it will take about 10 days to fix it so we can go on.

We had another baby come to camp yesterday morning. Mrs. Larson had a boy that weighed 10 lbs. You have heard C. talk about a Larson that was in Snowflake; it is the same man taking his second wife. They have been on the road 6 months. She wanted to get up this morning and come to our camp. Ellen Fielding waited on her.[2] I thought we lived poor on bread and meat but I don't think so now. We have got plenty of bread and that's what lots of them haint. Platt Lyman's folks have eat the last pound of flour and are now grinding wheat in a coffee mill to live on. We have got 7 sacks flour yet.

You want us to tell you what kind of a country this is but I don't know how. It's the roughest country you or anybody else ever seen; it's nothing in the world but rocks and holes, hills and hollows. The mountains are just one solid rock as smooth as an apple. Dixie is a good road to the side of this. They are just singing "Come let us anew our journey persue" before prayer. We are, I think, about 15 m. from the Colorado and they think it will take us 5 or 6 weeks to get to our journey's end. There is about a foot of snow here now, so you see we have had some winter as well as you. But we are all well and feeling good but we get lonesome and wish we were home some times. I wish I could see you all now.

Your Loving Daughter,
L. Decker

Excuse this scribling, I have done it by campfire.

B. Letter written at Bluff, May 10, 1880

Bluff City

May 10th, 1880

Dear Father and Mother,

I thought I would write a few lines to you to let you know how we are getting along. We are all well and as dirty as pigs living in the dirt. Pete and Hannah[3] are starting home in the morning and it just gives me the belly ache I want to go so bad. I am nearly dead to see some of you. Tell Will I want him to pack old Jack and ride old Jenny and come out here and see us, it wouldn't take only about 10 or 12 days. The water is not out yet and I don't know when it will be; it is a terrible job to get it out. Cornelius is talking about going up to Recapture, about 6 miles, to put some crop in and then go up to the mines and work a while: we got your letter from the Mancos and was glad to here from you. Willie don't do a thing but talk about that slate Dordy[4] is going to send him. You ought to see Genie; he is nearly as tall as Janie and fat as a little pig — and so is Willie. When Hannah gits there give her a pen if you have got one to spare. She let me have one this morning. I made some ink with powder and vinegar so never mind sending any.[5] The wind blowed my house down on me and Genie day before yesterday. I had a wagon box leaned up on its side and it fell over and shut me up under it and scared Willie about to death he hollered, "O Ma your screwed up tite under there and this things just came a flooming onto me and spilt butter milk all over me." I am getting used to this place so that I like it a little better, the trees are green and there is some fences and Corrals put up and it begins to look more like home. I'll tell you who my neighbors are Mrs. Rowly[6] is one and Harriet Ann[7] and Mrs. Holyoak[8] and a Cedar woman on one side and a Beaver woman on the other, so you see we have got more neighbors than we used to have. We live up in town now. Some of the folks have dug Wells and got splendid water at twenty feet. There was a funeral here last week an old Man over Seventy died he came out here with two of his Nephews and they went 80 miles above and left him here sick.[9] I don't think it is any place for old folks to come to yet a while. We are looking for Pete and Em[10] we heard that they were going to start about the 10th of April. You bet I was lonesome May day, I kept thinking about your gooseberry pie; did you have one? If you have any more send me one in a letter. I am tired of dreaming about good current cakes and coffee; I dream about being in your house and having something good every night. There are so many going back home that it makes me feel lonesome; there are seven starting in the morning and about that many last week so there is not Many men left to work on the ditch. You bet your boots if we stay here I am coming back before long to see you if it only takes too weeks. We have had two good messes of fish and now we have lost both the hooks so we can't catch any more.[11] Write as soon as you can.

Your loving Daughter,
Lizzie Decker

C. Letter Written at Bluff, June 22, 1880

Bluff City

June 22nd, 1880

Dear Father and Mother, I thought I would write a few lines. I won't have time to write much; there's been a man here taking the census and he is going back in a few minutes. We are all well. It is so hot here we can hardly breathe. The men have got quite a bit of corn in and some wheat and oats and barley and over an acre of potatoes. Our garden is in the field this year; they did not have time to fence the lots. Cornelius is going up to the mines to work in about a week or two as soon as he gets a house up. Pete is going to start home in about two weeks. Write soon.

Lizzie Decker

D. Excerpts from a Letter Written at Bluff during the Summer, 1880

. . . . the days are so hot here that I dont know how we will stand it. I never suffered so with the heat in my life. I cant eat a thing but I think I could if I had some vegetables. We did not get any garden in till late and it will be a good while before we get any thing green. Ide give anything for an onion or a radish. I have just weaned Genie, I did not eat as much at a meal as he did for I had to wean him. He is the best baby I ever saw. I have been takeing bitters for a week but Ive been telling Em that I guess it is the effects of liveing out in the cold all winter, now liveing out in the heat through the summer and its just thawing the frozen bread out that we eat last winter and no wonder we feel a fool. I am going to have a house this week and then it will take four yoke of oxen to ever get me out of it again. Write soon.

Lizzie Decker

Footnotes

1. This letter was written from the east end of Grey Mesa at a point usually called "Slick Rocks." I have not seen the name "Harrys Slideoff" used in any other letter or account of this expedition. There was a delay of several days here while the men blasted a road from the top of the mesa to the valley below.

2. The baby was the son of Mr. and Mrs. Mons Larson, born February 21, 1880, on top of Grey Mesa under most adverse conditions. This was the third baby born on the trek. Larson family records indicate that Mrs. Z. B. Decker, Jr., assisted with the birth.

3. Pete and Hannah: Peter A. and Hannah Mortensen.

4. Dordy: A nickname for George Morris, younger brother of Elizabeth.

5. If Mrs. Decker used her own ink, made of gunpowder and vinegar, to write this letter, here is positive proof of good quality, home-made ink, for the writing is still clear and unfaded after three-quarters of a century.

6. Mrs. Samuel Rowley.

7. Mrs. Joseph F. Barton.

8. Mrs. Henry Holyoak.

9. This was Roswell Stevens of Holden who died May 4, 1880.

10. Pete and Em: Peter and Emily Decker Mickelsen.

11. Cornelius I. Decker had used these hooks to good advantage at every opportunity; at Hole-in-the-Rock he had supplied two large fish for an exploring company, November 30, 1879.

APPENDIX IX

REMINISCENCES OF GEORGE W. DECKER

George W. Decker was a young man of fifteen years when the Hole-in-the-Rock trek got under way. Late in life he recalled some of the things he had done and the experiences he had had during that expedition and committed them to writing. Most of the writings presented here were loaned to me by his daughter, Mrs. Myrtle Janson, during the summer of 1955, some typewritten, some in Decker's own handwriting.

The first of these is a speech made at the Hole-in-the-Rock in 1941 as several of the original pioneers and their friends and families gathered there to celebrate the 60th anniversary of the original expedition. The other articles are excerpts from his writings which he recorded at various times as he recalled specific incidents and events related to his participation in the Hole-in-the-Rock expedition.

From these excerpts it seems quite obvious that the highlight of the whole expedition for young Decker was his return from Lake Pagahrit (or Hermit Lake) early in March 1880, and especially his crossing of the Colorado River at Hole-in-the-Rock on that occasion. However, his reports concerning the gathering and herding of livestock are very important since they definitely establish the fact that a large herd accompanied the main body of the expedition — a fact that has been questioned by some writers.

A. George W. Decker's speech at Hole-in-the-Rock, 1941

I find there are conflicting opinions as to who drove the first wagon down the Hole, or "Chute," as we all got to calling it. This is the way I remember it.

All December and January there was a wholesome rivalry between the men selected to assist at the Hole. Ben Perkins and his brother Hy were the chief men on the rock job. Much speculation went on as to who should take the first wagon down the Chute. There was not a dissenting voice when Ben was talked of as the man except Ben's own "No."

"Hy shall 'ave it," he said, meaning his brother Hyrum Perkins. Everybody gave way to Ben's suggestion.

On the morning of January 26, 1880, Hy's and Ben's wagons came to the Chute in this order. Hy's horses refused to face the Chute — too steep — and they had too clear a view of the river about two-thousand feet below. They tried another team with the same rearing and surging backward and still a third team — all too frightened and nervous to risk. Big Jens Nielson even was nonplussed. Then Joe Barton came to Brother Nielson and said, "Brother Nielson, I think I have a pair of horses that will go down the Chute."

"Vell, Broder Barton, if you haf, bring heem along," said sensible Brother Nielson.

Joe brought his big wheel horses and they moved off unconcerned but very slow and sure, feeling their way with their large careful feet for they were totally blind (had been for more than a year. An epidemic of "Pink Eye" had blinded hundreds of horses in southern Utah during 1877, 1878, 1879. Some of our best saddle horses were totally ruined.)

Joe took at least two wagons down at that time. Those wagons and Joe's horses, calm and sure, gave the other horses courage to go down. I, a lad of fifteen, was on the rock ledge at the side of the Chute when Joe gathered up his lines. "Be sure you don't slide off into the hold horses," I called. He showed me a rope in the other hand fastened somewhere back of him, and a crowd of men held to ropes back of the wagon. Joe, standing erect, as I remember, moved his wagon over the crest just as gently as if he carried a load of eggs; and the crowd at the top came to life with chatter, laughter, and a crazy explosion of hurrahs.[1] Then, giving proper space between outfits, the rest of the wagon train slowly made their way to the river. The first great obstacle was conquered; next was the river itself. You all know how the cattle and horses had to be forced to swim that turbulent stream and how wagons and people had to be ferried across. I won't go into that.

I want to say a word or two about the most unusual family I have ever seen, and how I got back alone the following March.

This family consisted of Tom Box, his wife, two sons with their wives, and two daughters and their husbands. They with their animals, caught us at the Hole.

Nature must have fed Tom on a solution of limestone down in Texas, and he had assimilated enough to make the giant of a man he was. To me, a mere kid, he was stupendous. All others of his group were built on the same plan. Mild mannered, all of them, they enthralled me with their conversation — thrilling tales and Southern drawl.

Tom, he told me, had started from southwest Texas with 1500 "cows" hunting better pasture. There had been a drought in west Texas as there had been in southern Utah. Tom trailed his stock up into New Mexico, crossed into Arizona, then northward into Utah where he caught us here. Someone in Las Vegas, Nevada, had told him of our Mormon Mission on its way to the head waters of the San Juan. He lit out and caught us just before the winter snows piled drifts ten to twenty-feet deep along all the divides blocking our return and also his own.

Tom agreed with us that there was not forage over the plateau for his 800 head of "cows," his draught stock and mounts, besides our animals. Since he did not care to turn Mormon, he took kindly to our suggestion that since all his party was horseback, it was his duty to get out of the country as quickly as possible so that our animals would not starve. He sympathized with our predicament, and made haste in getting his two-wheeled commissary cart into Colorado by the shortest route.

His cart was the greatest curiosity I had ever beheld, built even on larger proportions than its owners. Its two wheels were eight feet in diameter, had been cross-sawed from a very large tree, and were held together with thick tires having a tread of eighteen inches in width. The box reached ten-feet on each side of the axle; the front end reached way up on the bull tongue and about ten-feet behind the axle. The outfit, when ready for travel, was really ponderous, requiring twelve head of oxen to pull it through this wild country of no roads. He had ropes and chains galore; he could pack when he could no longer wheel; and pack he did. As the Tom Box party left, it was a sad farewell for me. We saw or heard no more of them.

As soon as we cowboys had delivered our stock at the present site of Bluff, (We were weeks ahead of the main company.) I was obliged to get back to Parowan as soon as possible for I had promised Mother to be back in time to plant the spring crops. She refused to sell her farm until she learned how things were to turn out in San Juan. So with my pony and one pack horse, I set out alone. Father was loath to let a fifteen-year-old go back alone in March facing the peril of snow and flood through the wildest portion of the United States. He offered me his gun, but I knew he was in more danger from Indians than I would be, so I refused it.

It will be 61 years next March (1942) since I faced alone the most rugged gorge, the most tempestuous river, the loneliest and most frightening country I have ever seen. My only thought as I came to the Hole-in-the-Rock Crossing was to get over the savage stream and find forage for my hungry ponies. Since we had so recently been fording animals at this point, I didn't even look around, but plunged right into the water fully expecting the Colorado River to be the same as when we left it only two months before. I was watching the riffle, as we called the crest of the waves, glinting over the surface of the river, near the mouth of Cottonwood canyon, when I was startled by the ice-cold water reaching the saddle. During all the twenty times I had forded the river, never had it come so high.

Now as I gazed dumbfounded, my horse disappeared from under me; only a couple of ears (on the top of his head) were visible; then his nose, snorting for breath, came up. Funny sensation! When the horse neared the crest of the plunging waves, he pricked his ears forward and turned down stream. I pressed the right side of his neck to turn him back toward shore, and after a long struggle made it all right. Then, believe me, I did some looking about to discover my predicament. The river had risen so much I could hardly believe it. "Ye Gods!" I said to myself; "I've got to cross this damned river, but how?" I was really alarmed. Alone in a wilderness and wet and cold! I looked up and down the stream to estimate the best place for fording. It was rising steadily. I looked at the crest — coxcomb form and so high that the water rolled back down the up-stream side of the crest wave. I thought if I could only cross that crest I was sure of reaching the west shore; and cross it I must.

My second plunge was maybe one-hundred yards nearer the falls which some of our animals had nearly gone over in the January crossings. Deeper and deeper my pony went into the water till the roaring of the rapids was very dis-tinct. When he again went practically out of sight, I nudged him to turn around and we reached the shore again just above where the water was plunging over the brink. Uh!

But I must make one more try. I went one-hundred yards above where I first entered the river. Same experience. The water was near my armpits and the pony became alarmed as we neared the crest. Again he turned and made for the east bank. Whew! I was the worst frightened kid that ever was in the Colorado Gorge. Not a human being, so far as I knew, within a hundred miles of either side of the river! No boat. Desperate, I wandered up the shore leading my ponies. Gosh! It was cold — wet clothes freezing in the bitter wind which poured down the canyon like a glacier.

Then I happened to think of some dead cottonwoods up from the ferry crossing so I slogged toward them. As I passed the old ferry crossing, I could see boats tied up on the further shore. I wondered if it would be possible to make a raft of the logs and cross on it.

I was reaching for a log, when a shrill whistle startled me. Sounded as if someone was trying to attract my attention. Holy smoke! I straightened up and scanned the west shore and all the slopes right up to the vertical cliffs. For some time I could see nothing. Then suddenly I caught sight of a moving object. Right at the base of a cliff was a man walking. But he apparently had not seen me, for when I called to him, he made a surprised halt. Was I tickled! When I called and motioned for help, he started for the ferry and was joined by a boy.

It was Charles Hall and his son who had spent part of the winter helping our missionaries get their wagons and belongings across the river. They had, by the strangest chance, just come from Escalante to the ferry that morning. My problem was soon solved, and I still had two hours of sun to partly dry my icy clothes, climb the cliffs and find my ponies some grass. I have often wondered what I would have done if those good Samaritans had not been at the river. My mother said they were there in answer to her prayers. Bless her dear old heart!

But that was the last I saw of the Hole-in-the-Rock until this trip, and I can't express my joy at seeing so many old friends and their children at this — shall I say Hallowed Shrine? To all that company of pioneers, it certainly is hallowed ground.

B. George W. Decker's reminiscences

Thursday 10-2-41. Sixty two years tonight since about 12 of us fellows from Parowan went into the head of Summit Canyon thru the Dry Lakes country to gather cattle & horses that had been ranging there and on the Mammoth, south of Bryan Head for the summer of 1879. That night a blanket of snow 3 ft. deep fell over the whole mountain plateau; deeper the higher we went. It appears today as if the natural forces are going to duplicate that stunt. It has been snowing since before daylight this morning.

On the 10-3-79 George Adams & I were assigned Bear-flat & Mammoth we run into a bunch of horses on Navajo Mt. Each caught a fresh horse & continued our search; didn't get to camp till long after dark: George [on] his favorite old white Colonel and mine was small but very spirited. Both stood the day's work well. Collected a bunch of horses, took them to head of Summit near Sugarloaf.

This fall from Sept. 16 to now October 20th. the weather conditions have duplicated the same period of 1879. I was riding the range every day during the spring, summer, & autumn of 1879 getting my fathers horses & cattle located rangewise so we could collect them when the word came to make the start. Finally the word came "be ready to move from the southern settlements not later than Oct. 25th." Jens Nielson of Cedar gave the word "start from Cedar October 22 morning." Twenty odd wagons, 70 loose cattle 15 loose horses.

Sunday-12-14-1941: 62 years ago today we at Hole-in-the-Rock on our way to San Juan to establish a Mormon outpost where "certain of our brethren can feel safe from persecution by the National officers" Whew! Anyway we were assembled there to select men and committees to establish an order of procedure to carry on the work which we could all see, who were there, was to stupendous! Rock-rimmed Colorado 2500 to 3000 [ft.] below us must be attacked: Well the men went to work in forming a group of committees and heads of committees: to be responsible for the task. The task *was* tremendous.

> Silas S. Smith was elected as captain
> Platt Lyman as assistant Captain
> Jens Nielson as Capt. 1st Ten & Chaplain
> George Sevy   " 2 "
> Benjamin Perkins " 3 "   That did not take
> Henry Holyoak   " 4 "   care of all the Workers.
> Z. B. Decker Jr.   " 5 "   Cow punchers were out of
> Afterward   " 6 "   it

Wednesday: 12-17-41. . . . I slept on the ground that winter from Parowan to Hole-in-the-Rock to Cotton Wood Wash where we left our spear-head bunch of cattle and horses strung from Cotton Wood Canyon on Colorado up over top at Cheese-Camp—Where Bill Hutchins of Beaver bid up hunks of cheese to twice their value so it made it cost some needy members of the company more; he never took a pound of it himself: I never like him after that. —

Cheese Camp; Paharat Lake, Slick Rock: Castle Gulch, Clay Hill, Snow Flat, Grand Gulch, Elk Mountain, Butler Wash, Cliff Dwellings, Comb Wash: Cattle and horses strung out: a pick nick for the Indians if they had only known it....

Wednesday March 1st, 1944. Just 64 years ago today I passed head of Castle Gulch (Green Water) on through cedars over damned rough country where Mormons were cutting a "road"? Got to Lake [Pagahrit] March 1st after night Had to spend the rest of the night telling men what I thot of the chances of getting thru to San Juan. I told them I had been clear thru to San Juan Valley where they were to go and we Dick Butts, Monroe Red & I had dropped about 100 cows & 125 loose horses over Cotton Wood wash where it was supposed by us they were to take their wagons: Some women listened with tears in their eyes: Especially Lizzie, Cornelius's wife. They all wanted to know why I came back to camp alone: I had made up my mind to leave the Camp on March 3rd for Parowan; No one else was ready so I had to make the start alone: hence Lizzie's tears....

Tried to cross Colorado river at the ford where had forded 1800 head of cattle & horses & had no trouble all thru December to the last of February: When I tried it Feb [March] 4th 1880 about sun down stream near to brink of the falls & I had to give up the idea of fording....

Friday 3-13-42: 63 years ago to day I started from my camp high on the south side of Little Creek Peak just before sunrise nervous with excitement: My last day on the snowey trail that I had been beating for 10 consecutive day — tho I was badly blind, snow Blind, I could pick out where the sun had caused snow to settle so I could get my two poor ponies along: it took me about 2 hours to get down from quite high on the Peak to Canyon edge opposite Ed. Tompson's saw mill site: coulden't go in bottom of canyon: snow too deep: When I got below Tompson's mill site I could see away off to North of me about a[t] Bear Valley road a black object: turned out to be George Ipson of Panguitch bogged in the snow, by occasional glimpses opening my badly inflamed eyes I reached his position with one horse drowned: get your other horse away! I yelled at him: the horse drowned had two new harnesses on ... George had to hold on to drowned horse I got into flood cut belly bands & hame strap threw each harness out on the bank then cut halter straps let him go under the snow covered stream: I think George followed my trail back to Panguitch. I hurried over to head of Little Creek Canyon built a fire dried my cloths some ate some raw meat for a dinner and hiked on down Little Creek Canyon. There was a clear sky as I emerged from the mouth of the canyon and I got a clear view of the valley clear out to Summit & West Mountains, gap & lake region I was told after I got to Parowan that there was two feet of crusted snow over most of the valley. I came d - - m near breaking down as I looked at Paragooh: so near & yet so far Parowan 8 miles: the heel of one spongy boot up in my instep: cloths all wet: but I trudged that 7 miles, driving my ponies before me: they were as nearly tired out as I was: but God! how my eyes did hurt: in one of the coldest sleet storms from paragonah to Parowan I splashed along urging my ponies ahead of me faster than they wanted to go, just as the sun was hanging for its plunge behind the west mts. I sprinted to Decker's gate: I lay in bed for three day before dear old mother would let any light to my bandaged eyes, Uh!

1. During the trek young George Decker spent most of the time with livestock. However, on January 26, 1880, he was on hand to witness the driving of the first wagons down through the Hole to the river below. Right to the end of his life he insisted that Joseph F. Barton had driven that first wagon, and he enjoyed telling friends about this memorable event, whenever occasion presented itself.

However, Decker was mistaken about the identity of the driver of that wagon; just how he became confused is difficult to say. It could not have been Joseph F. Barton for he was camped back at Fifty-mile Spring. Barton's own account of the event is additional and conclusive proof. See Appendix X, this work.

APPENDIX X

WRITINGS OF JOSEPH F. BARTON

The original of this document is in the hands of Mrs. Harriet Eliza Barton Hammond, daughter of its author. Mrs. Hammond was two and a half years old when the expedition went through the Hole-in-the-Rock. Shortly before her father's death she induced him to write an account of that expedition. He agreed to do this, but died shortly after the work was begun. The entire account — as far as Mr. Barton got with it — is reproduced here. In copying this from the original handwriting of Joseph F. Barton, I have found it advisable to add a few punctuation marks to clarify the text.

Writings of Joseph F. Barton

Verdure Utah May 10th 1914

In the early part of the year 1879 I was called by Erastus Snow to be one of a company of about fifty men to establish a colony somewhere across the Colorado River.

At this time was residing at my native town Paragonah Iron Co. Utah (I say native having been born only 4 ½ miles distant at Parawan) Was 24 years of age married and had family of two children. The company was made up mainly from Iron County Utah. As soon as spring opened about twenty men were selected from the company to do exploring work across the Colorado River in the Southeastern part of Utah which up to this time was a very wild and unexplored tract of country. The exploring party going out by way of Lees ferry and Moan Copy Ariz landed on the San Juan River about 25 miles down the River or north westerly from the noted four corners a very conspicuous point in the United States.

In the early fall 1879 the explorers returning to their homes gave good reports of Land Water & grass. Now came the busy time as it was the desire of Erastus Snow that the company proceed on their journey to the new land immediately. Consequently I with my family and brother Amasa M. Barton on the 3rd of Nov 1879 bid farewell to our Fathers Mothers brothers and Sisters and friends whom were very dear to us and joined in with the band of missionaries who were going out to Subdue a barren waste build homes and establish new colinies chiefly for the purpose of commensing the civilization of the wild and powerful tribe of Navajos who for a number of years had been raiding and committing many depredations in Southern Utah.

Reaching the Butler Ranch a few miles above the Town of Panguitch on Sevier River we encountered a heavy Snow Storm which lasted four days which put 4 ft of Snow on the Escalante Mt and made it almost impassable for the outfit. However our cattle were put to the front and the cowboys succeeded in leaving a fairly good trail. After reaching the Town of Escalante we turned to down the desert to the Sunny South Pulling in at 40 mile where we had the first general roundup of the whole company which was made up of some 80 wagons. We found it necessary to call a council meeting as we now find that our proposed route to the San Juan Country while Some Shorter than either of the routes traveled by the exploring party in the Spring and early fall in going to and returning from the San Juan Country is wholy unexplored. At the meeting a company of ten Young men were selected to do Some exploring work beyond the Colorado River.

Consequently the next morning the company of ten myself included having a Small boat that had been brot from Escalante by Chas Hall Started for the River arriving that evening at the Rim about 12 to 1500 ft above the River and about 2 miles from it by the trail we would have to travel. Next day we enjoyed considerable experience in getting our boat to the River by way of the ruff trail. Having accomplished this feat we took 3 days provision and our blankets upon our backs and commenced exploring for a route by which we could gain the Summit or main tableland. After exploring to our Satisfaction we returned to the main camp we [made] the report that without Shooting our way thru it would be impossible for the company to reach their destination on the Short cut road. This proved to be rather discouraging as the Company had not been provided with powder nor Steel whereby to blow too pieces the ledges that we might pass on. However another council was called and from the fact that the Escalanta Mt was now so full of Snow that it would be impossible to take the back trail any farther than the Town of Escalanta that it was resolved to Send pack animals back for powder & Steel and in the mean time move the camp to the Colorado rim. But on account of Scarsity of wood water & grass it was deemed advisable to divide the company leaving ½ back at 50 mile Spring 5 miles frome the rim, from which camp we would walk to our work Monday morning remain all week and walk back Saturday evening; this work continued for about two months.

It was here that we spent our Xmas hollidays in dancing Singing and merry making. For all that it was the hardest winter ever known in Utah everybody in both camps enjoyed the best of health and generally a good spirit prevailed. When the road work was so far completed that we could get out across the Colorado Some four or five miles a general break up of both camps was indulged in. Of course everybody was very anxious to try the new road down the cele-brated hole in the rock which is a crack or gat [gap?] thru the rim rock (barely wide enuf for the passage of a wagon) which led to a narrow ruff canyon that wound its way to the River. The first decent of the hole in the rock being 26 ft and which took sevrl days blasting to fill and even then was thot to be a very dangerous peice of wagon road. However by means of a long rope and 10 men the wagons were lowered thru the hole and set on their way for the River (¾ of a mile distant) before any of the teams of camp no 2 put in an appearance. The writer happened to be some distance in advance of the balance of company no 2 and reached the dreaded road just at Sundown and knowing that if he waited for the ten men and rope he would camp on the rim that night, but after taking a Survey of the cavity & putting on ruff lock and urging his team considerable finally got them to face what seemed almost next to death. However the next ½ minute landed team wagon and driver at first station about 300 ft down the hole in the rock right Side up, where upon examination he found that the chain to ruff lock had broken but thru a providencial act the chain had flipped a lap around the feloe in Such a manner as to Serve for a lock.

APPENDIX XI

THE GEORGE B. HOBBS NARRATIVE

In Chapter VII of this work George B. Hobbs tells of the experiences of himself, George W. Sevy, Lemuel H. Redd, Sr., and George Morrell who were sent from the Hole-in-the-Rock to scout the country ahead in an attempt to locate a possible route all the way to Montezuma. The narrative found on the following pages is a continuation of Hobbs' account in which he tells of his second expedition from the Colorado River to Montezuma, this time with provisions for the relief of the families which had been located there since the previous summer.

This account is copied from the San Juan Stake History, L.D.S. Church Historian's Library.

The George B. Hobbs Narrative

After working some time on the road, which the company at the Hole-in-the-Rock were making by blasting, etc., down to the Colorado River, I returned to my camp at Fifty Mile Spring to get supplies and my mules in order to join Dan Harris on a return trip with supplies for our people who were starving at Ft. Montezuma. Making inquiries from those who had promised to look after my mules while I had been away [on the exploring expedition] I discovered that they had neglected to keep their promise, and no one knew anything about my mules or where they were. Riders had been back as far as Escalante and had practically traveled all over the section of country lying between the Kaiparowitz Plateau and the Escalante Gulch, and no one had seen my mules since I had left. I started out to find them, going about 6 or 7 miles from camp. But finding no grass whatever I knew my animals would not stay in such a desert country. My belief was that they would try to make for their former home in Parowan. Returning to camp with this belief, I decided the next day that I would quit the camp altogether as I did not like the way the brethren had treated me in this matter, while I had been exposing my life to explore the road for them.

Therefore, I set out alone early one morning in February [January] 1880 with a supply of crackers and my blankets with the intention of returning to my home. After going a mile or so I was impressed to lay my griefs before my God, and kneeling on a smooth rock I uttered a few words of prayer, asking God to direct me in what I should do. The impression came to me that I should keep to the west side of all horse tracks. This I did, and after traveling a short distance I found some tracks leading up the steep barren clay hills toward the Kaiparowitz Plateau Cliff. I followed the tracks almost to the cliff where I found a narrow bench covered with abundant bunch grass, and here were my mules, fat as they could be, together with one other animal which the company had thought dead. This happy discovery came, as I always believed, as a direct answer to my prayer. Once before, when on my first trip, my prayers had been answered in a similar way, when I besought God to direct me which way to go, we having lost our bearings. He answered it by impressing me that I should follow the canyon to a certain place where I found a large cottonwood growing. This I did and found it was the only way we could get out. This simply meant the saving of our lives, as we were starving, being without food in the cold snow, after having lost our trail.

Dan Harris returned from Escalante with supplies, and as it had been pre-arranged that I should return with him to bring supplies to those at Montezuma, we traveled together to the Hole-in-the-Rock near the Colorado River and then crossed the river, I fording the river with my horses, his horses being already on the other side. Taking our supplies in a boat, we camped about three miles on the east side of the river the first night. A heavy snow storm overtook us, and as the indications were that it would continue I refused to go further until the snow abated, stating it was better to have the snow under feet than over head. Bro. Harris became quite angry at my suggestion to stay a day or so and went back to the river where he persuaded two California miners (father and son) who were with the party to accompany him.[1]

Some of the brethren had gone about four miles further ahead to work on the road in order to make it easier for us to get out with our pack animals. When Bro. Harris passed these men they asked where I was. He answered that I had refused to start in the snow storm, and he was glad of it, as I wanted to go by way of the Elk Mountain, and he knew he could go up the San Juan. He then said, "Tell Hobbs that I will go up the San Juan and come back again twice while he goes his way and I will meet him on the road." It pleased the brethren to think that a shorter way might be found, as I had held to my opinion that my way was the only way to get through.

I now stayed and worked on the road three weeks longer as I wished to get my wagons across the river.[2] The storm continued most of this time. When I got ready to start I asked for a volunteer to go with me but none would go. Bro. Sevy said no man could live and go through those cedars with the snow which must be on the ground. I said that I would go, as I would never live to know that women and children were starving to death for the want of an effort on my part.

The next morning I placed the packs on my mules, tying the head of one to the tail of the other and leading the first one. In this way I traveled the entire distance, going on foot myself. The second day, when I came to the slick rocks, I looked back and saw a band of horses following me with men driving them. When they reached me at the bottom of the rocks I found it was Jack and Adam Robb, formerly of Paragonah.[3] They told me they were going to leave their horses at the Lake and accompany me through, as they had been off their homesteads near Farmington, New Mexico, for six months and were afraid someone might jump their claims.

We made good time, following the back bone or dividing ridge between the Colorado and San Juan Rivers toward the Elk Mountains, the snow getting deeper every mile we traveled. The weather was so cold that the snow was not crusted. Five days I spent in these cedars and gulches with the snow up to my chin. I had to cut trees out of my way in order to get through and my mules did not have a mouthful of food during this time. On Feb. 22nd, 1880 (my 24th birthday), I got out of this deep snow into a branch of the Comb Wash where the ground was bare. Here my mules would eat a little grass and then roll in the sand, which seemed to give them much pleasure, after being in the snow so long. The next day was good traveling down the Comb Wash.

Passing the Harris camp[4] the following day I reached Montezuma. Geo. Harris rode out overtaking me,[5] asking me how long I had been on the road. I answered that this was my ninth day. He said, "You have made good time." I asked him when Dan Harris had got through. He said "Yesterday," and explained that he and his companions had eaten up all his supplies. He had been wandering in the deep snow 29 days[6] from our camp in the Hole-in-the-Rock. Geo. Harris desired to buy some of my supplies but I stated that no money on earth could buy them, as they were sent to relieve those who were starving at Montezuma.

George and his brother Dan immediately got ready to return on my tracks to the main camp, which they did, reaching the camp at Cheese Ranch, about 10 miles east of the Colorado river. Inquiries were made as to whether they had seen me. They answered, "Yes, he got through, and for God's sake if there are any of the rest of you that want to get through, you had better follow his tracks!"

It was a joyous moment for those starving Montezuma people when they saw me coming over the hill with the white sacks of flour on the packs. They had been watching for nearly a week, as the 60 days of promise were just expiring (my companions having on our first trip stated we would return with food in 60 days, they believing they could hold out that long).[7] They had but one pint of wheat left when I arrived and had not tasted flour bread for over four months. I stayed with these people 20 days while the Robb boys went up to Farmington and worked on their homesteads. Upon their return I joined them.

Just previous to our return a cowboy carrier [courier] had brought word to Montezuma Fort that the White River massacre (in which the Meeker family were massacred by Indians) had occurred and for us to be on the lookout as well as those at the fort.[8] Before leaving the camp at Cheese Ranch I had agreed upon a system of signals on any prominent ridge that I might cross to guide the company which way to come, my signals were three fires in a triangle. On the third day out we were making toward the Elk Mountains, arriving at a prominent ridge about noon. I made my first signals, which were immediately answered by a signal fire on the side of Elk Mountain. We were pleased to think that we would be with company again that night. No sooner had we started towards their fire in the afternoon and gone down into a box canyon than we came across the fresh trail of the Indians fleeing into the country west of the Elk Mountains. They had passed but an hour or so before. Not knowing whether the fire we had seen was an Indian's signal fire or our friends, made our going dangerous, as we expected to be shot from every turn in the trail, my companions preferred that I go in the lead, they keeping well behind. I still had confidence in my God that he would preserve us, as he had done before. We found by the sign which the Indians' horses had left that we were gaining on them as it made traveling for us much better than for them as they beat down the snowdrifts.

These Indians ran into our brethren's camp about an hour ahead of us, retreating into the hills immediately not knowing but what our people were hostile toward them. They sent a squaw in, and our people gave her some clothes and food. Then others ventured in, they asked about us, but the Indians said they did not know anything of our whereabouts, although we were behind them. The men immediately came to the conclusion that they had killed us as they seemed so ignorant of our whereabouts. Six men immediately started out back on their trail expecting to find our dead bodies. They met us about half a mile from their camp. I then told them of the Meeker massacre and that perhaps these were the Indians that were getting away. They immediately threw out guards to protect the camp and stock.

They had agreed to bring my wagon with them, but I learned it was where I had left it. This necessitated me going back after it. I met many different parties that were on their way to catch up with the main camp which was now at the Elk Mountain. The weaker ones were in the rear, some had an ox and a mule hitched together, some had cows and heifers in their teams, one I noticed was a pair of mules with an ox on the spike with a young girl riding the ox, to keep him in the road, all made inquiries of me how far it was to San Juan. The Robb boys accompanied me back as far as the Lakes staying there four days while I returned alone to Cheese Ranch for my wagon. In places where I could not get up the hills with my loaded wagon (having no help) I packed the supplies from my wagon onto pack mules, then came back for the wagon.

On April 4th, 1880, we overtook the main company at a place now called Rhen Cone on the San Juan River.[9] Next day we pulled up a steep dug way that had just been completed,[10] and the following day (April 6th, 1880) we arrived at the point on the San Juan where Bluff City now stands. Much disappointment was experienced by members of the company of about 225 souls on their arrival for they had expected to find a large open valley, instead they found a narrow canyon with small patches of land on each side of the river. Wm. Hutchings of Beaver was the man that named the place Bluff City on account of the bluffs near by.[11]

The next day (leaving camp here) I pulled up to Ft. Montezuma which was my destination. The company now began the general work of colonizing, taking out the water, building water wheels, putting in crops, etc. I had promised Silas S. Smith who was captain of our company who was home at Paragoonah that I would let him know when the company got through, I just had time to scribble a letter to him sending it to Mancos (125 miles away) by a cowboy who was just leaving, to that effect, this being the first news to get back to Utah of the company getting through.[12]

FOOTNOTES

1. Hobbs and Harris had camped on Cottonwood Creek when the storm struck. These California miners are mentioned in numerous accounts but are never given further identification.

2. During this time Hobbs did get his outfit across the river, probably coming across with the rest of the wagons from Fifty-mile camp late in January, 1880. He took his wagon as far as Cheese Camp before finally setting out with packs for Montezuma, as is indicated by later references in this account. Although Hobbs uses the plural "wagons" in this one place, it seems quite obvious that he had but one.

3. Platte D. Lyman's journal entry for February 15, states that four men started for the San Juan with pack animals that day. This number probably included Hobbs, and the Robbs. This checks about right with later statements by Hobbs, that he arrived at Comb Wash on February 22 and at Montezuma two or three days later, having traveled 9 days from Cheese Camp. James Dunton and Amasa Barton had also taken a herd of horses ahead of the main company from Cheese Camp, according to the Lyman record.

4. At the site of Bluff.

5. George Harris rode out of the Harris camp at Bluff and overtook Hobbs as he was passing by on his way to Montezuma.

6. Hobbs had spent nine days, having left Cheese Camp February 15. He and Dan Harris had originally crossed the Colorado to begin their trip together about January 23 or 24.

7. In his *Deseret News* (December 29, 1919) account Hobbs says: "I having on my first trip stated I would return with food in 60 days."

8. For an account of this massacre see LeRoy R. Hafen (ed.), *Colorado and its People*, I, 381–86.
It is hardly likely that the Indians Hobbs followed into camp three days later were members of the Meeker Massacre party.

9. Rhen Cone! — bend or corner. This is where the San Juan cuts through Comb Ridge. It is the site of the later Barton trading post where Amasa Barton was killed by an Indian a few years later.

10. San Juan Hill.

11. As far as I have been able to learn, this is the only account that gives William Hutchings credit for having suggested the name of Bluff City. I see no reason to doubt it. When the U.S. Post Office Department was preparing to establish an office there, the name was shortened to Bluff.

12. In his *Deseret News* account, Hobbs states: "My father, who lived at Parowan, had promised Silas Smith, who was still at his home in Paragoonah . . . that he would let him know when he got a letter from me saying the company got through. . . ."

APPENDIX XII

BRIEF HISTORY OF WILLIAM NAYLOR EYRE

The following excerpts from the History of William Naylor Eyre are taken from a typewritten copy given to me by members of the Eyre family — descendants of its author. Only that part of the history dealing with the Hole-in-the-Rock expedition is reproduced here.

Brief History of William Naylor Eyre

I was born on February 12, 1864, in Parowan, Iron County, Utah, to John Eyre and Sarah Ann Gillins. At the time of my birth Parowan was just a new pioneer town, the first south of Utah County. I was the fifth boy in a family of sixteen children.

Because of the danger from Piute Indians, Parowan was surrounded by a mud wall about ten feet high. Apostle George A. Smith was the leader of this pioneer settlement. The town started reorganizing in 1851, January 13. They settled on Center Creek and there built a little saw mill which was run by water power.

The imigrants had to go into the canyons for timber to build their log houses. Our house was one-half block south of the meeting house.

The first school I attended was Old Father Holmes', a log room fourteen by twelve. It was heated only by a fireplace, while the benches were made of slats. There were no books, so we learned to read from the black-board.

I next went to school in the West Log School House. My teachers were Dina and Ada Dalton. This school-room was larger than the previous one, being about twenty feet by thirty feet. This room also was heated by a fireplace. Our books were the Primer and the McGraph's Spelling Book. Small slates took the place of paper. They taught up to the third reader, and by this time, I was about sixteen years old.

My next schooling took place in the district school. Unlike the others this was made of concrete. My teacher in this district school was John E. Daly. The principal was Mary Hanson, assisted by Hulda Mitchell. I graduated from the fourth reader.

I had no high school education, but instead began herding sheep and helping with the farm work.

In 1880 I went to San Juan where I stayed until the following year. A colony of people were called to settle that country in 1879. The leader was Bishop Nielson from Cedar City.

We left the first of January, 1880,[1] for San Juan. Our route took us across the Wasatch Range from Parowan to Panguitch, from Panguitch up through Red Canyon, across East Fork Valley, and over the Escalanta Valley, and over the Escalanta Mountains. The snow was about two feet deep and it was extremely cumbersome. We passed through into the town of Escalanta, which had been settled for quite a number of years. From there on we had to make our own road for nearly two hundred miles. We went south east from Escalanta down to the Fifty Mile Spring, then a little to the south-east into very rough country.

The worst part of the road was the hole in the rock at Colorado River. We had to blast through a big cliff large enough to let covered wagons through. It was so steep going through that we had to use horses to help hold the wagons back.

We found, when we were down, we were on the worst [west?] bank of the Colorado, so we had to make a ferry to take us to the other side. It was a raft large enough to hold two wagons and a man on the back to paddle. When the raft was paddled to the other bank, four men would jump into the water and pull the raft to shore with the aid of ropes which were fastened to each corner of the raft. We would then unload it and the current would take it to the other shore once more. This continued until fifty wagons were ferried across the river. The cattle and horses swam across.

After all were across, we struck out in a south-east direction, up a seven mile slope over solid rock. When we reached the top of this incline, we found a beautiful lake in a rock basin.[2] We named it Henry Lake.[3] The water for the lake was supplied from rain and snowfall, as there was no spring which could supply it.

We went along the top of this range for about thirty-four miles — due east. The end of the range dropped straight down on a large bluff.[4] This necessitated making a dugway in order to get down.

As the mountain was very soft, ploughing was easier than expected and we soon had a dugway built.[5]

After about four miles of traveling across a flat rocky country, we reached Box Canyon.[6] We had to go around this canyon to evade the wash and instead hit the great Cedar Base, which was so thoroughly forested that we had to start work on a road through the trees. The water in this forest was of an extremely inferior nature; however, for want of any other we used it for ourselves and for our cattle.

Then, after leaving the Cedar Base, we continued eastward until we came within two miles of the Comb Wash where there were no cedars, but some favorable brush and pretty good grass.[7]

Striking another mountain [Comb Ridge], and as it was an impossibility to cross it, we turned due south and went down the Comb Wash for a number of miles hitting the San Juan River. We had to make another ferry boat here, or else a dugway around the end of the mountain which was practically straight off and the river ran against the end of it. So we decided that it would be best to make the dugway. We filled the river up with rocks and trees and dirt. We made this dugway two hundred and fifty feet around the edge of the ridge. We were up against it again when we got around, for we were in the north-east Butler Wash, but fortunately was not straight up and down. We decided that the best and only way we could get down would be to make another dugway up the hill. We went to work and built holes along the upper side of the road and made the dugway one-fourth of a mile up the hill.[8]

The San Juan River at this point was the line between Arizona and Utah.[9] We were on the north side; hence, in Utah. Along the bend of the river there was about two hundred acres of land laying to the west and north. On the north-east part of the flat we established the town of Bluff.

I first cut down cottonwood trees in order to get logs for our home. We then set to work to make a fort. Our houses faced each other in a square with the block houses on each corner and an opening for the wagons to come in and out. Each house left out a log in order to protect their house from any invading Indians.

At this time Bishop Neilson, leader of the settlement, set to work surveying an irrigation ditch, whose water would be supplied from the San Juan. It was a very difficult job. At the head it was about six miles from Bluff up to where the canal come out of the river. This required a heavy cut from six to maybe fifteen feet deep. Here we used our teams and the old Mormon scrapers.[10] They were easy to work, but hard to pull out. From there on, it was surveyed. The men made this ditch about fifteen hundred feet long. It became necessary to make cribs, also. While doing this we uncovered a den of reptiles. Rattle snakes, bull snakes, garter snakes, centipedes, triantlars, and scorpions. There were enough snakes to fill a good sized tub. We rolled them into the river and they were drowned. Some of them attempted to swim but the water was much too cold for that. After we got the cliff shot off and the ditch made, we filled it with water. But to our disappointment it ran through the cribs like through a sieve. The next bit of work was to dig out clay from the side of the mountain and dump it into the cribs so that they would be cemented enough to hold the water. Thus, we were able to get the water into Bluff.

FOOTNOTES

1. This date must be an error; it is two months too late. Other information contained in this account indicates that Mr. Eyre was a member of the expedition, under the leadership of Jens Nielson, that left Parowan and Cedar City during the latter part of October, 1879. His statement that they had to make their own road from Escalante to Bluff is an indication.

2. This is a very brief account of the trek up Cottonwood Hill, through the Chute and across Grey Mesa.

3. This must be a reference to Lake Pagahrit or Hermit Lake. I have seen no other account which gives it the name of Henry Lake.

4. Clay Hill Pass.

5. The emigrants carried scrapers and plows for use in road-building, canal digging and farming.

6. Grand Gulch.

7. Snow Flat.

8. This statement seems somewhat confusing. The expedition did have some road work to do in order to get from the bottom of Comb Wash up to the first bench on the north side of the San Juan River at the foot of "San Juan Hill." From that bench they cut a dugway road up the face of that hill. Were the holes referred to by Mr. Eyre made in connection with this road work? It is possible that his account refers to a road later constructed along the north bank of the San Juan into the mouth of Butler Wash, then up that wash and eventually out to the east.

9. Mr. Eyre is mistaken in this.

10. Mormon scrapers: tongue scrapers.

APPENDIX XIII

FROM THE MEMORY OF JAMES MONROE REDD

Sixteen-year-old James Monroe Redd was an active member of the Hole-in-the-Rock expedition. With most young men of the company, he performed valuable service in helping care for the livestock.

Two brief accounts of the trek have come to us from Mr. Redd's memory; they are included on the following few pages. The first of these was given to me by Kenneth Reed who had obtained it in Escalante. The circumstances under which it was dictated and who actually penned the account as it fell from the lips of its author are not known. The second

item was dictated to James McConkie in 1931, as explained in the intro-
duction to the document.

Everyone to whom I have talked who knew James M. Redd agrees
that he had a remarkable memory and that anything he may have written
or told about the Hole-in-the-Rock trek should be considered as a major
source of information.

A. From the memory of Uncle James Monroe Redd relating the emigration from Harmony, Washington County, Utah, to Bluff City, San Juan County, Utah, in the year 1879-80

On or about November 1st. 1879, L. H. Redd, Monroe Redd, Wm. Goddard,
Sid Goddard, Warren and Edmond Taylor, James Pace and family & Wilford
Pace left New Harmony and headed East for San Juan County. They traveled
the old road to Panguitch down East Fork to sweet water and over the Wasatch
Range down to Escalante.

Near Escalante the Party from Harmony caught up with a company of
about eighty wagons made up of people from all over the southern part of the
state. From there the party crossed the Escalante desert to ten mile spring. Next
camp was about ten miles farther, and the next was at forty mile spring. The
next camp was at fifty mile spring where the company found Silas Smith and
company who were camped waiting to find a way across the Colorado River.

The company sent scouts up and down the river in an effort to find a way
down the ledge to the water. Footmen finally dragged a wagon box down the
ledge to the river and made a skiff to cross the river. When they returned to the
company they reported that a million dollars would not possibly make a road
across the river.

The party from Harmony came along with the company, it was evident that
some move had to be made as there were far too many animals for the available
feed in that country.

George Hobbs of Parowan, a head strong old pioneer had faith that the
company could be crossed over the river: therefore, another outfit was rigged
up to prospect for a possible way to go. This party was made up of L. H. Redd,
George Morrill and George Sevy. They took four mules, two for packing and
two for riding and two men walked, ride and tie. They crossed the river went up
to the slick rock and prospected from one river to the other and decided just as
the other party had decided that the company could not be crossed. They camped
that night and were packing up the next morning to go back to the main company to report their findings when eight mountain sheep came into camp which
were so gentle that they would not move away from the party. No one in the
party had a gun, and only rope they had was the pack ropes on the mules. George
Hobbs unpacked a mule, secured a rope and attempted to rope a sheep but it
eluded him by keeping just out of the way He followed the sheep until it reached
the rim of the canyon where the sheep [climbed over] a shelf and rimed around

from shelf to shelf until it reached the bottom of the ledge. Hobbs followed the sheep for about two hours and the other men had begun to get worried about him. Finally they heard him call, "Boys I have found a road."[1]

These men packed up the mules and went down the ledge following the route that the sheep had taken, upon reaching the bottom of the ledge they traveled East to what is now Bluff. On the trip going over the cedar ridge three feet of snow fell and four men have never endured a harder trip. They ran out of provisions and were without anything to eat for a day or two before reaching what is now Bluff. At Bluff they found two families: George Hobbs' sister who had married a man by the name of Harriman and a Davis family of Cedar City. They were out of provisions living on what wheat they could grind in a coffee mill and jerked beef.

Hobbs and his companions were told that a trapper a few miles away had flour but would not sell it. This party went to the trapper who had packed 400 or 500 pounds of flour on burrows from Ala Mosa, Colorado about 300 miles away. L. H. Redd finally persuaded this trapper to let them have 50 pounds of flour for which he paid a twenty dollar gold piece.

These men bought two mules of Davis and Harriman for they [were] worn out riding and tieing as they had been doing in the deep snow. They started back to the main company, but somehow on account of the deep canyons which it would have been impossible to make a road through — we claim that by inspiration, these men were lead back on the only possible route to the Colorado river and the main company. Silas Smith, an Ex-legislature man, rushed to Salt Lake City, and the legislature being in session at the time explained the condition of the company to them, and obtained an appropriation of $5,000 to blast out the road for the emigrants, and ordered a ton of giant powder and the other necessary equipment delivered to the company at any cost, which was promptly done. In the meantime Charley Hall of Escalante hauled red pine timber from the mountains a distance of sixty-miles.

The timbers were skidded down the ledge, hewn and made into a ferry boat and by the time the last shot was put in, the ferry boat was ready to cross the wagons and outfits.

The wagons were let down the ledge and ferried across the river. It took seven or eight weeks to complete this task. James Pace's wagon was the first wagon down the hole in the rock which was so narrow that it crushed the water barrel on the side of his wagon.[2] (Uncle Monroe Redd says that at this point where Uncle Jim's barrel was crushed a man had to lie on his back to see out of the Hole in the rock.) George Sevy's and Jim Pace's wagons were the first wagons to cross the river — as they were both put on the boat at the same time. Wagons were rolled onto the boat by hand.

After the first trip across with the boat a gush of wind came as the boat was being taken back and drifted the boat down the river a mile. It took four horses to get it back and into operation. Meanwhile wagons were being let down all the time and by the time fifty or sixty wagons were down ready for the boat, but due to the many men available and the system used it only took about ten minutes to cross a wagon.

The last teams down the hill were ox teams and the head team being somewhat in head, the men unhooked the chain from the wagon, and went back to find out what was wrong with the others. Meanwhile the oxen could see the camp fires on the opposite side of the river and plunged into the river yoked together. The oxen excited in swimming across, blew and snorted so loudly that the camp became panic striken with the women rushing to the wagons fearing that a bear-like monster was after them.

The company moved slowly forward reaching Bluff City April 6, 1880, which is one of the most notable dates in the history of our church. This was a very remarkable expedition; the country crossed is the roughest part of Utah. There were no serious accidents and three babies were born on the trip.

B. An account dictated to James McConkie, 1931

(In about August, 1931, my son James wrote as J. M. Redd, Monticello, Utah, dictated the following: I was present when the writing began . . .

— Oscar W. McConkie)

I was born Aug. 24, 1863, at New Harmony, Utah. When I was seventeen I left New Harmony with a company that had been called by Pres. Brigham Young.[3] We were on the road seven months, and I was learning to be a cowpuncher that winter. We came up to Panguitch, then across the East Fork to Escalante and down to the Colo. River to a place now called "The Hole in the Rock," where we camped seven weeks. And you will soon know why.

There were 80 wagons in company, mostly young married men. Three babies were born on the trip. There was no trail we were trapped among snow and ice. To find a way to the bottom of the canyon was our problem. We used 3,000 lbs.[4] of dynamite on the road, mostly to let the wagons through that place now called "The Hole in the Rock." When working on "The Hole in the Rock" four men were sent out as scouts.

Twelve miles from the Colorado River they came to some slick rock which they thought the wagons couldn't get down. Camping there that night, they packed up the next morning to go back and give in the final report that they couldn't get through. They were just ready to go when eight mountain sheep walked into the camp. They had no guns, so George Hobbs, one of the scouts, unpacked a mule and tried to lasso one with the rope. One sheep wouldn't leave, until then. Then it jumped down a rim about two feet high, around a hill, and finally led him to the bottom of the canyon. They had found a way.

They went to Bluff (what is now called Bluff) then up to Montezuma. Two families lived at Montezuma and were grinding their seed wheat on coffee mills to make flour. While there, being out of food they [the scouts] bought a sack of flour from Peter Shirts, a trapper, paying a 20 dollar gold piece for that 50 lbs.

sack of flour. It had been packed 300 miles on mules from Alamosa, Colo. When they arrived back with the company, they stated that it was possible to get through but would be a hard proposition.

They sent the elected captain Silas Smith, back to Salt Lake where the Legislature was in session. The Legislature approved and appropriated $5,000 for road construction. The Mormon Church sent back a ton of giant powder and approximately that much steel in picks and crowbars to Panguitch with the orders to get it to the camp as soon as possible and at any cost, which they did. With all the munitions they soon blasted a way down.

A few fellows slid on poles to the bottom arriving there first. By the time the party had arrived they had constructed a ferry boat to get across the Colo. It was about noon when the wagons started to cross. The horses and mules were placed at the sides of the wagons in crossing. Most wagons were taken over two at a time. After the first two were safely landed, the boat on its return trip met with a difficult wind, and was blown down the river about a mile, but was finally stopped by huge rocks. Men were sent down and soon had pulled it to safety where the encampment was waiting to cross. It was just sunset when all the wagons had crossed except the last two which were drawn by oxen.

As soon as the oxen were released from the wagons they started to swim instead of giving the men a chance to place them on the ferry. The sun had set and the moon was just coming up when they reached the opposite shore, panting and puffing for about a half hour before having the strength to hustle to their camps, where the warm glow of the fires were awaiting them. At dawn they packed and commenced to move up towards the divide between the San Juan and Colorado Rivers.

There were so many wagons and horses that they had to scatter out in order to get grass for the horses. Sometimes they had to stop for two or three days along the way to fix places in the trails and roads in order to get through.

After a weary, tiresome, journey we arrived at Bluff, April 6, 1880. Apostle Erastus Snow of the Latter Day Saint Church told the people that if they moved on they would be blessed. But if they stayed they would be doubly blessed.

[James was ten years old, as well as I can remember, thus accounting perhaps, for his writing that it was President Young and not President Taylor as was actually the case. He undoubtedly thought it was Pres. Young so wrote it down, even though Bro. Redd undoubtedly said Taylor. I have written the account as James wrote it, but the type errors are mine.

                                                    S/ Oscar W. McConkie]

FOOTNOTES

1. See Hobbs' account, Chapter VII, this work.

2. For accounts of others who are said to have driven that first wagon see pp. 109, 110 this work.

3. See Oscar W. McConkie's note at the end of the document.

4. This estimate of the amount of blasting powder used at the Hole is too high. Most of the powder arrived after the company had crossed the Colorado.

APPENDIX XIV

EXCERPTS FROM THE LIFE HISTORY OF
HENRY JOHN HOLYOAK

Although Henry John Holyoak was but a lad of nine years when the pioneers built the road from Escalante to Bluff through the Hole-in-the-Rock he vividly remembered a few incidents that occurred during the trek. In later life he found time to dictate his account to a granddaughter, Lucille Mecham. I copied the excerpt printed below from that source.

Life History of Henry John Holyoak

I was born in Iron County: Paragoonah, Utah: 29 October, 1870, the second child of Henry Holyoak and Sarah Ann Robinson. We lived there till I was 9 years old. I left there with my folks to go to the San Juan 29 October, 1879. We were all winter on the road. They worked the road as they went. While crossing the mountain I frosted my feet. We went thru Potato Valley and down on the desert on to the place they called "Hole in the Rock." We were there till January 7[1] when they went thru the Hole and crossed the river (Colorado). There was ice on the river so they had to cut it so they could get the boat thru to the other side.

While crossing the river they had me on the back of the boat to watch the 2 pair of oxen yoked together. One was a mean ox so that's why they had them yoked and had him chained to the wagon wheel. About half way across the ox broke the chain loose and the mean one made a dive at me and I dropped down in the bottom of the boat and they went over the top of me into the water. We had to cut the ice so they could get out on the bank. Going up from the river the road was steep and the chain broke and the wagon turned over, the tongue went up in the air and lit upside down in the road so we had to take it to pieces and pack it up on top so we could put it together. We had a hive of bees and had to wait till we could sack the bees before we could start packing the pieces of wagon and the load up the hill. That took a lot of work to get things together.

I had to melt snow to have water to drink and to water the teams. While working on the road further on they sent two men back for supplies. They took six head of horses to pull the wagon; part way up they threw the wagon box off then they had to leave the hind parts. It took the team 100 pulls to take the front parts to the top with their bedding and grub, then they took the hind parts.[2] When they returned they had a load of cheese. (They afterwards called it Cheese Rock where we camped.) The cheese came from Bear Valley. The other team brought flour and other nic-nacks.

Silas Smith was their leader up to there. He went back to help get the supplies and go to the legislature. Platte Lyman led the party from there to Bluff.

They made the road as they went. We were all winter on the road when we struck the San Juan River the cattle got stuck in the quick sand so we had to watch them and drive them to a place so they could drink where there was a good place. When we reached the place they called it Bluff.

FOOTNOTES

1. The first wagons went through the Hole on January 26, 1880.

2. This is an interesting account of driving a wagon back up through the Hole-in-the-Rock.

BIBLIOGRAPHY

In addition to the major documents contained in the Appendixes of this volume, several other sources contain material regarding the Hole-in-the-Rock trek. The most significant of these are listed below.

I. Primary Sources

    A. Published Items

        Beck, Elden, "Mormon Trails to Bluff," *Utah Magazine,* October, 1940 through June, 1941.

        The author of this series of articles presents original documents, copied primarily from the San Juan Stake History. Most of the materials published therein had not been previously published; thus the writing constitutes a major item in the bibliography of the San Juan Mission. A major weakness of the series lies in the failure to copy some of the material accurately and in a lack of adequate editorial comment.

        Hobbs, George B., "First Exploration of the Forbidding San Juan," *Deseret Semi-Weekly News,* December 29, 1919.

        An account of the experiences of four scouts sent to explore the region between the Hole-in-the-Rock and Montezuma on the San Juan. The account is very similar to that contained in Chapter VII and Appendix XI of this work.

        Jones, Kumen, "First Settlement of San Juan County, Utah," *Utah Historical Quarterly,* January, 1930.

        Jones, Raymond S., "Last Wagon Through the Hole-in-the-Rock," *Desert Magazine,* June, 1954.

        An excellent account of the descent through the Hole-in-the-Rock as related by Joseph S. Smith.

        Lyman, Albert R., "Lake Pagahrit," *Improvement Era,* October, 1909.

        An interesting account of the lake and wildlife associated with it as seen by Mr. Lyman, who spent many seasons at the site as a cattle man.

    B. Unpublished Items

        Bastian, Lula R., History of John R. Robinson.
        This manuscript contains some important information about Mr. Robinson's participation in the expedition as recorded by his daughter.

        Collett, Melvina Duke, The San Juan Mission.
        This account is taken primarily from the Collett family records and demonstrates the role of Reuben Collett and other Escalante settlers in assisting the San Juan Mission.

Decker, Elizabeth Morris, Letter to her Parents, January 19, 1880, from Fifty-mile Camp. Original in possession of Edgar T. Decker.

Decker, Louis A., Brief Sketch of the Life of Zechariah Bruyn Decker, Jr., Son of Zechariah Bruyn Decker and Nancy Bean.
> As a boy Louis A. Decker made the Hole-in-the-Rock trek with his family. Many years later he compiled this brief account of his father's life and included in it a brief report of the San Juan Mission.

Jones, Kumen, The Journal of Kumen Jones.
> Preface to the Writings of Kumen Jones.
> The Writings of Kumen Jones.

Parowan Stake, Cedar Ward, Historical Record.

Parowan Stake Historical Record.
> This is a manuscript history of the Parowan Stake of the Church of Jesus Christ of Latter-day Saints. It is located in the L.D.S. Church Historian's Library, Salt Lake City.

San Juan Stake History.
> This is a manuscript history of the San Juan Stake of the Church of Jesus Christ of Latter-day Saints. It was compiled under the direction of Andrew Jenson during the second decade of the twentieth century. Many valuable documents and statements regarding the San Juan Mission are contained therein. The document is located in the L.D.S. Church Historian's Library, Salt Lake City.

Smith, Silas S., Journal.
> Subsequent to the first publication of the present volume, Edith Dibble located the journal of Silas S. Smith among some of his original papers. The journal is very brief but does add a few dates and other important information.

St. George Stake Manuscript History.
> Located in the L.D.S. Church Historian's Library, Salt Lake City.

II. Secondary Sources

  A. Published Items

Bailey, Paul, *Jacob Hamblin, Buckskin Apostle.* Los Angeles, 1948.

Birney, Hoffman, *Zealots of Zion.* Philadelphia, 1931.
> This volume is quite unreliable regarding details of the expedition.

Gregory, Herbert E., *The San Juan Country . . . Geological Survey Professional Paper 188.* Washington, D.C., 1933.

Gregory, Herbert E., and Moore, Raymond C., *The Kaiparowits Region, U.S. Geological Survey Professional Paper 164.* Washington, D.C., 1931.

In addition to a rich supply of geological information regarding the area, these two U.S.G.S. publications contain some information relative to the Hole-in-the-Rock expedition.

Jenson, Andrew, ed., *L.D.S. Biographical Encyclopedia.* Salt Lake City, 1901–1936.

Kelly, Charles, "Chief Hoskaninni," *Utah Historical Quarterly,* July, 1953.

Lyman, Albert R., "First Whitemen in San Juan County, Utah," *Utah Historical Quarterly,* January, 1930.
"Fort on the Firing Line," *Improvement Era,* October, 1948, through March, 1950.

Mr. Lyman has devoted more time than any other person to the collection and writing of San Juan history. This series of articles provides substantial background and purpose for the colonization of the Four Corners area.

Moore, W. Robert, "Escalante: Utah's River of Arches," *National Geographic Magazine,* September, 1955.

Redd, Anna Prince, "Hole In The Rock," *Improvement Era,* January, 1947, through January, 1948.

This is a semi-historical serialized account of the Hole-in-the-Rock expedition. Although it portrays the spirit of the undertaking, it does not stick strictly to facts.

"Where Trails Run Out," *Relief Society Magazine,* February, 1947, through January, 1948.

This is a semi-historical serialized account of the exploring expedition of 1879.

Redd, Charles, "Short Cut to the San Juan," *1949 Brand Book.* Denver, 1950.

This is a paper read by Mr. Redd before the Denver Posse of the Westerners and is one of the best short treatments yet published of the Hole-in-the-Rock expedition.

Richardson, Sullivan C., "Hole-in-the-Rock," *Improvement Era,* January, 1940.

In 1939 Sullivan C. Richardson traversed a major portion of the old route from Bluff to the Hole-in-the-Rock and briefly reported his findings by way of this short article. Several good photographs are included.

Roberts, Brigham H., *A Comprehensive History of the Church of Jesus Christ of Latter-day Saints Century I.* Salt Lake City, 1930, six volumes.

A first-class treatment of the doctrine and history of the L.D.S. Church.

B. Unpublished Items

Anonymous, Trail of the San Juan Mission.

Unsigned, typewritten article located in the files of the Utah Historical Society, Salt Lake City.

Atkin, Ellen, The Story of the Hole-in-the-Rock.

Paper read at Fifty-mile Spring before a group of persons then involved in a retracing of the old wagon road from Escalante to the Colorado River, Labor Day, 1952.

Barton, Morgan Amasa, Back Door to San Juan.

The author is a son of Joseph F. Barton of the Hole-in-the-Rock trek.

Fielding, Lydia Hammond, Biography of Joseph Stanford Smith.

Jones, Lenora, Life of Parley Butt.

Located in the files of the Cedar City Chapter of the Daughters of Utah Pioneers.

Lyman, Albert R., Benjamin Perkins, 1844–1926.

Manuscript on file in the Brigham Young University Library.

Nielson, Margaret, San Juan Expedition.

This manuscript is said to have been prepared primarily from information supplied by George W. Decker, who as a young man was a member of the Hole-in-the-Rock expedition.

Perkins, Beatrice Nielson, Hole-in-the-Wall.

Sherwood, Jessie M., Life Sketch of Mary Jane Wilson.

Mary Jane Wilson was a nine-year old daughter of Mr. and Mrs. Benjamin Perkins at the time of the Hole-in-the-Rock trek and was able to remember and have recorded in this sketch some interesting details of camp life as seen through the eyes of a child. Manuscript located in the files of the Utah Humanities Research Foundation, University of Utah.

Smith, Ellen J. Larson, Life Sketch of Mons Larson.

INDEX

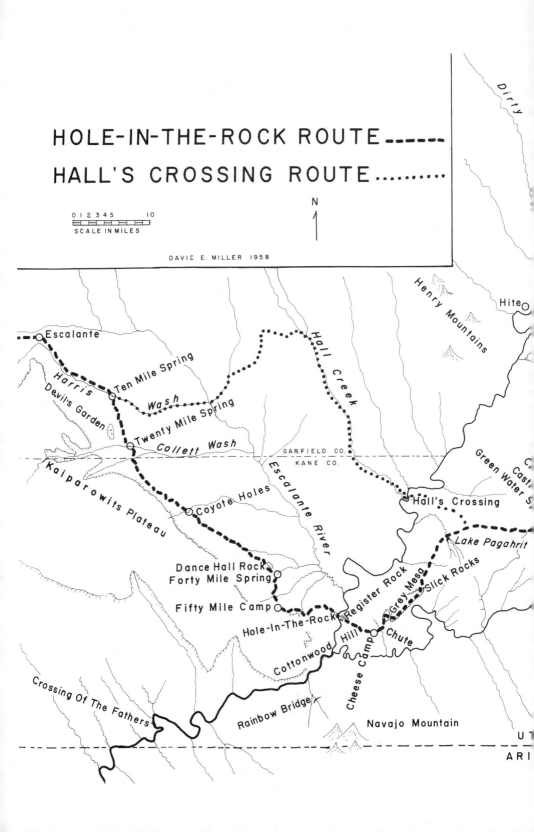

HOLE-IN-THE-ROCK ROUTE ------

HALL'S CROSSING ROUTE ....

N

0 1 2 3 4 5   10
SCALE IN MILES

DAVID E. MILLER 1958

Dirty

Henry Mountains

Hite

Escalante

Harris

Devil's Garden

Ten Mile Spring

Wash

Twenty Mile Spring

Collett Wash

Hall Creek

GARFIELD CO.
KANE CO.

Kaiparowits Plateau

Coyote Holes

Escalante River

Hall's Crossing

Green Water S.

Castle

Lake Pagahrit

Dance Hall Rock
Forty Mile Spring

Fifty Mile Camp

Hole-In-The-Rock

Register Rock

Grey Mesa

Slick Rocks

Cottonwood Hill

Cheese Camp

Chute

Crossing Of The Fathers

Rainbow Bridge

Navajo Mountain

UT

ARI

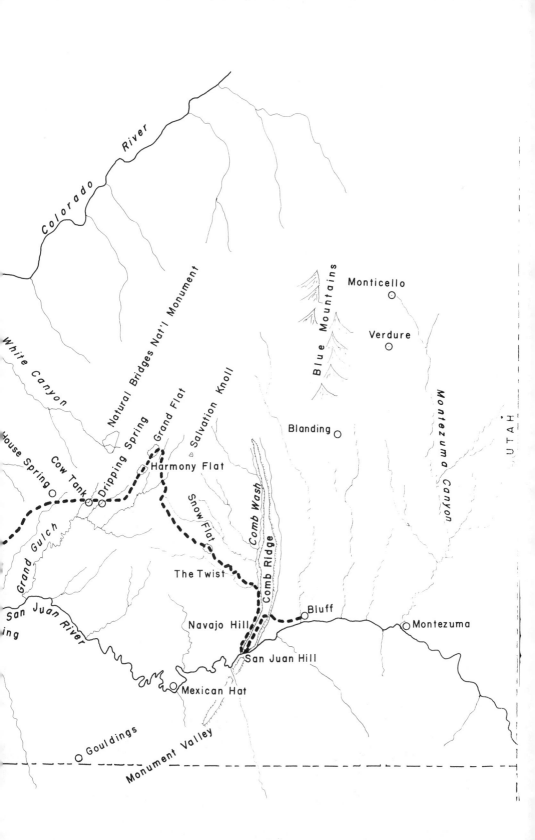